I'LL B[...] JUST [...] CHRISTMAS

Stories from four years on a bicycle

by
Matthew Blake

Foreword by Stephen Lord

Beaten Track
www.beatentrackpublishing.com

Beaten Track

First published 2013 by Beaten Track Publishing
Copyright © 2013 Matthew Blake

A CIP catalogue record for this book
is available from the British Library.

ISBN: 978 1 909192 23 2

Cover Design by Andrew Whitehead
www.1and9illustration.co.uk

Beaten Track Publishing,
Burscough. Lancashire.
www.beatentrackpublishing.com

For my Grandmother, Muriel Blake

Foreword

I remember meeting Matt some five years ago, a month or so before he set off, at a gathering in a London pub for past and future long-distance cyclists. He was instantly likeable, a good decent sort, I thought, not an urban sophisticate but an unassuming man from the heartlands and definitely a greenhorn when it came to travel. I wondered how long it would be before he became a hardened road warrior, sleeping under road culverts to escape desert heat, talking his way through army checkpoints in China and devising ever-more ingenious repairs as his bike and the rest of his gear inevitably fell to pieces.

Two years passed and I heard his tent had been stolen. I had one, but he wanted it sent to Guatemala. 'Guatemala? Are you mad?', I thought, but Guatemala proved to be a doddle for Matt, already inured to routine traveller hardships such as petty crime, floods, crashes, heat waves and hypothermia. I looked him up on his blog and didn't recognise him. In appearance, he now looked the part with the rock'n'roll looks of a world biker, one of those seekers of all that life has to offer. Jack Kerouac called such people 'a generation of wandering holy men'. But Matt wasn't just one of a kind, he came across as one of the best of his kind and had kept his calm, honest and incorruptible nature. He had outwitted bent cops and bandits, lived through endless goodbyes, love and heartbreak and yet avoided any delusions of self-importance a lesser person might have fallen for.

'Anyone could do this' is Matt's modest view of his four-year ride round the world, though readers will inevitably be asking themselves if they have the same level of determination after reading this account. That many thousands of people of all ages now set out on trips like this is telling. Round the world rides have become the new backpacking, the greatest adventure of our times, open to all starting at just a fiver a day, as Matt shows. I think he's trying to say that the rest of us have no excuses not to let go of whatever is stopping us - so pick up your bike and ride!

Stephen Lord
Author, *Adventure Cycle-Touring Handbook*

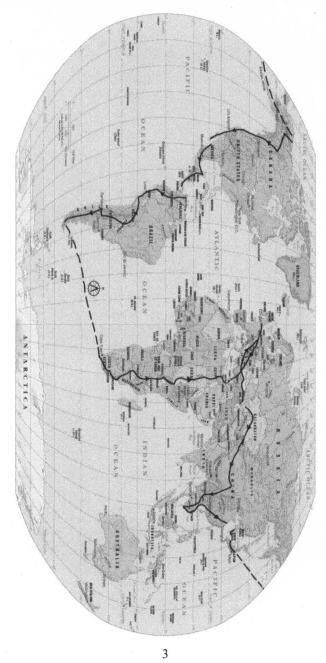

Prologue

It was in January 2006 during my second year of university that I first started riding a bike regularly.

I was living in south London and had just started playing football in the north of the city: the journey via public transport took an hour and cost £4.20; by comparison the bike was free and I could be there in less than forty-five minutes. Originally it was nothing more than price and practicality that attracted me to cycling; however, within a month I was an addict and the bicycle had become my primary mode of transport.

Meanwhile, as this love affair blossomed, I started to become disenchanted with my life in general. I had massively under-achieved in school during the previous few years, always aiming to do the bare minimum to pass rather than pushing for a better grade; outside of school I was content to wake up at noon, prioritise football on the weekends, subsist on a diet of cereals and had given no thought to a career or other such distractions, despite being only sixteen short months away from graduation.

I was happy enough, surrounded by family and friends, but when you come from an industrial town whose Wikipedia entry manages to list more infamous residents than famous, and a country where the state of popular culture meant that one of the biggest selling records during the year of my departure was a drug addict singing about her refusal to go to rehab, sometimes it's hard not to think that there must be more out there.

Two things happened in the first half of 2006 that would shape the next years of my life.

The first was that by chance I would run into an old girlfriend. We had dated on-and-off for six months of the previous year, at the end of which she made it clear she wanted me to make a commitment or else she would be walking away; I really cared for her but was unwilling to take on even the most basic level of responsibility, so I sat back and watched her go. Seeing how she had moved on and was now happy with somebody else flicked a switch inside and I realised that I needed to take opportunities when they came along, as by avoiding responsibility the only person I was holding back was myself.

The other occurrence came via an unlikely route: I joined an internet forum. I had just moved in as a lodger with a family that had two young children - they were lovely people, but we had precious little in common - a situation which left me craving conversation to fill the evenings. The forum provided this, to the extent that inside three months I had racked up over 10,000 posts. Topics could range from sport to politics to film, but the one that would ultimately affect me most was when someone started the discussion 'Name something you'd really like to do but probably never will'. By this time I'd been cycling daily for several months and commented that I'd have no idea how to go about it, but that I'd love to see how far I could get on my bicycle. In reply, someone who I'll only ever know as *Green Giant* sent me to the website of Alastair Humphreys, an Englishman who between 2001 and 2005 spent four years cycling around the world.

Alastair instantly became a hero of mine and in the days that followed his name was joined by others, such as Anne Mustoe, Ed Genochio and Stephen Lord, as I feverishly read blogs and websites, all of people who had made their own big bike trip and each with their own fascinating stories, experiences and pictures.

Whilst I had thought about it, I had never thought it possible. Now I saw it was and my mind was made up.

I was going to cycle around the world.

1: Small Steps But All In The Right Direction

So this was it.

The day that had been over two years in coming had finally arrived. Unfortunately, in contrast to the knowledgeable and athletic cyclist I had envisioned, the man about to leave home was nowhere near ready.

In every non-cycling aspect I was there: in the ten months since leaving University I had been working two jobs to save up what I thought would be enough to keep me on the road for a couple of years, had managed to arrange all my inoculations in order to stay healthy and, thanks to owning both a world map and permanent marker, had even managed to come up with a vague route.

On the cycling front, I'd planned to buy the bike and learn all about maintenance in the months prior to leaving, whilst drumming up some fitness on practice rides; this plan was on course right up until two weeks before the new bike arrived - and just four months from the planned leaving date - when I tore a ligament in my right knee. Thus, the next few weeks were spent having x-rays and MRI scans, before finally being given the news that my knee would heal with only a week or two to spare before I planned to leave.

By the time of my departure, I could fix a puncture but nothing else. I'd ridden only two practice rides and never cycled for more than two days in succession. Furthermore, three months out injured, combined with a desk job that offered frequent access to cake, had left with me a physique that could best be described as *chunky*. Overweight and with no knowledge of how to fix a bike, my own self-doubt was evident in the fact that whilst I harboured dreams of spending the next few years cycling around the world, I had told my friends and family that I would be going to Vietnam and then returning. And that was if I could get that far.

But this was it.

There was no big fanfare when I left: I had a quiet meal with my parents the night before, and despite three hours of stalling, Dad finally waved me off just before midday. No grandstanding, no big emotional goodbyes, just a hug and a 'have a good time'.

This was now definitely it.

I took one final look at the house I'd lived in for most of the last fifteen years, pulled out into the road, detoured through Banbury town centre one last time and was off; destination: Reading, for a night at my cousin James'. Prior to leaving, my knee had healed in time for only four days of practice riding, two of which were spent doing the very same ride. It was a route I knew I was capable of, on roads that I could easily navigate without a map, but this did not stop the first day from being an unmitigated disaster. I'd hoped for little more than to get through the day, and anticipated that my mind would be wandering the whole time, reflecting on the life I'd left behind, but also focusing on the hopes I had for the ride ahead.

Instead, within half an hour of leaving, the skies opened and my mind flipped between hoping that the rain would stop, wondering how far away in the distance the rolls of thunder actually were and the sudden realisation that my *mac-in-a-pac* brand waterproof would probably not be up to the task of cycling around the world. I pushed on regardless, through the small towns of Bicester and Thame before arriving at Watlington, coming out of which there's a large hill that on both practice rides I'd had to walk the bike up. This time, however, if only to prove to myself that I could, I was desperate to ride it. I failed terribly, walking the bike up most of the hill. As if to seal a miserable day's cycling, just four miles from my bed for the night I felt a deflating in my back tyre.

Cold, soaking wet and tired, I phoned James to let him know I'd be late. By chance it turned out I was outside his canoe club and he suggested that as he'd be driving past shortly anyway, I might like to put my bike in the back of his truck and get a lift to his.

To my shame I gave in and on the four mile drive to James' house, I sat, quietly contemplating, as the challenge I'd set myself sank in. Sat beside me, James found it hilarious that after six hours I'd already cheated on my ride.

A warm shower, a hot meal and a good night's sleep were the perfect antidote and feeling refreshed, I set off the next morning for Kingston-Upon-Thames, the town in which I'd studied and where my love for cycling had begun. Despite the still-pouring rain, thirty-five miles proved a far easier distance to cover and aside from an accidental 400 metre detour onto the M25, it went smoothly. Upon arrival I met up with some old friends and far more importantly, bought a better waterproof.

Leaving town the following morning was a big moment for me: up until this point I had been on roads that I knew, doing routes I had cycled before. Now, coming out of the other side of Kingston, it felt as though the trip had truly begun. I vowed to myself to never again take another lift and pedalled out into the world. With the rain still lashing down, I left town and pulled up at a traffic light, where a dog-walking pedestrian looked at me, evaluated the bike and mumbled miserably under his breath "*I'm glad I'm not you,*" before walking off. He was welcome to his opinion, but with a renewed energy level, a waterproof that now worked and new pastures to explore, there was no-one on earth I would have swapped places with.

9

My aim for the day was Dover - or as close to Dover as I could get - and despite the rain finally stopping that afternoon, the hills of Kent meant that I ended the day about twenty miles short of the ferry. To keep costs to a minimum I had planned to spend the majority of my evenings wild camping and cooking meals on my brand new petrol stove.

Like most things in life, you never forget your first time and this was no exception: Super Noodles, accompanied by hot dogs boiled to perfection. I took the pan off the stove, eager to enjoy my first real meal 'on the road', but as I was carrying it the pan-handle slipped and my pot rolled off down the road, spewing its contents all over the pavement.

The second meal I cooked was a mere ten minutes later; super noodles again, minus hot dogs. It had not been quite as I'd planned, but at least I had eaten. Now I just needed to find a place to sleep.

That first night of roughing it was a petrifying ordeal. I knew I needed to learn to feel comfortable sleeping by the side of the road, but even after finding a secluded spot well away from the street and having locked my bags safely inside the tent, I still slept with one eye open, every noise amplified by a million, whilst in my mind every car that drove past was coming for me. For the next eight hours I wished I'd never seen *28 Days Later*.

Of course, nobody found me and I was up early and on the road to Dover, easily covering the last twenty miles in time to take the 12:05 ferry across the Channel to Calais. Pushing the bike on-board was one of the most spectacular emotions I would ever feel. For the previous ten months I had been working in an office, which was vital for funding the trip, but each day had seen me sit in front of a computer for nine hours, with very little human interaction, knowing that the following day would be exactly the same. Before that, I had chosen which university to attend, so knew what I would be studying for the following three years and most of the people with whom I would be learning and socialising. Now, for the first time in my life, I had absolutely no clue as to what the future held. Would I make it around the world? Would I make it past France? What would I do if my things were stolen? What would I do if the bike had a more serious problem than a flat tyre? Where was I going to sleep tonight?

I couldn't answer a single one of those questions, but knowing that I would soon find out felt beautiful. We left port and I looked back on the White Cliffs, a big smile creeping onto my face as it dawned on me that I had absolutely no idea how long it would be until I saw them again.

On-board, I purchased a road map and worked out a route; I had now been on the road for three days and reckoned I could get to Brussels, where I had planned to have my first rest day, in another two if I pushed it. I rolled off the ship, stocked up on bread at the first patisserie I saw and was on my way to Belgium.

Things went well until I got forty miles down the road to Dunkerque, at which point it became apparent that the map I'd bought only covered main roads, and not all of them. I rode for the next hour in what I thought was the right direction, only to end up on a motorway. None of the places I was visiting appeared on my map; none of the roads led to anywhere that I had heard of and to compound matters it was getting dark. I saw the lights of a town up ahead and rode hopefully towards them. To my dismay, I was back in a town I had been in an hour before: I had effectively drawn a massive number '9' on my map, adding around thirty miles to my journey.

Veurne, a place where signposts lead nowhere and cycle paths stopped without warning. It would be another half an hour before I finally found Highway 8, the route which would lead me all the way to Brussels.

I stopped to evaluate the situation.

OK, it's pitch black, you're stressed and you've spent the last four hours riding in circles. But on the plus side the bike's fine, it's not raining for once and as much as you don't trust the map, you're now only ninety miles from Brussels, on a road that goes all the way into the city centre, meaning that you really shouldn't get lost.

I looked at my odometer. I'd been averaging fifteen miles an hour that day.

Nineteen miles divided by fifteen miles per hour is six hours of riding. It's close to ten o'clock now. If I carry on riding I should be there by six am, at the latest.

I decided to ride through the night.

A driver stopped to ask if I was OK and upon hearing my plan warned me to take care on the dark roads. He needn't have worried, as for the next thirty miles I had the pleasure of a well maintained tarmac cycle path, parallel to but well away from the road. I passed through several small towns and villages, all unique in their own way, yet all connected by having their own mass graveyard from the First World War, and for the first few hours of the night my adrenaline was soaring.

I'd spent the best part of the last year staring out of an office window, dreaming of being outdoors and now that I was, I wasn't prepared to stop. I was on a sensory overload binge, with every sound, sight and smell enhanced and enlarged. All that I saw was new. The way I was living was new. Everything I owned was new! Stopping at midnight to cook a tin of ravioli and boil a pot of coffee was unbelievably liberating.

I felt free.

But after every binge session, there is a crash and in this case it came at just gone two a.m.. The weariness caught up with me and it was all I could do to crawl into an opening by the side of the road and unpack my roll mat. I woke up a couple of hours later, covered in slugs.

I was back on the road before dawn, now accompanied

by road markers which were counting down the distance to Brussels. I was still about fifty miles from the city; however, since arriving in France I'd cycled for nine hours, with only two hours' sleep. The adrenaline that had seen me through the night was disappearing fast and I was cycling very slowly. Around nine a.m. my body crashed completely.

On the outskirts of Oudenaarde I propped the bike against a tree and sat down for what was supposed to be five minutes' rest. Body aching and eyelids drooping, I was out like a light. The next thing I remember was being woken by a local woman who had been out doing the school run. She had stopped her car after seeing me flat out on the pavement next to a bicycle and immediately ran over to see if I was OK. Somewhat embarrassed to have fallen asleep in such a stupid place, I reassured her I was fine and grateful for her stopping, but not in need of medical attention.

I knew I had to move, but my body was struggling. I managed to shift into a more upright position, to make it look more like I was resting, as opposed to being the heap of bones I truly was. It didn't work. The noise in the distance was getting louder and it was a siren. 'It won't be for me', I told myself, but then why was it getting closer? *Please dear God, don't be for me.*

It was. Someone had seen me and called an ambulance, without bothering to stop and see if I was alright.

The siren was now about 100 metres away - a realisation that got me up like a bolt. I was on my feet and by the bike as the paramedics approached.

"You called the ambulance."

"No, I have no phone."

We stood for a few minutes scratching our heads, me apologising for what had happened and the men wondering who would call them out for something like this. Needless to say, I left very quickly, an overriding feeling of guilt and shame that I'd allowed my own fatigue to waste the time of others.

But the fatigue didn't go away. I was still thirty-five miles from my goal when a puncture delayed me by a further half an hour, and as the clock ticked round to four in the afternoon, I was still twelve miles from Brussels.

I'd had enough: no sleep, no energy, legs in searing pain. I knew that this was not what cycle touring was meant to be like, but I also knew I had to get to Brussels. My mind had been riddled with self-doubt before leaving home, and with the farce of having to accept a lift on my first day, I knew that if I was going to succeed on this trip, I needed to cycle into Brussels, for myself if nothing else.

The last twelve miles took two painfully slow hours, but my relief upon seeing the 'Welcome to Brussels' sign was insurmountable. I had done it! In five days I had cycled the 340 miles from Banbury to the Belgian capital.

OK, so it meant nothing in the grand scheme of things and in comparison to what I had planned, 340 miles was no distance at all, but in just seeing those words - 'Welcome to Brussels' - so much of my self-doubt disappeared. From having never really cycled before, I had now done five days straight. Yes, my poor map reading had made it harder, yes, my refusal to rest properly had made it harder still and yes, my lack of physical fitness meant I was in for some tough weeks ahead. But I'd overcome the challenges I'd faced and best of all I knew I was nowhere near my limit. Before, I had the dream, now I was certain I could do it. From this moment on, I would never again doubt that I could complete my journey.

I rode to a hostel, had a shower and contentedly climbed into bed. I slept for sixteen hours.

2: Learning Curve

Brussels is a perfect representation of Belgium: friendly enough, aesthetically pleasant, but overall just a bit dull. So, after a day spent resting my legs, I was well and truly ready to get going on the Monday morning. I was eager to leave Brussels better prepared than when I'd arrived, so looking to stock up on a couple of bike tools and a map before leaving the city, I was frustrated to find that none of the shops opened until 11a.m..

This annoyance soon disappeared when, whilst waiting for a bike shop to open, I was approached by Vinz, a bicycle mechanic on his day off, who just happened to be passing by. Seeing my gear he asked me where I was going and told me he himself was off on a day-long ride to Holland and back, on a 'weed run'. He was also a big cycle tourist who had done most of Europe and he talked of the kindness he'd received on his travels. After a brief conversation he insisted on passing some of this kindness on and he did this by guiding me three miles out of his way to a specialist cartographer, where I could pick up detailed cycling maps for most of Western Europe. These maps covered my ride all the way to Austria. I thanked Vinz, we exchanged email addresses and I was off on the road again.

Whilst I had learned plenty in my first week on the bike, my sole focus had been on getting to Belgium, and with that monkey of self doubt off my back, I now felt far freer to take in my surroundings at a more relaxed pace. I had never quite been sure what it was that attracted me to cycling, but as I headed in the direction of Munich via Luxembourg, riding outdoors with hot sun overhead, large forests on either side, conquering big hills, pulling off at the end of the day to a lake or a river for a swim, I began to find my answer; it was a lifestyle I easily fell in love with.

Luxembourg proved to be small but scenic and the glorious landscapes carried on into Germany, where eight days after leaving Brussels, I arrived in Munich.

It's fair to say I was feeling pretty pleased with myself: in fifteen days I had cycled from my own home all the way to the Bavarian capital. More than this, I learned something new at every corner and in doing so was coming outside of my old safety zones. In contrast to the person who had left England, I was gradually learning what all the different parts of my bike did, could now cook a palatable meal and, despite a pair of aching knees and a sore backside, my body felt the healthiest it had in as long as I could remember.

Of course I was happy with all of these things, but what I was most proud of was my sleeping arrangements: my first night's camping on the road had been a petrifying ordeal, my own paranoia preventing a good night's sleep, to the extent that I'd still felt so scared when I left Brussels that I had wimped out and stayed in cheap campsites for the next two evenings. Whilst the odd night of luxury was always a possibility, after coming out of Luxembourg, I knew I had to get into the habit of sleeping where I could and vowed to start spending the evenings outdoors.

Considering it's a country in which wild camping is illegal, it proved surprisingly easy in Germany and each day, just as the sun was starting to disappear, I would pull off to the side of the road where nobody could see me, put up my tent and crawl inside. It wasn't all plain sailing: on the first night, waking up to the sound of a deer with his head stuck in the porch, eating my leftover pasta, was a bit of a shock, whilst on my third evening I inadvertently discovered that camping at the foot of a hill that is hosting a rave atop is not much fun. Nonetheless, at the end of each day I would go through my evening routine; each night I would fall asleep and each morning I would wake up, always without any major problems.

16

To begin with I had felt it necessary to take my bags into the tent to prevent them being stolen; over the days into Munich I realised that even if anyone attempted to steal my things, there was absolutely no way they would be able to lift, let alone run off with, a fully loaded touring bike weighing over thirty kilograms without disturbing me, so from that moment on I rarely locked the bike when in the tent at night.

I now felt comfortable outdoors: my sleeping demons had been conquered.

Munich was fun and another rest day beckoned, the time spent enjoying the city's wonderful bike paths, sipping on a couple of cold beers and laughing childishly at the Englisher Garten's naked sunbathers, before the road out towards the River Danube beckoned.

The Donau-Radweg is a bike path that runs 1,700 miles along Europe's second longest river, beginning at the source in Germany and going all the way down through Bulgaria and Romania, to where the river meets the Black Sea. To me it sounded like the perfect route out of Europe and it didn't disappoint: after the hills of Germany, the terrain over the following days was as flat as a pancake. Ninety miles per day with lots of other cyclists sharing the path, some of whom would come and talk, others who would try to race me; it was a lot of fun.

By the time I crossed from Germany to Austria - a border marked only by a 10"x10" sign saying 'Welcome to Austria' on one side and nothing on the other, where I amusingly got to watch an Austrian dog walker stroll his dog into Germany, get it to do its business on German soil and then walk casually back into his own country as if nothing had happened - I'd had nothing but sunshine since leaving England nearly three weeks previously, but my good luck with the weather was about to run out. About fifty kilometres from Vienna the skies suddenly blackened, the heavens opened and due to not getting my waterproofs on in time, I got soaked. The temperature had plummeted, and after an embarrassing fall on a slippery wooden bridge as I came into the city and despite my hard work on toughening myself up for camping, I wimped out and went to a hostel.

The following night the rain still pounded down, but I made a point of sleeping out in my tent.

Austria soon became Slovakia and five short hours along the river later, Slovakia became Hungary. A few days rest in Budapest visiting Sophie, a friend who was studying in the city and who was also the first familiar face I'd seen since leaving home, and it was off on the road to Serbia.

In setting out, one of the things I had most looked forward to was crossing borders; I wasn't sure why, but I just liked the idea of passing from one country to another with just a flash of the passport or crossing an invisible line on the floor. Alas, the borders I had crossed so far were somewhat of an anti-climax: Germany had no marker indicating where their country finished or began, whilst in Luxembourg half of the letters had eroded from their sign. Indeed, the only official looking border post I had come across had been Hungary, where the officials waved me straight through because they were too busy hiding indoors from the rain. I was now entering my seventh country and my passport hadn't been checked once, although this is where Serbia made a great first impression; not only was there a proper border post, but I got the first stamp in my passport and as I came into the country I was greeted by a large signpost for the Danube Cycle path, which read 'We wish you a nice ride with the wind at your back :)', the colon and close bracket used to emphasise the smiley face. I instantly liked the place.

Now though, as I entered this new country, there was one specific encounter I was looking forward to: hospitality networks. The most well known of these, CouchSurfing and

- specifically for cyclists - WarmShowers, are internet-based communities where the simple premise is reciprocal hospitality: I put my location and contact details on the website and when people are in my area and need a place to stay they email me; in return, when I'm out on the road I can email people around the world asking them if I can stay. We had been members in England but our location meant we'd never had any guests, so I was keen to see what other sorts of people were offering their houses up as places to stay and in Serbia I had an offer.

I had been trying to find hosts since leaving home, but every one of the fifteen emails I'd sent had been met with a reply that the person was unable to host me at that time. Nevertheless, as I came into Belgrade, a city that'd hosted Eurovision the week before and still appeared to not quite have recovered from the hangover, I received a confirmation from Marco, who lived about 250 kilometres south of Belgrade, that I would be a welcome guest at his apartment.

I'd already received great hospitality in Serbia. The people were quick to stop and chat and, more often than not, offer me a roadside beer with them, or give me little extras, such as a box of strawberries or a bar of chocolate, when shopping at the market. So, with a good opinion already cemented in my mind, I made my way to Marco's and was delighted to find he continued this trend.

Half-American, half-Serbian, Marco had grown up in the States and was now living in Nis, supporting himself via web-design work. In the States he'd been a barman at a strip club and showed me pictures of himself with some of their celebrity clients, his most prized of which was a photo of him arm in arm with Andre Benjamin of the band Outkast. Fluent in both English and Serbian, he was a smooth-talking, confident young man who was more than happy to talk and as we walked around the town, his sociable nature was wholly apparent, in that he knew around

99% of the population. He was a wonderful host and after we'd been to a café (where, of course, he knew the owner) and he'd shown me around, upon discovering that I liked my history, he took me to a friend of his who owned an antiques shop. The friend in question turned out to be a former Serbian Army Officer who showed me his medals and brought out a book of photos he'd taken in 1999, whilst on duty during the NATO bombings of Nis. They were graphic images: one picture showed a woman of around seventy, flat out on the floor in a pool of blood, her hand still holding on to her grocery bags; another showed a heavily pregnant woman limping away after being injured by a cluster bomb. I was old enough to remember the troubles in Serbia in the late nineties, yet I'd been too young to take much of an interest. Now that I was here, it was shocking, not only to see what had taken place, but also to feel just how close to home these events were. I looked back in the direction of England and realised my bicycle had already begun to make the world seem a much smaller place.

Seeing these pictures was strange; stranger yet was how delighted the man was to spend time with us, enthusiastic to talk openly about his experiences. We spent a good hour chatting - a Serbian war veteran, a half-American and an Englishman - without ever a moment of tension in the air.

If this had been an unexpected afternoon, my final evening as Marco's guest was something I certainly wasn't prepared for. As we returned home, he told me that we were off to meet some friends of his who happened to be Christian Missionaries. Marco himself wasn't a Christian, but he'd been asked to go along to one of their meetings that night and he wanted to invite me as well. We prepared to leave, and just as we were doing so Marco pulled me to one side to ask quick favour.

"These guys are Christians, they don't know about me

working at the strip club. Please don't tell them."

I promised him I wouldn't.

The evening was fascinating. I am not from a religious background and have never shown an interest in joining an organised religion. It's not that I have a problem with religion as such, more that as someone with friends from all different races and religions, each faction seems desperate to tell me that unless I join their group then I and my non-believing friends will go to hell, and so from my point of view it appears that whichever religion I choose, significant numbers of those I care about are destined for misery. Not wanting to prioritise one friend over another, I simply choose to stay away. However, here I was, at what turned out to be a meeting to discuss how to spread the word of Christ throughout Serbia. The group was made up of mostly English as well as a few Serbs and the agenda consisted of first talking about why it was important to spread the word of God, then how best to accomplish this, before finishing off with a Q&A. I must confess I didn't agree with a lot of what I heard - one idea that certainly didn't sit right was when talking about how to convert people, the speaker said that they'd found that when meeting new people if they introduced Christ straight away it put people off, so instead it was best to befriend someone first and then bring religion into the friendship several weeks down the line, an idea which to me seemed to be a sort of *conversion by deception* - but they were a friendly group and I found it interesting to be there.

At the end, I was asked by one of the young Englishmen, a polite young guy in his early twenties who was clearly very eager to speak about his faith, if I had any questions about what I'd heard during the evening. I am far too polite/too much of a coward to have asked any of the more provocative questions I had, but the one thing I'd noticed throughout the night was that one of the groups they were focused on converting to Christianity was young Muslims,

21

without any reason or logic being given as to how. Against my better judgement, I asked about this and after it was explained to me that people who already belong to a faith are the most likely to convert, I enquired how you go about converting someone from Islam to Christianity. Whilst I feared my questions sounded foolish, he was brimming with enthusiasm as he explained that the way he would approach the task of converting someone from Islam would be to go to them and ask that for the next two weeks they pray only to Jesus: this would be all he asked and if they did this, in this two weeks of prayer, the Lord would work his ways to bring the convert over. I probably should have shut up at this point, but this instantly led me to my next question.

"OK, what if after two weeks a Muslim came back to you and said '*Yes, praying to Jesus is great, but Jesus is just one of our prophets. Imagine how great it would be if you prayed to all our prophets. What if, for the next two weeks, as I have prayed to Jesus, you go away and pray to Allah and then see if this changes anything?*' Would you do it?"

"No," he replied, with a chesty laugh, "I couldn't do that."

Over the coming years I would stay with several missionary groups that recruited new converts, not just for Christianity, but for varying religions around the world. Throughout my time with them - as long as I avoided talking religion - we always got on well, had lots in common and I made some great friends amongst the groups. Yet, no matter how much I tried, I could never quite get myself to agree with what they were doing and whenever I tried to work out why, I came back to what this young man had taught me: that missionary groups go around the world asking people to change their way of life, without having any intentions of changing their own.

It was something I simply couldn't respect.

We all said goodbye that night and the following morning it was also time to say goodbye to Marco. I'd had no idea what to expect from the hospitality networks, but if each stay was to involve drinking with war veterans and being a fly-on-the-wall at missionary groups, accompanied by an undercover lap-dancing club barman, then I looked forward to more experiences like this. I left Marco, departed Nis and headed through the mountains for Bulgaria, making my way via Sofia - quite possibly one of Europe's ugliest capitals - to Samokov, a small town at the base of the Rila Mountains and a place used in the winter as a feeder to the Ski Resort of Borovets. The town is high up in the hills, not particularly easy to get to and quite a detour from the main road. However my reason for going was simple: when looking to fund this trip, I had gone to a recruitment agency and told them I was looking for a job. As a twenty-one year old with a degree in Criminology and Psychology, their job offer of a position selling holiday apartments in Bulgaria was certainly not what I expected, but it was what I'd been given and through this I had met Nik and Kiko, two locals who lived high up in the resort town and whom I went to visit. They'd thought it crazy to attempt to cycle from England to Bulgaria, let alone further, so their faces, when I showed up a day earlier than planned and knocked on their office door, were a sight to behold.

The following morning, as I cycled away, a thought occurred: I'd been so focused on leaving home that I'd rarely reflected on what I'd left behind, and as I left their company, it dawned on me that I had no more contacts from here on in. I'd seen Sophie. I'd seen Nik and Kiko. Now I had no idea how long it would be until I saw somebody - anybody - that I knew again. That night, for the first time on this trip, a tear rolled down my cheek, as I thought about all the people I wouldn't see for a long time.

Descending from the mountains, the cruise into Turkey

was simple until coming into Istanbul. I knew it was a big city, but I'd had no idea just how big, until I rode under a sign which read 'Welcome to Istanbul' and asked a local how far it was to the city centre. I thought his reply of 'forty kilometres' must have been some mistake, but it was getting late and I was on the outskirts of the city, so I went to the coast and decided to wait until morning to find out if what he was saying was true.

That night I slept rough on the beach and as I rested, I looked back through the photos on my camera, focusing on the ones of myself from the opening day of the ride. I smiled. The person in the pictures didn't know what a derailleur was. The person in the pictures had never wild camped before. The person in the pictures had never cooked a meal on a petrol stove.

The man now holding the camera let out a big laugh: I was unrecognisable from those photos. Seven weeks since leaving and here I was: over a stone lighter in weight, learning new skills every day and tucked up in a sleeping bag on nothing but a roll mat, watching the stars over the city that is the gateway to Asia.

In the morning I would be there.

I woke at six a.m. and embarked on what I thought would be an easy ride into Istanbul. Sure enough, the man's guess of how far it was to the city centre had been wrong: it was more than forty kilometres.

3: The End Of The Beginning

The kilometres into Istanbul were some of the most dangerous I would ever endure. Drivers came from all angles down the busy streets; two lane highways would have three cars roaring side by side, with pedestrians spilling out onto the road as they waited to clamber onto their Dolmus - the minibuses that served as the major form of local public transport. From the edge of the city to the centre proved to be over forty-five kilometres and as I neared my destination, tired of getting lost on back streets or having altercations with the passing traffic, I decided to ride in on the freeway. Fortunately the police didn't care and, after much stress, I made it to the city centre, where I would remain for the next week.

During this week I confirmed in my own mind that I had absolutely no interest in partaking in tourist activities whilst on my ride; I had known this before arriving in Turkey, but had always made an effort to go and visit the famous local sites. However, when I arrived in Istanbul I found going anywhere near a tourist zone would result in constant hassle, with cries of "Hey my friend, where you from? England? Come to my restaurant, lovely jubbly", "You come with me, I have best shop in Istanbul" and, perhaps best of all, "I shine your shoes, only 25 lira, money goes to children's hospital" following me everywhere. I had cycled five straight days to get to Istanbul and all I really wanted was some quiet and relaxation. Realising that tourist zones only resulted in further stress, I made up my mind from this point on that unless I really wanted to visit something specific, I wouldn't bother. Thus, whilst the Blue Mosque, Dolmabahce Palace and Saint Sophia all looked impressive from the outside, I have no idea what they look like closer up and found it far more fun to go to the places the tourists weren't. I was aided in this by Ozhan.

My dad works for a company with offices around the world and as his job involves communication with each branch, he'd written to the Istanbul team, mentioning that I was passing through and could use some help around the city. It had been Ozhan who had replied and whilst I had originally only sought advice about seeing a doctor to obtain malaria pills for Asia (the one thing I'd forgotten to do before leaving home), upon hearing that I was currently staying at a hostel, Ozhan invited me to stay with him and his family for as long as I wished.

I had already been in Istanbul for three days by this point and I bit his hand off at the offer, for one reason and one reason only: football. The European Championships were in full swing and the Turkish national team had just made the quarter finals in extraordinary fashion. After an opening game defeat to Portugal, they had beaten hosts Switzerland with a last minute goal, before, when needing a win in their last group match against the Czech Republic, they had overturned a two goal deficit, scoring three times in the last twenty minutes, including two goals in the final three minutes of the game.

Not just the fact that they had got through, but the dramatic way in which they had done so, had set the country rocking and with their quarter final match against a fancied Croatian team just three days away, I asked Ozhan if it would be OK to watch the match with him in Istanbul.

He welcomed me into his home and a couple of days later we found ourselves in a tea house in the suburb of Bakirkoy with a group of his friends as the game kicked off. If the way the Turks had got to this point had been special, it was nothing compared to what was about to happen: the game was a fairly dire 0-0 draw that went to extra time when, with penalties looming in the 119th minute, Croatia took the lead. The game didn't even restart until the clock had ticked past the allotted time, but with the very last kick

26

of the game, from a hopeful long punt forward from their goalkeeper, Turkey scored an equaliser, sending the game to penalties. Within two and a half minutes a nation had gone from despair to elation and with the stuffing knocked out of the Croats, there was only ever going to be one winner of the shoot-out.

As the final Croatian penalty was saved, a city of twenty million people erupted. An Ozhan bear hug was my reward and within minutes thousands of people lined the streets, chanting as cars joined the procession, honking their horns and flying ten foot tall Turkish flags from their backseats. The crowds grew, and as we watched the scenes from a vantage point way high up, all we could hear was the anthem of 'Turkiyee – Turkiyee' being sung in full voice down below. The chants wouldn't stop until morning.

So this is what it feels like to actually win a penalty shootout.

The celebrations would continue for a further four days until the Turks would lose 3-2 to Germany in the semi-final. Regardless, the following morning, the city was still buzzing and it was time for me to get back on the bike. I thanked Ozhan for my time with him, promised to come by again in a couple of years, and took the boat across the Bosphorus, in doing so saying goodbye to Europe and arriving in Asia with my next target being Trabzon. Trabzon was 1,200 kilometres away: I generally aimed to ride 100 kilometres a day, and with my birthday thirteen days away and my parents having booked me a hotel as a present, this seemed like the ideal next stop.

I had read much about travelling in Muslim countries before, with people often citing how kind and generous the people are, although this didn't stop me from being surprised at just how much hospitality I received throughout Turkey. Of course, whilst the strictness of religion in Turkey can be debated (just how Islamic can a country that

27

has its own beer - the excellent Efes - be?), the culture of hospitality is still deeply ingrained into Turks both young and old, and as such I found myself constantly being barraged by kindness. Wherever I went, a cup of tea was never far away and watermelon vendors by the side of the road would often flag me down to offer me a free slice on my journey. Even the drivers - who, it must be said, were by quite some distance the worst drivers I'd ever come across - would cut me off and then stop to offer a cup of tea by way of apology.

The ride along the coast was beautiful but brutal. I had envisioned coastal riding as something that would be easy, riding along at sea level on a road parallel to a beach. Instead, I found the road was carved into cliffs overlooking the sea and would often cut inland over the large hills and rocks, meaning my day would consist of riding seven kilometres uphill, descending straight back down again to sea level, before being faced with yet another seven kilometre climb ahead of me. Repeating this cycle in the thirty degree heat, fuelled on a diet of kebabs, wasn't easy, but to my surprise I found the last 300 kilometres into Trabzon to be entirely flat. Suddenly able to travel 150 kilometres a day without problem, I arrived in Akcabat, a town just fifteen kilometres short of Trabzon, a full day before my scheduled arrival.

With nowhere to stay until the following day, I felt a bit lost and sat myself down on a bench overlooking the beach, trying to work out what to do next. Within minutes, I was approached by two young men who introduced themselves and explained that they were twins of Turkish descent, but who had been born and raised in Belgium. They were twenty-three and I told them I would turn twenty-two in two days' time. They found it funny that a man younger than them had already done something like my bike ride and not only were they impressed, but they, like so many others in Turkey, pointed out that as a guest in their country, it was

28

their duty to buy me lunch. As we sat eating, them asking about my life on the bike and me asking about how life is in Belgium ("It's OK, it's a bit quiet sometimes but we like it." *I knew Belgium was boring*), my mind wandered and I began to question both my own behaviour and how we behave collectively in England. Here were two twenty-three year olds who, upon seeing that I was foreign to where I was, had instantly come over to speak to me, to make sure I was OK and to buy me lunch, all without any agenda or motive other than their culture. Would we behave that way at home? Would I have behaved that way in the same situation in my English village? At that moment, I honestly could not say that I would have.

Not for the first time in Turkey, I felt humbled.

They left after lunch and I returned to pondering where I was going stay that night. Once again, I would be fortunate enough to have my problems solved by the kindness of Turks. As darkness set in, I met a group of students at the beach, shared tea with them and, after only a brief conversation, was invited to sleep the night in their dorm.

Whilst my opinion of the locals was growing daily, it became apparent as we spoke that the outside view of the English wasn't quite so high, and perhaps a little misguided: when my hosts found out that I would spend my birthday in Trabzon, their response was *"Ah! So you will have much beer, get very drunk and maybe a few Natashas?"* True, I may have been looking forward to having a beer or two, but a 'Natasha' - the colloquial name for the Russian prostitutes who operate in the city - was certainly not something I would be getting involved with. I did my best to explain that pretty much 99% of westerners, including me, didn't do this, but even when I left the following morning I still wasn't sure they believed me.

Two days later on my birthday I would bump into them again in Trabzon. It was ten at night and I was making my way home for an early sleep after a meal and a beer (*one beer*) when our paths crossed in the main square of the city. They asked how my birthday was and after a short chat, I told them I was off home. Again, they looked confused that I wasn't 'looking for a Natasha', pointing out a couple of the women on street corners, most likely of that profession, that maybe I'd be interested in. Laughing to myself, I gave up trying to explain that this wasn't the social norm in England and went back to my hotel alone.

As well as the hotel, my parents had also sent out a birthday package for me, which was held up at customs and meant I was forced to spend six days in Trabzon awaiting its delivery. This was more than enough: it was a pleasant enough city but on my way in, everyone I'd met had raved about how great a place it was to visit. 'Ah yes, Trabzon is the most beautiful place in Turkey; we have beautiful beaches, the best fish restaurants and of course the amazing Sumela Monastery'. Unfortunately this wasn't strictly true: the beaches were six kilometres out of town in one direction, the restaurants were four kilometres out of town in the other direction and the monastery was a forty-four kilometre, hour and a half long bus ride away inland, so by the time I finally got my parcel I was all too happy to be on my way and made tracks for Georgia.

The further I'd travelled through Turkey, the more religiously conservative it had become. It hadn't really occurred to me, even when a couple of days short of Trabzon I'd seen a woman in full burka struggling in the sea with her child, desperately trying not to be pulled under the waves by what must have been a ridiculously heavy garment. But as I looked around, I found less beer being sold and more people observing the call to prayer the further east I went. With this in mind, it made crossing into Georgia - a border post that contained nearly as many free roaming cows as people - a bit of a shock, as less than three kilometres down the road I came across a beach where young Georgian girls, scantily clad in bikinis, were partying with their macho boyfriends, loud music booming out of the overhead speakers and, despite the early hour, the liquor flowing freely. If I looked over my shoulder I could still see Turkish beaches in the distance and I got the impression that not only did they want to have fun here, but they wanted their Turkish neighbours to see them having fun.

But beach and booze was not why I was here. I turned inland, about to hit my first real challenge of the ride.

The Goderdzi Pass, at an altitude of 2,025 metres above sea level, is a mountain pass that is mostly unpaved and in such bad condition that several of the trucks which passed me got stuck on their way up. From the turn-off to the summit was around 100 kilometres. Having camped a part of the way up on the first night, I aimed for the pass on the second day and was within a couple of hours of it when I stopped for a rest. Within seconds, I was approached by a couple of local people who lived opposite where I was sat and instantly ushered me into their house for a meal, before force-feeding me the Georgian staple of *Chacha* - home brewed vodka.

They were a wonderful family and one of the sons proudly showed me around their Georgian home. The house itself was made almost entirely of wood, with two bedrooms upstairs accessible only by a ladder (one room for Mum and Dad, another for the six children) and two rooms downstairs, one being the kitchen, in which several women were currently preparing food, whilst in the other - the dining room - men sat talking around a large table. All of the rooms had window frames, but not one of them had any glass.

Oh, and in the dining room they had a flat screen TV.

It seemed crazy to me and I couldn't imagine how cold they must have got up there in winter - even if they did fit glass for the seasons - yet despite living in conditions that we would consider cramped at best, unbearable at worst, this family had still somehow come to own a television that was far better than any I'd ever possessed, presumably by prioritising this over other amenities. It appeared a strange choice to me, but it was not my place to judge; they were a wonderful family and after a hearty meal and one too many *Chachas* I was back on the road.

The family had told me the pass was fourteen kilometres from their house. After cycling fourteen kilometres and with still no sign, I asked a passing driver, who told me I was still three kilometres from the top. A further eight kilometres on darkness began to set in.

It had been a long day; I was somewhat surprised at how well I'd coped with the uphill nature of the ride and I had begun to understand just how fit my body had become, but due to the terrible nature of the road my speeds were well down on what they should have been. My body could have carried on but as the sun dropped, given my altitude, so did the temperatures and it became very cold, very quickly. Giving up for the day, I set up camp and huddled in the tent.

The following morning I woke to the sound of something close by outside. I stuck my head out the tent door and saw a cow, its nose in my food pannier, chomping away on my breakfast. I shouted at it to go away; the startled animal took two steps backward and trampled right over my bike. Up like a flash to inspect the damage, I was relieved to find that aside from knocking the front mech slightly out of place, she'd done nothing significant.

I was even more relieved that the pass was only a further 500 metres up the road and from atop I could look down both sides of the mountain onto the clouds below; it was an exquisite view. It hadn't been easy getting there but, nearly forty-eight hours since turning onto the climb, I had finally made it to the summit.

It was the highest altitude I'd ever been.

Happy just to have made it, I descended out of the

mountains through Gori (a town famous for being the birthplace of Stalin and a place where, despite being credited with the deaths of at least twenty million men, women and children, a statue of the man who murdered far more people than Hitler still stands proudly), before I made my way in the pouring rain to Tbilisi, from where I would head to Baku to get a boat across the Caspian Sea to Kazakhstan.

Azerbaijan proved a bizarre country to travel through. At first glance, it has a very authoritarian feel about it, with the face of their president and/or dictator Ilham Aliyev everywhere, from the billboards at the side of the road, to the money that the Azeri people spend every day. Add to this that rather than the names of their favourite sport stars, young Azeri boys run around in t-shirts emblazoned with the faces of various mobsters - Tony Soprano, Scarface, The Godfather, to name just a few - and on the face of it you have a country where the message appears to be all too clear: 'Don't mess with us'.

Get past this though, and you will discover, as I did, that it is a country with a highly contrasting population: on the one hand, yes, I found that somewhat disappointingly, for the first time I was being ripped off in certain places, with a few vendors seeing me as little more than a walking wallet and some sections of society clearly caring about money and little else. But on the flip side of this I came across far more people whose welcome and hospitality surpassed that of the Turks and Georgians, often to an almost overbearing level.

One afternoon I stopped to check my email at a net café and no sooner had I sat than it became apparent that their internet was down. Despite this, the store owner demanded money from me and with five Azeris telling me to pay, in the end I was forced to hand over the equivalent of 40p - not a massive amount, but it was the principle that bugged me. I left and went a few hundred metres down the road to use the internet at the next cafe; I spent two hours there and was served piping hot cups of tea throughout, at the end of which the owner refused all of my attempts at payment.

Experiences like this were frequent in Azerbaijan and whilst I appreciated the generosity of some, I have to admit I really struggled with the people. Being ripped off was frustrating but I quickly learned to stand up for myself; far harder to deal with was the complete lack of personal space. The Azeris were some of the kindest people I'd met but the social boundaries I was used to did not exist here and often, when people were trying to help or being naturally inquisitive, they would go a bit too far, get too close, become too overbearing, and I would end up more stressed than I would have been if left to my own devices.

An experience which summed up this aspect of life here occurred the night before I arrived in Baku; with the sun going down and me a short twenty-three kilometres from the city, just north of the excellently named James Bond oilfield, I decided to camp for the night. A local man who'd seen me go into the forest where I'd planned to sleep insisted I couldn't stay there and should come to stay at his house. I'd cycled 120 kilometres in thirty-five degree heat that day and just wanted to sleep, but instead I was taken in and told to shower.

Not asked to shower, told to shower.

We ate and with me doing my best to stay awake, he then insisted on his sons giving me a tour of their farm. By eleven p.m., I was desperate to sleep. He pointed to my dirty riding clothes. I didn't understand. After some miming it became apparent he wanted to see if I wanted to clean them.

After some further miming it became apparent he expected me to clean them.

I was twenty-three kilometres away from my host's house in Baku, a location with all the cleaning facilities I'd need, but no matter how hard I tried to explain he wouldn't let me go to bed without doing my laundry. Spending another hour having to hand-wash my clothes, it was gone midnight by the time I was finally shown where I would be sleeping and things didn't get more comfortable here either. Entering his son's bedroom, a box room that barely held a single bed and which already contained his sleeping nineteen year old offspring, it was shown to me that I would sleep on the narrow stretch of floor between the bed and the wall. As I lay down in this gap I could see used condoms underneath the bed.

For reasons I'll never know, the son insisted on sleeping with the light on and this kept the temperature above thirty degrees. There were mosquitoes in the room and despite my tiredness, even if I distracted myself from the heat and the bites, I still had a bright light shining in my face.

Sleep was near impossible and as I lay there that night, an unknown teenager on the bed to my right, a light shining bright into my eyes and mosquitoes feasting on my body, I realised that rather than a comfortable room in a hotel, or my own bed back in England, the place I most wanted to be - the only place I wanted to be at that point - was my tent. It may just have been a tiny canvas dome, but that tent offered me somewhere to go at the end of the day, a place where no-one could come and talk to me in a language I didn't understand or make me do things I didn't want to do. It was a place where I could shut myself off from the rest of the world, if only for the hours that I would sleep. At a time when everything around me was constantly changing, the view of the inside of the roof of my tent was the one thing that stayed the same.

For the first time it occurred to me that my tent was now officially my home.

The following morning I woke up after three hours of sleep, groggily thanked my host for his hospitality and descended into Baku.

4: Testing Times

Despite a week with my wonderful host Ali and his family in Baku, I was still unsure of my feelings towards Azerbaijan. However, as I went to collect my Kazakh visa from the embassy, I was once again hassled for bribes by the Azeri police force (the Baku constabulary are little more than organised beggars) and then forced to pay extra to be allowed to board the boat to Kazakhstan. This settled the matter in my mind once and for all: I had met some wonderful people, but I needed to get somewhere else.

This 'somewhere else' would be Aktau, a Kazakh port on the western edge of the Ustyurt desert and my route into Central Asia. My way of getting there would be via the boat whose name ended in the moniker *II*, due to the fact, I found out later, that the original sank in 2002, killing everyone on board.

The boat was a cargo ship which sporadically ran the route between the two cities, leaving port only when it became full. I waited patiently and when the time came for me to leave, I was happy to find that I would not be the only European aboard. The Mongol Rally is an adventure race which has been held annually since 2004, in which participants drive from London to Ulaanbaatar, the capital city of Mongolia, and as I arrived at port I found that several sets of competitors would be joining me on the voyage over the Caspian Sea. It had been just over three months since leaving home and during this time I had rarely met any native English speakers, so an evening with not just some fellow countrymen, but also fellow overlanders, was something I was thankful for.

After speaking with them I also became more grateful than ever for being on my bike rather than in a car, as whilst I'd been frequently asked for bribes throughout Azerbaijan I

36

had only ever paid one - ten pence to a police officer in Baku - the only reason being that if I hadn't then my host's father would have done so on my behalf. In contrast, the ralliers' reported that most of them had been stopped by police at least twice a day. Some were down in excess of $500 and of course, there were no receipts to go with these fines.

As the boat pulled out of port we were all glad to be going, and with the discovery of cold beer available in the ship's canteen a party atmosphere ensued. The following morning the discussion turned to more practical matters, in particular, just how long the boat journey was going to take. I had heard that the average was eighteen hours, the Spanish teams had heard twenty, whilst the English competitors said they'd settle for anything around those times; I don't think any of us were particularly surprised when we finally docked thirty-eight hours later.

From Aktau to Almaty was 3,500 kilometres. With three days of my thirty day visa having already expired and with me needing to obtain a Chinese visa in Almaty before departing the country, this effectively left me needing to cycle 150 kilometres per day in order not to overstay. This seemed like a tall order, although the flat Kazakhstan terrain gave me optimism. Alas, this unlikely task became an impossible one when I met Slava.

We had arrived in port just after 6 p.m. and having got through customs I made my way to the beach to look for somewhere to sleep; it was here I was approached by Slava. He was a twenty year old Kazakh of Russian decent who was at the beach for a family barbecue and was someone, he was very keen to tell me, who would be moving to England within six weeks to start studying at Sheffield University. Hearing about what I was up to, he insisted that I should not to sleep at the beach, but instead should be a guest at his house. Furthermore, as his friend ran a vodka bar down town, he would, he assured, look after me for the evening.

What happened next I have no idea, although waking up with a splitting headache and money missing from my wallet suspiciously parallel to the cost of three rounds of local vodkas, I could probably just about piece it together. The desert road and my race against time to Almaty were calling but my body was beyond function, with me physically incapable of riding the bike until gone noon.

I lost the best part of that day and as I left Slava, wishing him all the best for his time in England, the realisation of what I was up against hit me: Kazakhstan is the ninth biggest country in the world, but with a population of just fourteen million, the majority of the place is a big desert. Somehow I had managed to arrive in said desert in August and as I pulled inland from Aktau the temperature rose above fifty degrees. With vodka streaming from my pores I could literally smell my hangover sweating out of me, and it wasn't just the heat causing problems, as the wind was a strong headwind. To top it off, despite this being the one major road in and out of Aktau, it wasn't paved and as I left that afternoon it was apparent that I would not be able to cover the distance in time. All I could do was vow to give it my best.

The next five days were pure hell: the only break from the constant sun came from either hiding in the drainage ducts under the road, or stopping at the roadside shacks dotted every sixty to seventy kilometres. The headwind was relentless, meaning that instead of my targeted 150 kilometres, I was lucky to manage 100 and was getting through about fourteen litres of water per day simply to survive. With no wells, rivers or shops, often the only method of obtaining this water was to stand in the road as long distance truck drivers drove past, waving my water bottles around in the air to indicate what I needed. Thankfully most would stop and carried plentiful supplies of water for themselves, so were only too happy to help out.

The only exception was a driver who got out of his lorry, walked over (with me clearly desperate for water in the baking heat) and placed a cassette tape in my hand, before getting back into his vehicle and driving off without a word. When I got to the next town I asked a shopkeeper what was on the cassette tape: it was the Koran.

Shattered from riding eight hours per day, drained from the heat and smelling terribly due to not being able to shower with such a limited supply of water, I accepted my fate and trudged miserably to a train station, where for the first time I would have to officially 'cheat' over a large distance of the ride. The train would save me well over a week of riding and a stint in whichever place the Kazakhs send people who overstay their visas, but I hated every moment of it.

I had not gotten an Uzbekistan visa, as the application process would have meant sitting around for a week twiddling my thumbs and with me impatient to get going, I had instead set myself the cross-Kazakhstan challenge. Having failed at this, the train journey - during which my wallet was pick-pocketed and I was forced to spend fourteen hours lying in a luggage rack - taught me that if a week sat around doing nothing meant I didn't have to use public transport again, then it was definitely worth it.

Once I accepted that I would not be able to cycle the whole of Kazakhstan, I made up my mind to at least cycle the mountainous part of the country and disembarked the train at the town in which the contour lines began on my map. Those final few days into Almaty were far more pleasurable: running on a diet of delicious Manty - a Central Asian staple food consisting of ground goat meat wrapped in pastry and then steamed to perfection - I flew into the Kazakh capital, covering 160 kilometres per day. As I arrived there were two things I had to do.

The first was simple: be thankful I was no longer in Georgia. I hadn't seen internet in nearly two weeks and when I did finally log on I found that the country I had been in less than a month ago was now a warzone. I worried for the Georgians I had met but was also selfishly grateful to have missed being there for these events.

The second would be far trickier: obtain a visa for China.

Chinese visas are difficult to obtain in Central Asia as it is, however as the Olympics were currently being held in Beijing, seemingly not wanting anyone to actually attend, the Chinese government had made getting into the country even more difficult than usual.

I had been told the best bets for getting a visa in the area were at the Chinese embassies in Baku, Tashkent and Almaty. I wasn't going to Tashkent and in Baku I had tried to get help from the British embassy, only for the sole English speaking employee I could find to use the F word as a noun, an adjective and a verb in his first sentence. Thus I decided against pursuing the matter further and instead put all of my eggs firmly in the Almaty basket. I arrived at the embassy at 9 a.m. to discover a queue of 130 people and a guard who informed me that not only was I too late to be served that day, but that I also couldn't apply for a visa without a letter of invitation or a visa for onward travel.

Letters of invitation had been barred for the Olympic period (a policy which made about as much sense as it sounds) and so I decided to change my planned route. Instead of travelling through China I would transit from there into Pakistan, before heading south into India. A transit visa for China would give me just enough time to cycle to the Pakistan border and as there is no such thing as a letter of invitation for a transit visa, there was theoretically no reason not to give me a visa.

Two days later, at seven in the morning, I arrived at the embassy to be number eighty-four in the queue. Finally getting in to the embassy at five to twelve, I was told that despite having my Pakistan visa in place they could not consider my application because it was handwritten rather than being printed and that I should come back on Monday morning.

By now I'd learned that the organisation here was shambolic and the embassy were doing their best to make it as difficult as possible for people to get inside the building, let alone obtain a visa, so I wasn't taking chances. I spent the entire weekend perfecting my application, including creating a copy in Cyrillic, and arrived at 3:30 a.m. on the Monday morning. I was number ten on the waiting list and by five there were thirty more names on it, by six there were sixty-five. When the embassy finally opened at nine, there were already one hundred and twenty-six people waiting to come inside.

But I was one of the first in and was excited to finally be served.

I entered, sat down and gave the clerk my application.

"OK, you are from England. I don't think you can make this trip."

"Why not?"

"You have no letter of invitation."

"It is impossible to get a letter of invitation for a transit visa."

"I know."

"I also have proof of onward travel."

"I know."

"So what is the problem?"

"You have no letter of invitation."

"I don't understand the problem."

"I know."

There was a pause before he spoke again: "But just so you know, it is not me who decides, it is this man."

He pointed behind me. I turned around and my heart sank.

Facing me was a man of about five foot eight, pencils

41

tucked into top pocket alongside a fifteen centimetre ruler, not a hair out of place and his name badge at exact right angles to his top pocket - the kind of man who had never been in love but whose heart had never stopped beating since the day he first held a clipboard. If the man who had served me enjoyed telling people that they wouldn't be entering China, then here was a man who clearly *loved* doing it.

From the first moment I set my eyes on this Chinese version of 'Rimmer' I knew that I would not be getting my visa.

He took great joy in rejecting the two people in front of me, both of whom somehow had the required Letter of Invitation, and then happily had one of them removed from the building by security because 'we cannot have any more than eight people in this room at one time'. Deflated, I handed over my application. He took one look at it and laughed directly into my face before smirking the word 'nyet'.

I could've taken politeness: a 'we are very sorry Mr. Blake, but you cannot make this journey at this time', or a 'It is a regretful situation but there is nothing I can do'. but to be laughed at by a jobsworth I couldn't.

I don't quite know how, but I left quietly and went back to my hotel where I lay on my bed. After the anger and frustration had subsided, a deep depression grew; I had cycled 5,000 miles and aside from four miles on the first day and the train I had just taken, I had pedalled every inch from England. The train ride was now, of course, a waste of time and with the week I'd wasted in Almaty I would've been better off staying on my bike out in the desert.

The original aim of my trip was to go to South East Asia and I was desperate to go there overland, but with no Chinese visa, a Russian visa not possible and with all other directions pointing back in the way I'd come I had no idea what to do. I checked online and the only other person I found who'd had the same problem had been forced to fly over China.

So this was it: 5,000 miles overland, but rather than cycle into South East Asia I would have to fly there.

I was devastated.

Almaty is a good city to feel sorry for yourself in; it's visually beautiful, with the whole place set on the side of a hill with a stunning snow-capped mountain overlooking. The infrastructure is modern enough, and whilst the old Communist architecture isn't much to look at, some of the more traditional places don't look too bad. But what makes it exceptionally good for the fed-up traveller is that the one thing their citizens love to do above all else is moan.

Everywhere I went I would ask people if they liked living in their country; most took pride in where they were from, yet the people of Almaty consistently replied in the negative with the generic responses of 'there's nothing to do here' or 'it's too expensive', or in another case the highly racist 'it's ok but there are far too many Asian faces'; in fact, in the week I spent in Almaty, the only person who had anything positive to say was a young girl who told me how much she loved her country whilst she was in the process of filling out a visa application to live in China for the next two years.

So yes, when you've no idea in what direction your own journey is heading, it can be really helpful to be around people who wish nothing more than to moan.

I spent the next day and a half moping before finally getting around to looking for solutions to my own problem. The choices didn't look great: there was either a plane across China, a route down to India via Central Asia and Iran (which would see me double back on myself in a direction I had no desire to go) or there was the offer from Johannes, a German tourist I'd met at a hostel, who invited me to travel with him overland on buses into and through Afghanistan. I appreciated his offer, but my mother had been so supportive, despite her obvious reservations for my safety, that I wasn't about to make her sit nervously as I traversed the most dangerous place on earth.

Just as all options had me leaning towards a flight, two cyclists arrived at the hostel - a young couple who introduced themselves as Matt and Mary. Matt was English, Mary was Australian. They had met in England and fallen in love, were now married and were moving back to Mary's in Australia. For their honeymoon, rather than a holiday they had decided to cycle their emigration path.

More importantly from my point of view, they were heading in the same direction as me.

They told me they'd had the same problem regarding visas, but a friend had contacted a UK travel agency on their behalf and found a solution: It had cost them £200, they had had to send their passports back to the UK and the process involved getting certain people to book and then cancel fake flights to China, but for the price this travel agency had obtained for them each a two month China visa which was now in their passports ready for them to use.

When living off £5 per day on the road, £200 is an astronomical amount of money, but I was elated; it would be quicker and ultimately cheaper than the route via Iran and as such it was a 'no brainer'. With time running out on my Kazakh visa I decided to organise this once in Kyrgyzstan and after buying Matt and Mary a beer as a way of saying thank you, I left Almaty the following day.

It had been a miserable experience getting to this stage, but I was back on the road.

5: Growing Up

I was not sad to leave Kazakhstan.

A frustrating month, which had begun with the horrible desert riding and culminated in the China visa hell, had left a sour taste in the mouth. As I crossed the border into Bishkek (in doing so leaving the confines of UEFA and entering the AFC - using the zones set out by FIFA is a far easier way to divide continents than any geographical feature or map) I was delighted to find that not only did Kyrgyzstan benefit from not being Kazakhstan, but also that there was much to love about the country itself.

My passport was on its way back to the UK, so I had a week to kill - a task which proved simple when accompanied by some wonderful hosts and several Baltikas (the national beer, coming in varieties helpfully named numerically from Baltika 0 all the way up to Baltika 20). It was an easy country to settle in, my only regret being that I didn't manage to attend a game of Buzkashi, the national sport of Kyrgyzstan and essentially a game of basketball played on horseback in which the 'ball' consists of the beheaded carcass of either a sheep or goat. It was something I had been desperate to witness; tragically, a plane crash meant that all matches were cancelled for the week I was in Bishkek. I was disappointed to have missed out on the one thing I came to see and in such sad circumstances, although as I rode off into the country, I realised that it was also a perfect reason to return in the future. I would fall easily in love with Kyrgyzstan: if the organized chaos of Bishkek had been fun (and it had, for there aren't many capitals in the world where you'll see a brand new multi-story shopping mall opening whilst a farmer grazes his goats directly outside) the mountains were about to leave me in a state of awe.

By the time my passport returned I had cycled just two days in the previous twenty, so both body and brain were eager to be back on the road. A flattish day to Lake Issykol got the cobwebs out of the legs, before a hilly road en route to Naryn culminated in a 2,800 metre pass, a new 'highest altitude' for the tour. As I descended to town, little did I know that these climbs were nothing in comparison to what I was about to come up against and that the onward road to Kazarman would be far, far worse.

I had left Naryn with what I thought would be enough food to get me to the next villages on my map, but after a day of riding two things became apparent; the first was that none of the three villages on my map, in which I planned to buy more food, actually existed. The second was that the road surface was now a combination of sand and lumps of rock, meaning that riding up these hills was beyond tough. After camping at the foot of the biggest mountain, the next day would be the slowest of the ride, a combination of a drawn-out, twenty-five mile climb and the woeful road conditions meaning that despite a full day's pedalling, I only covered a measly thirty-eight miles. Realising that (on the assumption that it existed) I would not make the next town that evening, I set up camp as the sun went down and for both dinner and the following morning's breakfast I ate the last of my pasta: I was now officially out of food.

As I awoke I encountered two local shepherds, dining on their traditional Kyrgyz breakfast of vodka and cigarettes, who assured me that the next village did exist and that I was just a couple of kilometres away. They proved to be right; I eventually hunted down the village shop, which had an inventory of just four items; super glue, pick-n-mix, biscuits and around ninety-six varieties of vodka. I settled on a kilo of biscuits and a kilo of pick-n-mix, wolfing the majority of it down straight away.

Given the brutal riding of the previous few days, the

descent into Kazarman would have proved an anti-climax, were it not for the surprise I received at the bottom. Each day I had come across bicycle tracks in the dust in front of me; I was sure they were relatively new and that whoever was making them wasn't far in front, but whilst I had seen them I had never managed to track down their owner; that is, until I rode into Kazarman and finally caught up with the makers.

I was so pleased with myself at having conquered what was by quite some distance the hardest ride I'd done and, for what was genuinely the first time, really feeling special about what I'd achieved. Then I discovered the owners of the tracks I'd been following belonged to Ewald and Ingrid, two Germans, who were a) both lovely people and b) both in their early seventies.

My ego instantly disappeared at the discovery that people fifty-nine years older than me had just done the exact same ride, but in place of my overblown pride were two new friends. Ewald and Ingrid had travelled the world extensively, living all over Asia and Africa, and now that they were retired they were on a six week trip to cycle a circular route around Kyrgyzstan. We shared an excellent lunch of Laghman - thick noodles covered in peppers and spices - and as they told stories from their amazing life, I was in awe at both some of the things they had done and - this is probably highly patronising but still impressive to me - the fact that they were still out here now. My ego also got to recover slightly when Ewald told me he'd cycled in Tibet and the roads we'd just done were in far worse condition.

After lunch we said our goodbyes: whilst I was on the road towards China, due to the poor road conditions, my new friends were going to take a taxi to the next town. I loved Ewald all the more for his brilliantly macho statement of 'I could cycle it but my wife wouldn't make it' while Ingrid was stood directly next to him.

I met some truly inspirational people in Kyrgyzstan; Ewald and Ingrid had been eye opening, Birgit and Martin, an Austrian couple who were on the home leg of a three year trip and who had chosen to conceive their first child whilst still on the road had certainly introduced a different way of life to me, and Coreen, a French woman who was spending her summer holidays cycling the Tajik-Afghanistan border solo seemed a wonderful mix of the fantastic and the crazy. The next cyclist I met though, would be on a whole new level.

Alvaro, a former lawyer, had left his home in 2001 and since being on the road had become known by an altogether different moniker: the Biciclown. Travelling with a clown costume, Alvaro's aim was to ride until at least 2014, plodding around the globe and bringing 'miles of smiles' to children via the clowning performances he gave for free. By the time we met, he had been out on his bike for over seven years, had already covered both South America and the whole of Africa (having cycled down the west and back up the east) and was now heading into Asia and China.

We had met briefly in Bishkek but he had left the city before me. We were both heading the same way, so we knew there was a likelihood our paths would cross and as I cycled up the rocky track coming out of Kazarman, I saw Alvaro sitting in front of me. We smiled a hello, and it was Alvaro who spoke first.

"These fucking roads, eh?"

We spent the next few days together, riding over yet another high pass (this one over 3,000 metres) on more abysmal roads to the city of Osh where, due to my visa nearing its end, I had to push on to China.

We arranged to meet again in Kashgar in a few days' time but I was still sad to leave Alvaro behind. It had been the first time I had ridden with someone else, and I was fascinated by his routine, with its daily shower and fresh eggs for dinner each evening. Here was a man whose quality of life was far ahead of mine. I had learnt so much from him in the days we travelled together and I was sad that the lessons were about to stop.

Another ride in Kyrgyzstan, another mountain pass, another new highest point (3,600 metres this time) and another absolutely horrendous road led the way to the Chinese border. It was now the end of September and on my last morning in Kyrgyzstan I woke up to water bottles that were frozen solid. That afternoon, as I approached the border, the first snowflakes of the season began to fall. Arriving at the frontier to China I once again had the feeling of excitement in my belly; the borders in Europe had left me with a sense of melancholy, mainly due to their closeness and lack of actual border posts. As I moved further from home, getting to the limit of each new country led to places with even more exotic and far-off names, and to things I'd never seen before. In Kazakhstan it had been the desert, in Kyrgyzstan it had been the mountains and now, as I arrived at the border into China, I had no idea what to expect. But what I did know was that whatever I was going to find, it would be different to anything I had seen until now.

When I arrived, the crossing was closed for the evening; I wasn't sure what to do with myself and made my way to a café. I ordered a pot of tea from the owner, a large Kyrgyz lady in her forties, who asked where I would be spending the night. Following a short explanation, I was told in rudimentary English "You cycle here from England, you no pay for bed."

Grateful just to be indoors, I spent the following few hours and my last few Kyrgyz Soms on more pots of tea that were shared with Atsushi, a Japanese tourist who was also crossing the border in the morning. Just as we were about to go to bed, the husband and sons of the family returned to the café, carrying with them the skinned carcass of a goat. My hopes that this would become an impromptu game of indoor Buzkashi were dashed when the three of them produced an axe, a cleaver and a hacksaw and began to chop up the dead animal, whilst the wife organised the meat into portions that would feed the café's customers the next morning.

In the west we are so detached from our food that the thought of doing something like this would be unpalatable to most, yet that night I watched in amazement as a skilled team of four hacked, sawed and sliced off section after section, until forty minutes later all that was left of the full-sized goat was a batch of meat and a pile of discarded bones. And as the whole scene was played out under the shine of a single forty-watt bulb, it looked like something out of a horror film. It was mesmerising.

While this happened in front of me I began to think about how my time in Kyrgyzstan had changed me as a person. When planning my journey I had met several people who had done big trips before and it was as if I had my face pushed up against the glass, peering in at their lives, wanting to be like them. I would listen to their stories and wonder what it would be like to live that life. Then in Bishkek, I had met an assorted group of cyclists; we spent the day together and as they spoke of the different things that had happened on their tours, not only could I relate to what they were saying, I could also jump in with my own stories.

At that moment it dawned on me that I was no longer merely someone who dreamt of being a cyclist; I was one. Better yet, I was loving it.

Each day, I woke up knowing I would see new things, do something I love and learn continually about the world around me. On top of this, in the previous month I had begun using my ride to raise money for the orphan charity SOS Children's Villages, so now I was enjoying what I was doing *and* was proud to be doing it to help others.

That night, after the axes were put down, the poor goat was all prepared for the morning's customers, and the light went out on that brutal but amazing scene, I went to sleep with a real sense of privilege - for what I was getting to witness on my bike - and pride in the person I was becoming.

It was a beautiful moment.

I woke sharply at 1:30 a.m. in a panic.

I'd hoped to sleep through the night but the instant I woke I knew exactly what was up. When I arrived at the café at 4 p.m., I'd had enough money left over for precisely eight pots of tea and nothing else. Now, at 01:30 in the morning, it had caught up with my bladder and the litres and litres of fluid were looking to escape my body.

I ran to the door and attempted to open it: it was upon the discovery that, for some unknown reason, my host had felt the need to padlock me in the room, things became problematic.

With no way out I had to find an alternative. The only window was eight feet off the ground, so this wasn't an option, and my bike had been left in the main hall of the café, so I had no access to anything on it such as empty water bottles which may have been of use.

After thirty seconds of frantic hopping around the room I spied a glass bottle underneath the wardrobe; I reached under to grab it, only to find it was full.

'*Hmm, maybe I could drink the contents and then relieve myself in the empty bottle?*'

As soon as I opened the bottle, the pungent smell confirmed that a) I wasn't the only person who'd been in this situation and b) I wouldn't be drinking what was inside.

More hopping followed and as I began to start leaking I grabbed the only thing I could find; a child's toy bucket - the sort you get when you go to the seaside to make sandcastles. Filling it to the brim and still needing to go at

51

the end of it was a thoroughly degrading experience, but I managed and somehow drifted back off to sleep, leaving the full bucket on top of the wardrobe.

The next thing I heard was a banging on the door at 6 a.m. the following morning. I grabbed my barbag (the only thing I'd managed to take with me into the room) and ran outside, relieved to get the last few pots of tea out of me. When I returned, the padlock had been replaced. I asked if I could go back in, but seeing that I had my possessions with me, the owner of the café couldn't understand why I needed to and, with a cafe filled with truckers wanting their breakfast, she didn't seem particularly interested.

I took a step back.

Well, you were thinking to yourself last night about how you've become a responsible, proud man. Well the responsible thing to do here is to explain that you've forgotten something and then try to find a way to sneak out that bucket you've left in there. Failing that, the decent thing would be to explain what you've done in there and that you need to get rid of it. And failing that, as a man you should at least try to do something as a way of a heads up and make an apology.

A decent, responsible man would have done any one of those things.

A very small, embarrassed boy with a severely reduced ego got on his bike and descended down into China.

6: No More Soy Sauce

Kashgar may have been only 245 kilometres away from the border, but as I arrived (in doing so seeing my odometer tick over the 10,000 kilometre mark), it was apparent I was now in a completely different world to the one I had been in just days before. On the western edge of the Taklamakan desert, I was now out of the mountains: gone was the quiet countryside, the terrible dirt roads and the market shacks, in their place a vibrant metropolis with asphalt pavements, car horns and department stores.

After the peace and tranquillity of the mountains it was quite a surprise - also surprising, in the most positive way possible, was where I would stay during my time in Kashgar. The Chini Bagh Hotel, a building which used to house the British Counsel, is a Mecca for cyclists; all the blogs that I'd followed, all books that I'd read and all the cyclists I'd seen on the road had mentioned their time here. Furthermore, with Kashgar being the junction for routes into Central Asia, China, Tibet and Pakistan, it was a hub for cyclists to meet, so I knew that with cheap rooms and a good location, the Chini Bagh was the place they would be.

It was an experience not to be missed. Often, when you are looking forward to something as much as I was, it can lead to an anti-climax, but the Chini Bagh didn't disappoint and after cycling straight past the palace-like building once, sceptically thinking that there was no way such a fancy looking place could offer rooms for £3 per night, I was delighted to be proved wrong and shortly after arriving was joined by Alvaro, a mere hour behind me on the road. The following days were great; the hotel was populated with twelve other cyclists, as well as several backpackers, and aside from enjoying the company of others and a chance to let the body rest up after the Kyrgyz mountains, the majority of my time was spent eating, either at restaurants and cafés in the day, or at Kashgar's famous food market at night.

If £3 for a hotel was cheap, then the food was even cheaper and I spent the next few days living like a king.

But, as per usual, I couldn't get too comfy and as Monday came around it was time to get back on the road and say yet more goodbyes. Alvaro was heading to the Karakoram Highway and Pakistan; a few others were hoping to get over into Central Asia before the snow became too heavy, and Sabine and Uli, an Austro-German couple who were on a three year trip and the only other cyclists going my way, had enjoyed Kashgar so much they'd decided to stay for another week.

So I was off into China on my own.

Usually this would have been fine, except that throughout my ride I had vowed to drink the tap water wherever I went in an effort to save money. So far, aside from a few quick dashes to the toilet in Georgia, this had been no problem; that was until I got a couple of hours' ride outside of Kashgar.

Having uncontrollable dysentery is unpleasant. Having a migraine is head-crackingly painful. And having the two at the same time is unbearable. But this is what happened and I spent my first night back on the road sleeping rough in a small clearing, repeatedly vomiting whilst desperately trying not to soil myself.

I didn't always succeed in this task; realising the filth I was surrounding myself with, and in order to stay at least the tiniest bit hygienic, I created a system: in my mind I created a clock and every time I knew another wave of illness was coming I would go to the next number on my mental timepiece. So, for example, the first time I could tell something was about to come out I would run five steps to one o'clock and back to bed, the next wave I would run five steps to two o'clock then back to bed, the next bout would see me run to three o'clock and so on. It seemed fool-proof, although the downside was that this plan would only work if I could keep my bowel movements to less than twelve per night. By the time daylight came back around I was up to seventeen o'clock on my system. It was not a pleasant night.

Foul smelling and still feeling terrible, I planned to ride on to the next town, but found I was too weak to pedal. Unable to cycle, I decided the next best strategy would be to lie by the side of the road in the hope that a local would stop to help me. It took an eternity to crawl back with my possessions to the verge and for the next six hours I lay flat out. Not a single vehicle stopped (I don't think I looked as conspicuous as I had hoped) and the few people who did walk past, having realised I couldn't speak their language, simply carried on with their lives, leaving me where I was. At some point in mid-afternoon a local field worker came over and put his hand on my forehead; almost wincing at the temperature coming from me, he shook his head and walked away. He didn't come back.

I was on my own here and I decided to try and push on to the next town. Despite not having any appetite, I forced myself to nibble at my provisions throughout the day and by the end of the afternoon, with my body noticeably recovering, managed to get on my bike and cycle a further sixteen miles. I stopped for the night in a ditch by the side of the road, successfully ate and kept down a large pack of super noodles, and I woke the next morning to find myself a changed man. Yes, what was coming out of me wasn't solid, but my legs had strength again and my body felt like I could ride. Yangshuo was the next town on my map and I arrived in mid-afternoon. I still wasn't 100%, but I was gaining strength by the minute. I decided to go against my better judgement and carry on riding, surmising I was over the worst of my illness.

Big mistake.

The day I left Yangshuo and the following day were fine, but then I was awoken in the night by the dysentery, vomiting and sweating, all back with a vengeance. Since becoming ill, and for the first time on my ride, I really started to notice my struggle with the language barrier and given how bad my condition now was and that the nearest town was a mere twenty miles away, I decided to try and get there to rest. The road may have been flat, there may have been no wind, but with my body in such a bad state, I was forced to give up when the sun went down, an entire day's effort yielding just fourteen miles travelled.

Another night by the side of the road, another night of dysentery, another night of severe headaches. As the sun came up the following morning, I got back on the bike and slogged out the final nineteen miles to town in just over six hours. Finding that it was a further thirteen miles than the map had stated was a particularly low point.

Having not washed properly since the start of my illness, my misery was complete when I checked in to a hotel only to find that they currently had no running water. The last meal I'd had in Kashgar had been heavily doused in soy sauce and now, as the smell of that, mixed with my own faeces, enveloped me and my clothes, I realised just how sick I had been over the previous days.

Over the course of the next few hours I carefully washed my body with a bar of soap and the small remaining contents of my water bottle before changing clothes, hosing myself down with deodorant and going to find an internet café: I was sick. If I'd been at home I'd have wanted a mother's love; just because I was 10,000 km away this wasn't any different and I wanted to e-mail Mum.

This should have been simple, but during the 2008 Olympic period, in a move that was essentially so they could spy on and monitor every single bit of online activity from outsiders, the Chinese government had passed a law which meant that until they said otherwise, all foreigners who wanted to use the internet were not permitted to do so, unless they registered their passport details with the owner of the internet café and this person then registered them on a government database. It's not a policy I condone, but in the condition I was in I wasn't going to argue. To my extreme frustration, the owner (of the only internet café in town) and his friends had no idea how to read my passport. They called several other people, tried putting each separate number into each separate box on their computer, but none of what they entered matched what the government database wanted to see and after an hour of trying I was told I couldn't use the internet.

I gestured to ask if I could send simply one e-mail; it was made clear that without my name on the government database I wasn't allowed anywhere near a computer.

I went back to the hotel. I'd not slept more than four hours a night on any of the previous days, the whole time projectile vomiting, crapping myself and smelling like a sewer; all I wanted to do was speak to my mother and now I couldn't even do that.

As I entered my room the smell from my clothes of rotting soy sauce that had already been through my digestive system hit me and I instantly felt sick again. I got into bed and cried my eyes out.

For the next three days I did as little as possible and, with the aid of some medication and a few good meals inside me, my strength grew and grew. By the time I woke for my fourth morning in town I was well and truly ready to get back on the bike and ride off into the desert, where over the next twenty-two days I covered 1,700 miles non-stop to Xining, the eastern outpost of the Taklamakan. For the most part a flat desert road and mild weather combined for an easy journey, whilst the vast open spaces meant that at the end of each day I could simply pull off to the side of the road and sleep rough under the stars. With no people or animals around and the nearest town usually at least thirty miles away, to be able to lie outdoors at night and know how alone I was was a freedom I never grew tired of.

As the days went by, desert turned into desert plateau, warm days turned into cold nights and as I got closer to Xining the people began to change as well. Xinjiang region in the west of China - with legitimate claims to being its own country - is historically home to the Uyghur people and despite the recent influx of Han Chinese, the area maintains a very Central Asian feel. However, the further from Kashgar I got, the fewer Uyghurs I saw and with a population of two million, Xining was what I counted as my first proper *Chinese* city.

I hated my three days there.

As I arrived in town, a group of young men shouted 'Hey Laowai (foreigner), FUCK YOU' before throwing a rock at me and things didn't get much better when, after having checked into the second hotel I visited (having been physically pushed out the door of the first due to their 'no foreigner' rule) I went for a walk around town. A high level of pollution left a disgusting layer of smog hanging over the city, whilst at street level the local population constantly spat on the floor of public buildings and threw any bit of litter they had either onto the street or into the town's river.

It was a sharp introduction to what would prove to be recurring themes in China - spitting, littering, pollution - and whilst over the next few weeks I grew accustomed to ordering meals from waitresses who would hock up large amounts of phlegm as they wrote down what I wanted, and no longer batted an eyelid when I saw mothers encourage their young children to literally crap all over their own doorstep, and even once I got past the complete lack of regard for their own environment, what I struggled with even more in China was the people's attitudes towards me.

Having been gone for over half a year by now I was used to the reactions that both my skin colour and my bicycle drew, but the Han took their inquisitiveness to a whole new level. During my two days in Xining, everywhere I went people would stop and stare; turning a corner would lead to someone making the shout of '*Laowai*' to let everyone know I was coming; even when simply trying to be alone I would get hassled. Sitting in a café for lunch, I had one man come up to me and grab my beard, seemingly to see if it was real. Twenty minutes later, a different man came up and started pulling at my arm hair, apparently for the same reason. Trying to start a conversation or even saying 'hello' in Chinese would result in either fits of laughter at my expense or the gazers simply glaring at me like I was some sort of alien, before walking off with their back turned.

I tried so hard to be polite throughout my time in Xining and put in real effort with the locals, but when I saw that the majority of people had no interest in speaking with me and that for many I was simply an object of fun, for the first time it felt like there was a wall between me and the people whose country I was in. It made me sad.

It was a divide I would feel all the way throughout China.

This is not to say I disliked China. I will not hide my disdain for the big cities, but once outside the more populated areas, I found - as is the case anywhere in the world - the people of the countryside were far more relaxed. In the mountains I discovered the landscape to possess a striking natural beauty and on the road, my journey was supplemented with some of the best local food I'd had yet; restaurants sold meals consisting of all kinds of varieties of noodles and soups which were mine for 50p or less, whilst outdoors, hardy street vendors would brave the cold, light fires in oil drums and fry potatoes mixed with spices which retailed at around fifteen pence per bag and were a perfect snack for carb loading.

I welcomed both the spicy food and the numerous cups

of green tea I was drinking, as the further into November we got the colder the weather was becoming. On the road into Xining I had woken several times to frozen water bottles and speckles of snow on the tent; now, leaving a city that already had an altitude of 2,275 metres and heading south towards the mountains of Sichuan, the elevations grew, the mercury dropped and the first heavy snow of the year began to fall.

My first night above the snow line was spent indoors, thanks to two students from a local university - a Chinese girl and her Tibetan friend - who, after professing their love for David Beckham, had felt the need to kindly buy me a hotel bed for the evening. However, the following day I was on my own again, climbing higher into the mountains, before camping on around fifteen centimetres of snow. That night, as inside the tent I hugged my hot-water bottles, outside a further batch of snow was coming down, so that when I rose the next morning everything as far as the eye could see was covered in a glorious white.

Marvelling at the scene in front of me, I struck camp and made my way to the road, the asphalt covered in a layer of sheet ice several centimetres thick. I thought I would try to ride anyway… the time on my odometer for my first fall of the day was zero minutes and seven seconds; it was the first of many.

The morning was slow progress, but as the sun came up and the time approached midday the ice gradually melted away, meaning I could at least ride on the tarmac again. This, though, created a different problem when, as I gained speed coming downhill, the now defrosted ice flew up off my tyres onto my gears, freezing both the cables and the mechanisms solid, meaning I couldn't change gear. In areas as hilly as this, where gear changes were frequent, I had to find a solution quickly. Continually boiling fresh snow to pour on the frozen cables would take too long, so I settled on a far simpler fix: being a logical thinker it dawned on me that the best method for getting a warm supply of water was to drink a large supply of cold water, let nature take its course and when needed, simply urinate on the bike.

With the bike heavily dowsed in remnants of yellow snow, I found riding through this weather enjoyable, even if a Laowai on a bike made a perfect snowball target for children. As I came through several Tibetan villages, I basked in the novelty of being in the wonderland conditions; the sun beaming down on me, the numerous Pikas - small gerbil like creatures - running around and the temperature barely above zero. Alas, the novelty soon wore off that evening.

Of course I was prepared for cold weather, but I never thought I would see snow on my ride and so the previous night, unbeknownst to me, I had made several mistakes in my camping location, the consequence of which was that the end of my sleeping bag was drenched. As I camped that night the temperature plummeted to minus twelve degrees and the end of the sleeping bag froze, along with large portions of my socks and toes. Cold weather, if you're prepared, is something that's easily dealt with; I was massively unprepared and saw that night through shivering in my tent, smacking clenched fists at the ground as the first symptoms of hypothermia set in and whimpering as the three biggest toes on my left foot froze. It would be six weeks before I regained any feeling in them.

Thankful isn't the word for when the sun came back up, although my gratitude was short-lived. After I'd pushed my frozen feet into my frozen shoes and it had taken an hour and a half to get the tent down, the cold finally got the better of me when, back by the side of the road, I tried to boil a cup of tea only to find both of my cigarette lighters refusing to work. The rational response would have been to get on the bike and carry on to somewhere warm. Instead I was far more primal; I smashed the cigarette lighter into tiny little pieces and then stood in the middle of the road, shouting at

the top of my voice to the deserted mountains:
"I WANT MY FUCKING MUMMY."

Getting back on the bike that day gave my body enough warmth to continue on to the town of Zoige, where, thanks to hotels costing only £1.60 per night, I was able to thaw out over the next two days. Not wanting to get caught in the snow any longer, I crossed the final pass of 3,885 metres with great relief and descended down below the snowline to Chengdu, the biggest city in Sichuan.

I have always loved my food, but in China - with both its quality and its price - I had begun to cross the line from 'food enthusiast' to 'comfort eater' and as I arrived in Chengdu, still with no feeling in my toes and stressed from the previous week's endeavours, I ate until I threw up.

Frozen, sick and struggling with the local population, my health - both mental and physical - was at an all time low.

7: Listening To The Rice Grow

Just how much of an effect China was having on my mental health became apparent when ten days after leaving Chengdu my chain snapped, taking with it my rear derailleur. For the first time my bike was completely immobile and although I was fortunate enough to be taken in by the police that evening (who kindly hosted and fed me), I did have to take the bus to Kunming the next morning in order to get the necessary repairs done. I had jumped 200 kilometres in one go and now the bike was fixed I was left with a dilemma: should I turn around and go back to where the bike had broken, or simply continue my journey from Kunming?

On the one hand I had set myself the challenge to cycle as much of the world as I could. On the other I was aware I was doing this trip for my own enjoyment; thus, if I hadn't been happy in a place, then it made little sense to go back. After much deliberation I decided to carry on from Kunming, writing off the 200 kilometres I had skipped.

With that, China became the first country to officially defeat me.

The following days towards Laos I kept myself to myself. Having struggled so much with the Chinese people I had become insular and instead of looking for social occasions I spent more time than usual on the bike. I was anxious to stay on the move and seldom bothered with the tent, instead choosing to sleep rough in lay-bys or abandoned buildings. The climate was now almost tropical and whilst the ride in Yunnan - with its continual thirty kilometre climbs and descents, interspersed with signs warning to watch out for wild elephants - was aesthetically beautiful, I was mentally beaten and just wanted to be out of the country. My final day in China saw me cycle ninety miles up and down mountains, before arriving at the Laotian frontier at 11 p.m., where I slept rough on the doorstep of a shop. The next morning I made sure I was the first to cross the border when it opened.

Never has a border crossing symbolised the difference between neighbouring countries more than that between China and Laos. On the Chinese side, the heavily armed border patrol performed drills in a disciplined manner with military music blaring overhead. Meanwhile, a couple of kilometres down the road the relaxed nature of Laos was on full display, as their border consisted of a lone guard, no blockade and an immigration office which opened half an hour later than scheduled for no discernable reason.

After the commotion of China with its noise, population density and pollution, coming into laid-back Laos felt like breathing a massive sigh of relief. After two months of having 'Laowai' shouted at me wherever I went, entering Laos to shouts of 'Sabbadee' (hello) from local children felt indescribably good; I was seen as a person again.

The first night I spent camping at a local monastery before the following morning, when 110 kilometres from Luang Prabang - a Unesco World Heritage Village and my next planned rest stop - the chain broke again. I had feared this might happen when it had gone originally in China and I had considered buying a new chain tool (the piece of equipment that puts links back into chains). I hadn't done so, as I knew that for Christmas (now less than two weeks away) my parents had sent out a parcel containing new tools to Vientiane, the Laotian capital. Thinking I would be fine without one for a mere ten days, I had ignored the golden rule of cycle maintenance: whichever tool it is that you don't have, that's the exact one you're going to need next.

True to form, the chain link broke again and, just as it had done previously, snapped my derailleur. This time it had gone one better, as aside from just snapping, my

64

derailleur bent into the wheels, ripping part of the rear hub.

For the second time in two weeks I yet again had an incapacitated bicycle. With little other option I thumbed down the next bus heading to town, had the bike lashed to its roof and climbed aboard to Luang Prabang.

Whereas in China I had been devastated when this had happened, in Laos I really didn't mind; given that I could get a hotel room with a double bed for £3, and that it was rapidly approaching Christmas, I decided to treat myself to a few days off. I arrived at a guesthouse and was delighted to find that two of the other guests were Matt and Mary, the Anglo-Aussie cyclists who had come up with the solution to my Chinese visa problem all the way back in Kazakhstan and a happy reunion followed.

A couple of days' searching took place, but in truth I needed roughly about half an hour to know that I would not find any decent bike parts in this sleepy town, so with no other solution I took the bus to Vientiane, spent four days hunting down a spare rear derailleur, before making the twelve hour bus journey back to Luang Prabang on Christmas Eve.

Due to delays our bus arrived at midnight local time in Luang Prabang. In Laos, pretty much all businesses close at eleven and the streets are dead by eleven-thirty, so settling for what I could find, my first Christmas on the road began by waking up at 06:30 after a night in a £2 bus station box room, to a breakfast of day-old sticky rice, after which I sat under my mosquito net, opening the presents that had been sent out from home.

With a fixed bike I was once again faced with the same decision I'd had to make in China; did I go back to where the bike had broken or carry on from where I was? This time it was easy. Laos was a country I loved being in, so, not only did I go back to where I'd stopped riding, I cycled there as well, adding an extra 110 kilometres to my journey.

Feeling slightly better about my Chinese cheating, the ride that followed from Luang Prabang to Vientianne would become one of my favourite stretches of road. With beautiful scenery and three separate climbs of sixteen, twenty and eighteen kilometres over four days I was in my element and as I did this - exactly eight months to the day since leaving home - my odometer clicked over 10,000 miles. I stopped the bike, inhaled a deep breath and took in the scene of where I was; tropical weather, jungle on either side of me and brightly coloured birds flying overhead. I had come a long way.

New Year's Eve was spent in the vile party town of Vang Vieng before returning to Vientiane - a city which history will note for its impressive collection of internet cafés and little else - this time managing to arrive on my bike.

During my first visit I had asked the bike shop's owner to order me in a new rear hub and frustratingly I returned to find that he hadn't done this. Unable to get the replacement part anywhere else, it will come as no surprise that four days later my rear wheel locked up completely and infuriatingly, for the third time in a little more than a month, I had to take a lift to the next town. This time it was just fifty-six kilometres to Savannahket - a small town located on the Mekong river - but it was immediately apparent that I wouldn't be able to get a new hub here. Given that the only other alternative would have been to return to Vientiane for a third time, I chose to fork off in a new direction; I took a bus over the bridge of the Mekong to Mukdahan, Thailand.

In 1964, as part of their attempt to destroy the North Vietnamese army (parts of which had joined forces with groups in Laos), the USA chose to spend the next nine years dropping over 2,000,000 tonnes of explosives on the Laotian countryside. As a result of this continual assault, Laos gained the dubious honour of being per capita the most bombed country in the world and, with an estimated 30% of these bombs dropped failing to detonate, it also means that there are still somewhere around seventy million unexploded bombs littering rural Laos today. Stories of people, particularly children, being injured or killed by these as they are stumbled upon remain depressingly frequent.

Knowing this, I had felt nervous as to how I - as a westerner - would be received upon entering Laos.

Of course finding the Laotians to be some of the kindest and - especially given what they'd been through - most peaceful people on earth had been a wonderful discovery, but if I had been slightly apprehensive about entering Laos because of something that had happened forty years ago, I felt far more conscientious entering Thailand because of something that was going on in the present day.

Before I go any further I should state that I know that many people go to Thailand and behave responsibly and respectfully and leave the country having been excellent guests. However from my experiences, both from people at home and fellow travellers of the eighteen to twenty-five demographic, I knew a lot of people in my age group saw Thailand as little more than a playground in which they could indulge in booze, drugs, one night stands and prostitution. It certainly wasn't everyone, but if you think it's a small minority then you're quite frankly kidding yourself and - prostitutes aside - it wasn't gender specific: when you hear firsthand accounts from backpackers listing the numerous drugs they have done, or an Australian girl telling you how many times she's had sex in public during her six weeks in Thailand, or an English man telling you how much he paid for a Thai hooker to do indescribable acts with a goldfish and a banana, then it's hard to not feel a bit embarrassed to be from the same culture as these people.

As I entered Thailand - a place I had not planned to go to - my main thought was '*what must the locals make of all this?'*

I knew I was being stupid in this and much like with Laos my apprehensions were misplaced. Yes, there were things that depressed me greatly and seeing drunk westerners, not to mention countless men in their forties, fifties or even sixties with Thai girls who could not have been past their late teens, was depressing, but the sight of the locals not batting an eyelid was also noticeable. After getting my bike fixed at one of the numerous shops in town and riding an extra fifty-six kilometres in order to make up for the cheated stretch (I was still feeling guilty over my Chinese bus ride) I found a country with friendly people, high quality food at the street markets and a warmth that left me often feeling humbled.

One of my favourite memories of Thailand was when, after having got caught out with nowhere to camp, I stopped to sit in a bus shelter. A local policeman came past, saw who I was and asked me to follow his car. Thinking he was going to take me back to town to pay for a hotel, I was overjoyed to find that instead he took me back to his own house, where that night his family erected a mosquito net for me to sleep under. A night under the stars on his balcony was blissful and the following morning he, his wife and I dined on a traditional Thai breakfast of Johk - a thick rice soup containing cuts of pork - before I set off towards the Cambodian border.

My own preconceptions of what Thailand would be like were moronic; I knew that before I'd even entered the country. But I hadn't expected the people to have been as welcoming as they were and as I headed towards Cambodia and the famous temples of Angkor Wat, I was slightly sad to be leaving.

Forty kilometres short of Cambodia's proudest location I was joined by Bella and Jean, two people who had become integral to my life during the first three weeks of 2009.

68

I had first met Bella and Jean several weeks previously on New Year's Day. For New Year's Eve I had been in Vang Vieng, Laos, the disgusting tourist town known for its TV cafés and the activity of tubing, a pursuit which consists of being driven up river and floating back down to town via numerous riverside bars. I'd had no desire to stop here - a town seemingly filled with people who had flown halfway around the world to get as drunk as possible as quickly as they could - but, not having had a night out since Slava had attempted to marinade my liver in Kazakh vodka five months previously, and realising I would be here for New Year's, it had seemed logical to stop for the night.

I hated the place and was looking forward to leaving the next morning, but as I was about to depart I was approached by Bruce, a Canadian cyclist in his fifties. Bruce invited me for dinner with some other cyclists he'd met and whilst I usually would have said no, my hangover got the better of me and I decided to cancel my journey and stay for one more night. It was at this dinner that I met Jean and Bella, a French-Canadian father and daughter who were spending four months cycling together to celebrate Bella's graduating university.

Bella and I hit it off instantly and over the next few weeks would be continually finding ways to see each other; we met up again in Vientiane and when Bella and Jean had left a day earlier than me I had ridden into the night the following evening to track them down at their hotel. In turn, when my bike had broken in Savannahkhet and I'd gone to Thailand, unbeknownst to me they had changed their route and followed me towards Siem Reap.

In the time since I'd gone to Thailand I'd resigned myself to the fact that I'd never see her again; something I'd come to accept about pretty much everyone I was meeting. With Bella though, it was different; in her I'd met someone I wanted to see again, so finding that she'd put in the effort to come and find me left me feeling elated.

They finally caught me about forty kilometres from the city and we spent the next three nights in a hotel. Siem Reap was four days from Phnom Penh and despite having spent the best part of three weeks growing ever closer, we knew that in the Cambodian capital our paths went in different directions and that it would be the last time we would see each other on the road. On our last night in Siem Reap, Bella came to my room and didn't leave again until morning.

Being a man who has just spent the night with a woman for the first time in close to a year, the last person you want to see the next morning is the girl's father. Luckily for me, Jean understood our feelings and with them off on a pre-booked boat across the lake, we agreed to meet again in a couple of days in Phnom Penh.

I rode to Phnom Penh with a spring in my step and as we spent more time together, we realised, yet tried to ignore, the reality that soon we would be saying goodbye: neither of us wanted to, but we both knew we had to and after a teary-eyed farewell, I watched Bella ride off (knowing that I'd successfully hidden a present for her in her panniers that she would find several hours later), feeling terribly sad that we had had to part ways, for I knew the chances were I'd never see her again. And yet, as she disappeared out of sight, a warm glow spread inside of me; after having spent nine months alone, for the first time I had met someone with whom I could share my adventures and to whom I could listen in return. For those three brief weeks, I had not felt like I was travelling alone anymore.

During my first few weeks in South-East Asia I had begun to feel... not lonely, but isolated, in the sense that I often found myself on the outside looking in at other people's groups and social circles. I was welcomed by fellow travellers and would spend evenings with them

70

discussing whatever came about, but it seemed like to every non-cyclist I met I was nothing more than 'the bicycle guy': I wasn't better or worse, just different.

During this time I had also started to become jealous of other people's relationships. I had become so independent in my lifestyle that I was used to being on my own; even so, watching couples travel together, absorb experiences together and even argue together made me realise that whilst I loved what I was doing, it did leave me very much alone.

Whenever I would get this feeling over the coming months, I would look back at the pictures of myself with Bella, see how happy I was in those pictures and be thankful for the time we spent together.

These memories would see me through some very dark days.

8: Why I Came

In 1975 the Khmer Rouge, led by the son of a rice farmer named Saloth Sar - a man more commonly known as Pol Pot - came to power in Cambodia. With the dream of creating a self-sufficient agrarian society devoid of money, the main obstacle to this goal was that Cambodia had a lack of food, a large population and in Phnom Penh, a large city. Their solution was simple; move people out of the cities, create large work camps in the countryside and kill anyone who raised even the slightest question about what was going on.

Shortly after coming into control the Khmer Rouge followed through with their plans, beginning by performing a mass evacuation of Phnom Penh. The reign of terror continued over the next four years and accompanied by the slogan 'To keep you is no benefit, to destroy you is no loss'; the regime would be responsible for the deaths of an estimated 2,000,000 people in one of the most severe genocides the world has ever seen. The killing would only stop four years later, when the Khmer Rouge lost control of the country and their leaders fled to the jungle.

Thirty years down the line, for those who want to try and understand the scale of just what went on, visitors are today invited to visit several of the sites where these atrocities took place. The Killing Fields - mass graves in which those executed were killed and buried - and Tuol Sleng - a former city-centre school which upon the evacuation of the capital became the regime's torture centre - are both now open to the public and during my ten days in Phnom Penh I visited both. They were harrowing trips and through statistics such as, that of the 17,000 people who came through the doors of Tuol Sleng just twelve are known to have survived, it becomes obvious just how dark the tragedy was here.

However, as shocking as these places are when trying to visualise what had happened, the aspect that hit me most was the idea of the ghost town: at just over 2,000,000, Phnom Penh's population is similar today to that prior to the genocide of 1975, and as I rode in I tried to visualise the whole place being completely deserted. Mentally removing all aspects of life - children playing, tuc-tuc's buzzing up and down the streets, car horns blaring long into the night - and replacing them with nothing but streets and streets of abandoned buildings, I began to appreciate the scale of what had taken place during the time of the Khmer Rouge's rule.

The added thought that the number who had died would be roughly the same as the population of the city today added extra context. It was a chilling introduction to what is nowadays a beautiful city.

Another constant reminder of the Khmer Rouge's rule comes in the form of land-mines; in their efforts to control where the population could and couldn't go, the regime had mined the countryside to the extent that even now, thirty years on, there are still thought to be around 6,000,000 explosive devices in rural Cambodia. It was, indirectly, because of this that I came into contact with one of the most inspirational people I have ever met. It came about because my dad is a regular poster on a QPR message board and, having spotted another user with the location of Phnom Penh, he had e-mailed to explain that as I was a QPR fan and would be cycling through, the fellow supporter might be interested in meeting up. That person was John Honney, who at the time was working at ground level for the Cambodia Trust Charity, an organisation which gives prosthetic limbs to land mine victims. He had replied in an instant, with an offer for me to stay with him for as long as I wanted and we instantly hit it off.

With an easy-going nature and what is best described as a very *English* sense of humour, he was not only a fun person to be around, but also a highly impressive individual. Aside from the humble nature of his work, I was in awe as he told me stories of how, before he'd ended up in Cambodia, he'd travelled the world several times - including a stint working as a death row lawyer in Atlanta - and as a side project had also set himself the lifetime challenge of running the five major world marathons - London, Berlin, Boston, Chicago and New York - a challenge of which he had only New York left to do. I was even more impressed to find that he'd done all of this on one leg (his left leg was amputated from the knee down in early childhood), but John was not someone to let something like a prosthetic body part get in the way of achieving what he wanted in life and over the next ten days as his guest I found myself in a continual state of amazement at what he had achieved in his years on earth.

Leaving Phnom Penh wasn't easy. In the days I'd been there John and I had gotten on well, spending the evenings watching movies, sharing meals and discussing QPR's greatest moments (depressingly short conversations), so having already said one emotional goodbye to Bella it proved just as difficult to say goodbye to John - another person who had become a true friend.

Leaving at 6 a.m. I dipped out of the city before it awoke - visualising the ghost town one last time - and made my way towards the coastal town of Sihanoukville, where en route I met a mango farmer named Chanlor who insisted I stay the night with him. Being one of the few Cambodians I came across who spoke English, I was delighted to accept his offer and the opportunity to find out about his life.

"Four years ago," he told me, "I had a very good job in Phnom Penh; I studied there and got a job working for an international technology company. I got to travel to China and to Singapore, it was a good job but I did not like it as I was indoors all day. I was not happy. And now look at me; I live here on the farm, I spend all day with my brothers (in Cambodia your co-workers are your brothers), we all sleep in the same room and I am poor. But I am happy."

Despite his education, he had chosen to live the quiet life on the mango farm.

The following morning, with a pannier full of mangoes, I carried on my journey to the coast, dipping a ceremonial toe in the Gulf of Thailand, before turning left towards Vietnam and the Mekong Delta.

As I left Cambodia I looked back on my time in the country and thought about what Chanlor had said. Along with Laos, Cambodia had been the poorest country I'd been to. Both of these places had seen death and destruction on an almost unimaginable scale and both had a population with legitimate reason for disliking and distrusting foreigners. And yet both had been filled with the kindest, most relaxed people I'd met.

On my way into Phnom Penh I had gotten a puncture outside a local's house just as dark was setting in; despite his lack of English, the man instantly assumed that I would need a place to stay for the night and without even so much as a formal invite ushered me into his house. That night I had joined him and his family, as we sat in candlelight around a radio - the only piece of technology they owned - listening to music and sharing a supper of rice and fish before we all slept in the one large room of his house, each under a separate mosquito net.

This was just one example of the many kindnesses I received in these countries and be it in the form of offering a place to stay, a bit of fruit to keep me going on the journey or even a swig of the awful homemade Tequila that one Laotian car mechanic insisted on me, throughout these places the local people had a smile on their faces and a welcome in their hearts.

"I am poor, but I am happy."

The poverty levels in both these countries are hard to

conceptualise, but that one sentence summed up so much of life in Laos and Cambodia.

As I crossed into Vietnam I thought about Chanlor and his brothers, sleeping out under the stars in their hammocks on the mango farm. I smiled.

When I first came up with the idea of my ride, Vietnam was the one place more than any other that I had looked forward to visiting; I don't know if it was the history, the food, or the travel shows I'd seen on TV, but for whatever reason, I'd been desperate to visit the country. With this in mind, it was something of a disappointment to find that pretty much everyone I'd met who had been to Vietnam absolutely hated the place. Their complaints were varied, ranging from the noise to the pollution, from the aggressive street vendors to the overcharging shop owners, but the one thing all these people had in common was that they wouldn't be going back.

With my enthusiasm dented somewhat, I found my first few days in the country to be surprisingly relaxing. In Ho Chi Minh I stayed with Jake and Mai, a young Anglo-Vietnamese couple who had married just three months previously and as they told me the story of how they had overcome obstacles to be together, I felt happy to be around a couple whose relationship had worked out, especially as until this point, particularly in South Asia, the main romances I'd seen hadn't had happy endings.

Back in Laos I had met a Chinese lady who was having an affair with a Laotian girl and she had told me how she was sneaking behind her partner's back for the weekend by coming across the border. When I saw her again the following week she was distraught, as the girl she'd been seeing had wanted to meet to tell her that in turn, she had been having an affair and wanted to break things off. In an unrelated set of events, I had come back to my guest house on Christmas Day to find an Australian man in tears. When

76

I asked what was wrong he opened his heart and told me how he and his girlfriend had been together for eight years and had planned their current trip as one last hurrah before settling down to get married. Now, two months into the trip his girlfriend had had enough and - of all days - had chosen Christmas to tell him that she would not only be leaving him, but would also be carrying on travelling for a further six months without him. I've rarely seen a man look as distraught as he did and he confided that as there was no way she would change her mind, he'd spent the rest of his remaining travel budget on the first flight home, which left the following morning. I had felt even more sorry for him when two days later I saw his former girlfriend in a beer garden, arm in arm with another man. Worse yet, a week later I saw her walking the streets with another man in Vientiane. By the time I saw her in an embrace on the lake front in Phnom Penh with yet another man, I decided that he was probably best off without her.

But having seen all of these relationships try and fail, meeting Jake and Mai was a breath of fresh air, for their story was far more uplifting; they had studied together at university in the UK and when Mai had gone back to Vietnam, fearing he would never see her again, Jake had flown to Ho Chi Minh and proposed. A little over a year down the line here they were, settling happily into married life and I enjoyed a wonderful few days with them, as despite the crescendo of motor bikes and car horns I found Ho Chi Minh City to have a vibrant charm.

Leaving the city, with 1,800 kilometres between myself and Hanoi, I had two options: one route would take me along the coast, the other would take me through the mountains. I decided on a route that was a mix of the two, cycling through the mountains for 1,000 kilometres, before coming down to the ocean at the city of Danang and along the coastal road until Hanoi for the northern section of the country.

This seemed like a good plan and everything went smoothly until I arrived in Dalat, where the rear hub I had purchased in Thailand broke. Now in need of another new part, for the first time I noticed the Vietnamese attitude towards money. I had always laughed it off when people had warned me; but when the only place in Dalat I could find demanded $150 for a piece of equipment that should cost no more than $35, I realised that there was some truth in it. I refused to pay that much, trying to point out that for that price I could fly to Bangkok, buy the part there and then fly back. I was told that if I didn't want to pay his price then maybe I should do that. Instead, I took a $6 night bus back to Ho Chi Minh, where after six days of searching I finally managed to locate a new hub; I got a new wheel built for a mere $50 and promptly got the bus back to Dalat. If having a broken bicycle is the most depressing feeling you can have as a cyclist, getting mobile again is without doubt one of the best and I left, ecstatic to be free again.

Dalat is a disgusting little tourist trap of a town, but I loved the mountains. The hills stretched my legs, the people of the countryside were friendly and the altitude meant that despite the ever rising heat, at night time it was cool enough to not have to worry about annoyances such as mosquitoes.

As much as I loved the rolling hills of the highlands, I despised my time coming along the coast in equal measure.

Things didn't begin well: after descending to sea level and arriving in the ode to concrete that is Danang, on my way out of town I had the first serious road accident of the tour. A little girl (who couldn't have been older than ten) had cleverly tried to balance five litres of water on her bicycle handle bars; this clearly wasn't going to work, but it hadn't stopped her trying and as she pushed off, the weight of the water swung her bike out into the road, meaning that unless I swerved I was going to wipe her out completely. As I made my evasive action, a motorbike came from behind and crashed into my rear pannier, sending me and the bike skidding uncontrollably into the middle of the road.

I've been hit once before (much more seriously, in West London, when a van had pulled out into me), but the feeling is still the same: for that split second your life is no longer in your own hands and what happens next depends entirely on what else is happening around you.

Fortunately for me the collision had left enough time for the traffic behind us to stop and after somehow landing on my feet I managed to quickly pick up the bike and scurry back to safety. The motorcyclist who had hit me took one look at what had happened, decided he wanted nothing to do with it and sped off into the distance. This didn't surprise me, although it was slightly disappointing, as the crash was in no way his fault. Meanwhile, the girl who had caused the crash simply stood sheepishly by the side of the road.

So, with my first accident under my belt, things had already started badly on my coastal journey and didn't get much better over the next few days, as I found that for the first time in a while I was no longer a man on a bicycle; I was a walking wallet. As a tourist, particularly in less economically developed countries, you expect local business owners to try and squeeze every penny they can out of you and as a rule if you're paying close to what the locals are paying then you're doing OK. This is frustrating, but understandable, and it's usually only in specific tourist towns and cities. Instead, along the Vietnamese coast it was ubiquitous; every single stall or shop owner would squeeze every penny they could out of you. It wouldn't just be small price rises either - attempting to be charged four, five or sometimes even six times the correct price became something of a norm at local markets. It became frustrating very quickly and meant that long after leaving the country, one of the most vivid memories I have of Vietnam is of a shopkeeper publicly chastising his assistant for selling me a bunch of bananas at the correct price.

I didn't enjoy the next few days and although I did meet some friendly people, most notably a local motorcyclist who rode beside me to chat for a few hours whilst joyfully pointing out every roadside prostitute we saw along the way, and then a restaurant owner who let me sleep on his eatery floor when a storm outside made the roads unrideable, for the most part I had found the people cold towards me.

The final straw came on the day before Hanoi, when I asked a group of local farmers if I could camp near their fields. They had welcomed me in and after I had cooked my dinner and spent an hour entertaining some of the local people's children, I set up camp and prepared for bed. Fifteen minutes later - and with no clue as to why - the farmer came back with a very changed tune, ordering me to get off his land. Confused as to what was going on, I protested, but it was made clear to me that if I didn't leave he would be chopping my tent up with a pair of scissors. I slowly packed up my things and left, eventually sleeping a few kilometres down the road.

The whole issue had left a sour taste in my mouth; I had no idea what I'd done wrong, I had been friends with both the man and his family and also had several pictures of his sons that they had insisted on taking (pictures I soon deleted after the confrontation), so to have had my possessions threatened for no obvious reason was not a nice experience.

A brief rest in Hanoi and it was back to the Chinese border.

Having been so desperate to leave China the first time around, I was surprised at just how keen I was to get back there, such had become my disillusion with Vietnam. I had spent six weeks in the country and other than the mountains and my time with Jake and Mai, I had hated nearly every moment of it; the noise of the road, the people over-charging and the constant shouts of 'GIVE ME A

DOLLAR' from the local children wore me down. After having spent such a relaxing time in Laos, Thailand and Cambodia, in my own ignorance I had expected a similar welcome in Vietnam.

I hadn't got it and whilst I could understand the reasons behind the hostility from certain locals given the history - this was, after all what I had expected in Laos and Cambodia - I had not expected people to be as cold or as money-centred as they were.

A statistic that stands out to me is that of the people who visit Thailand, 50% will return again in the future. In comparison, of those who visit Vietnam, only 5% will ever go back.

Vietnam is and always will be a significant place for me personally; aside from being the first place where I was hit by a motorbike, or the first place where a local would threaten to cut up my tent with scissors, it will also always be the first place I ever dreamed of cycling to. Back in early 2006, when I had first started riding, it had been the idea of rolling into Ho Chi Minh City that had been the mental goal of any challenge I was going to set myself. Now three years down the line, I realised that things don't always pan out quite as you hope, and that the vision of Vietnam I had in my head was far different to the reality of the place.

As I crossed into China I was glad that I had been to Vietnam. At the same time I knew I was a member of the 95% who wouldn't be going back.

9: 'But If There Was Hope, It Lay In The Proles'

Since leaving the UK I had decided to grow my hair and as a result of nine months of barber avoidance, I now looked nothing like my passport photo. As I tried to enter China, the border guards took exception to this and it needed a full twenty minutes of identity checks before I was allowed to enter. Thinking I was finally through, I went to take back my documents, only for something else to catch the guard's eye.

"Oh Mr. Blake, you have already been to China?"

The fact that I'd been to the country before and yet still wanted to return seemed to set alarm bells ringing and I was set a barrage of questions: Where had I been? Who was I with? What pictures did I take? Where would I be going this time?

My answers were pretty dull, but they ate up more time and having been so desperate to leave Vietnam, I now wanted just to be free to cycle into China. Eventually I was granted entry and as I went to ride off I heard another voice shout after me.

What now?

I turned and the sight that greeted me was a completely unexpected one; a short Chinese man in his sixties, riding a folding Dahon bike.

My grumpy exterior disappeared instantly and we began chatting. He introduced himself in perfect English as Mr. Liu Wang and told me he was a retired maths teacher from Hubei Province who, having recently stopped working, was now on a three month ride from Phnom Penh to Chengdu via Vietnam. With the energy of a ten year old and a personality which could best be described as 'firecracker', we agreed to ride to the next town together. Right away I

82

wondered what I'd let myself in for, as he pulled out onto the highway, the only road in sight, and managed to get on it the wrong way, in the process taking us back to the Vietnamese border. But I enjoyed his company and as we cycled on the shoulder of an empty four lane road he gave me my first impromptu Mandarin lesson.

One of the biggest struggles I'd faced on my last visit through China had been language; I'd met approximately five Chinese people who both spoke good English and hadn't been in the process of trying to sell me something, whilst for my own part, due to its tonal nature, Chinese had been the language I had struggled with the most. As we arrived in Pingxiang, the next town along, I could already speak more Mandarin than I'd picked up in the prior three months of Chinese travel and as we stayed together for a further three days my learning continued to the point that by the time we said goodbye I could count, greet people politely and order sweet and sour pork - my staple food in China - confidently in restaurants.

Liu's acquaintance made my own journey far easier; his company when we were together was a delight and feeding off of his energy levels, I had learnt many skills that made travelling through the country more enjoyable. As we said our goodbyes in the city of Nanning, the heavens opened and the rain began. It would stay for the next three weeks.

As for me, I was headed for Guilin, a city many other travellers had raved about. On arrival I discovered that what these people had meant was that the areas around Guilin were beautiful, whereas the city itself did its best to follow the Chinese model, which itself was following the British rule that each city centre should look exactly identical, have exactly the same shops and have as little character as possible.

I was disappointed to find this theme continued throughout China; the countryside was pleasant but the cities were disgusting. Over-populated, polluted and often soulless. In the west of the country, and even around Sichuan and Yunnan province, the ride had been tolerable due to the beauty of some of the rural areas. Now as I entered the east, where most of the 1.5 billion Chinese people lived, the population density was heavier, the countryside less frequent and the ride unpleasant.

In Changsha, the fourth city in my first two weeks of returning to China with a population of over six-million, I was knocked off my bike for a second time, as a local student decided reversing blindly down a cycle path would be a good idea. I suffered nothing more than a grazed knee but my urge to get out of the country only grew and as I rode, whilst it was never in anger, I was also finding the constant shouts of *Laowai* and the over-interest from the local people merely exacerbated my desires to get out.

With green areas having been replaced by industry and smog - at one point I cycled for 200 kilometres without a break from factories shadowing the road - I found locating places to sleep difficult and with the rain seemingly not wanting to stop, I often ended up sleeping rough in bus shelters and shop doorways.

I cycled every inch of the way and when, after six weeks (during which I was able to mark my first anniversary on the road) I made it to Qingdao, it was a moment that encapsulated little more than relief. I had made it, but I would be lying if I said that I had enjoyed it.

My irritation with China ran deeper than a few stressful days on the road and as I sat in Qingdao, I began reflecting on what was now the best part of five months that I had spent in the country, trying to piece together why and how the place wound me up so much. The issues could be seen from the moment I'd entered via Kyrgyzstan.

In the unlikely event that you're ever at the Irkeshtam Pass, the border between Kyrgyzstan and China, do yourself a favour and see if you can get your eyes on something I regretfully couldn't. As you enter the Chinese side there'll be two or three small huts on your left - from what I've been told it's the middle one you'll want - and if you're there just see if you can get a look inside.

What's in this fabled room that's no larger than a garden shed?

One thing and one thing only: books, books and more books. The Dalai Lama's Book, Wild Swans, anything to do with the spiritual movement Falun Gong, numerous other titles and probably around a thousand copies of the China Lonely Planet.

No, not some canny businessman who had thought the border would make the perfect place for a bookshop; this is a room for all the banned literature in China. The books that, heaven forbid, if the people were to read, would lead to the implosion of society. Apparently.

I had managed to get my own books into China successfully, but this was due to having met others who had had theirs confiscated. These people had passed on to me what was and wasn't allowed in and so all those months previously, feeling slightly ridiculous, I had crossed into China with a Lonely Planet that had the Tibet section removed and a world map that had Taiwan ripped off, as anything that shows it as an independent country is a no-no. The border guard had given me a wry smile as he examined these books, before letting me through.

As I say, I didn't make it inside this special room, but I've heard stories of many people who did, so whilst tales on the road are often exaggerated and it's easy to speculate as to whether this place exists or not, having crossed China for a second time I was in absolute certainty that it did.

But at the end of the day it's just books. Nothing that ever began by banning books ever ended badly, did it?

As a rule I refused to get involved in politics on my travels as it simply wasn't worth it; however in China it was impossible. China is the world's most populated and - if predictions are correct -soon to be richest country.

The place also represented everything I find depressing and embarrassing about the world today; the country is led by a thuggish dictatorship, freedom of speech is non-existent and whilst the human rights abuses pile up, the outside world supports China in its policies as it is financially viable for them to do so.

Dejected at the current state of affairs, from my time in the country I tried to see if I could work out how a regime that has either directly or indirectly caused the deaths of tens of millions of its own people over the years is not only still in control, but is also very popular within the country.

The answers weren't pretty.

The first and most obvious answer to the government's success was propaganda; in short, it's everywhere.

The Xinhua News Agency has a monopoly on journalism in the country, whilst the ironically named CCTV (at least someone in the government has a sense of humour) is the television broadcaster. Both are run by the State and have strict controls over what is transmitted. The reach of these agencies is huge and as the majority of Chinese people cannot function without a TV on in the background, it's fair to assume that these newspapers and TV stations are the only source of news for many.

But how reliable are they? For obvious reasons I wasn't able to read any of the newspapers but there were two occasions when I did manage to sit down and watch CCTV9, the English language channel.

On one occasion it was the news. I had already managed to witness Chinese censorship firsthand when, as I was watching CNN and a report about China came on, the sound mysteriously disappeared, returning again only when the news was no longer about China. After realising that this wasn't a fault with the TV, the complete lack of subtlety in what had just happened dawned. But whilst foreign broadcasters were silenced, the CCTV9 channel's news certainly had its voice as I tuned it and watched a report on the recent worldwide outbreak of swine flu.

The report began with the sentence *"The World Health Organisation has today said that China is the country best placed to fight the recent outbreak of Swine Flu"*, before going on to show how the US was not well placed, that the US government had been slow to react, endangering the lives of its citizens and, luckily for China, its government had moved swiftly and strongly to protect its people. This was the main story, but over the course of the bulletin the themes became clear: everything the government had done was fantastic, every idea they had come up with was revolutionary and people should be thankful for the Chinese leaders.

Having been highly patronised by the news, the second programme I watched was a showcase discussion celebrating the thirty year anniversary of China opening its doors to foreigners, a broadcast that consisted of four Westerners who had moved to China and them telling the entire world how great China was. As the interviews began, the Chinese host asked a woman who had moved to China from the US at the end of the seventies "How did you find the quality of life here compared to the US when you first moved?"

Her answer about having moved to a country where the cultural revolution had just seen the deaths of thousands, where political demonstrations were brutally suppressed, and a place which in the coming years had the Tiananmen Square massacre to look forward to? Not to mention the mass starvation that had happened fifteen years before, a population crisis so bad it had led to the 'One Child Policy' and a critically weak economy with widespread poverty?

"How were things here compared to America?"

"Oh life was the same, if not better in China."

I wasn't buying it.

Everything on TV had an obvious message: life under the Communist party has always been fine, it's brilliant now and it's going to be great for everyone long into the future.

But if I wasn't buying into this idea the local people certainly were and a perfect example of how the Chinese authorities successfully manipulated the news was through the government's use of the Olympics.

The decision to award China the Olympics was nothing short of a disgrace and, as predicted, the Games were used as one big orgy of nationalistic propaganda. So, as the rest of the world got reports of the numerous protests about the Chinese government on the torch relay, the displacement of two million Beijingers who were made homeless for the Games, two women in their late seventies being sentenced to a year of 're-education through labour' for applying for a 'protest permit' due to having lost their homes, the government telling injured hurdle superstar Liu Xiang if he didn't win gold then all of his achievements so far counted for nothing and perhaps best of all, the dubbing over of a nine year old girl's voice during the opening ceremony as the child who actually sang was deemed 'not pretty enough' to be shown on TV, in China these things were either ignored or barely mentioned.

Instead, the quote that was used far more often, and the one which several Chinese people I met could recite from memory, was that "Jacques Rogues, Head of the IOC, said Beijing was the best Olympics ever". When people said this, you could see the pride in their eyes and if there was any question as to whether the Olympics had achieved its goal of increasing national sentiment, then as I rode through China nine months after the actual events and could still in some places genuinely not tell if the Games had finished due to the amount of Olympic paraphernalia all around towns and cities, then it was safe to say they had.

The Olympics weren't just a good example of propaganda, the period during the Games is also an excellent display of how the Communist party suppresses opinion in a method separate to the banning of books; internet censorship.

Prior to the Olympics, China was known to have a team of 30,000 full time internet police who were employed to monitor online content, remove unwanted articles and track down those responsible for the postings; however, one of the provisions of China being awarded the Games was that they relax online controls and let all content be free to internet users.

Rather than relinquish these controls, the government increased them drastically and in the run up to the Olympics not only were local sites banned, but English speakers and Westerners were hired to trawl through English language websites and block anything that could be seen as even vaguely suspicious. To indicate just how bad the paranoia was, my own personal website, which merely mentioned the fact that I would someday like to cycle through Tibet, was barred before I even arrived in China; just how terrible my account of cycling through their country would have been for Chinese people to read I wasn't sure, but it's something we'll never know.

But what if you broke these rules? Or posted something you shouldn't have? Well, back in Kashgar I had met Steve, an ex-pat who lived in Shanghai, and in the run-up to the Olympics his friend had sent a news article from Reuters - an organisation banned in China - and he'd quoted it in his blog. Five days later, three fully armed members of the Chinese army showed up at his door, took his computer and he was arrested. His business was threatened with closure and the man himself threatened with deportation.

All for reposting a newspaper article.

Better yet, not only were the government blocking websites during the Olympics, they were also spying on what foreigners were viewing, as throughout the entire Olympic period - all the way up until the end of October - if a foreigner such as myself wanted to use the internet, I would have to register my full name and passport details with each individual internet café owner. This meant that the Chinese government has a record of not just what foreign visitors to their country had been looking at, but also who had been looking at what, what issues in China they have been searching and perhaps, which websites they would need to restrict in the future.

This may sound harmless, but to put it in context, if I were to look at the wrong page online, the Chinese government, in a matter of seconds, would be able to pull up a file of who I was, where I'm from, what I looked like, which hotel I was staying in and, with the passport details, even my home address in the UK.

In the same way that I have no doubts as to the existence of my 'book room' at the border, I have absolutely no doubt whatsoever that after the Olympics the web records of all foreigners have been stored and tooth-combed.

I also wouldn't be surprised if a list of people who wouldn't be welcomed back to China has been made.

So with a highly censored media, little freedom of speech and a policeman on the doorstep if you took one step out of line, one of the things it took a while to understand is just why the people accepted life like this. The answer is simple; for many people in the country life has never been as good as it is right now.

China's GDP has grown by a minimum of 7% (usually much more) for every year since 1992, so particularly for the older generation who have lived through the Cultural Revolution, seen purges of friends and family, and been in the country during mass starvation, to see the current situation is a beautiful sight. Sure, from their point of view they may not have everything they want, but things are certainly better and with only growth forecast, there is no reason to be upset with a little loss of freedom of speech.

As for the younger generation, having grown up in an only-child environment, where they have been showered with all the love and attention they could desire since birth, being part of China's famous generation of 'Little Emperors' is hardly going to lead to creating people who are going to complain about freedom of speech. Add to this that a trip to school each day - a day that will last nine hours - will involve entering a building past numerous murals and paintings of Chinese leaders and subsequently consist of numerous lessons teaching just how great their government is, then logic says that after sixteen years the students are going to believe the hype.

I struggled with the loyalty to the government in many Chinese people. I have no problem with pride or nationalism, but the real problem I had was with the level of ignorance that many of the people I met portrayed.

Due to staying with primarily ex-pat English teachers, I came into contact with several students and the general consensus could be summed up by one student, who told me "Our government has no reason to lie to us". Whilst this was sad, the person it really hurt me to see come out with sentences similar to this was Mr. Wang.

He was an amazing man and I had instantly liked his happy and welcoming nature, but on our final day he stopped me when I suggested we visit the local Carrefour supermarket to pick up some food.

"We do not shop here. We do not like France because of President Sarkozy meeting with the Dalai Lama, so now we do not like France - and Britain, Italy and Germany are all very angry with Sarkozy over this. But we must not shop here because of Sarkozy."

The previous year President Sarkozy had met with the Dalai Lama in a move which had caused outrage in China and led many people to boycotting French business.

Hearing these words from Mr. Wang was disheartening, as he was unlike the majority of people in China; he was old enough to have lived through the Cultural Revolution, he knew what suffering was and, as someone who had travelled, the likelihood was he would have had other sources of news, but not even he could see any reason for questioning what the government had told him.

The idea that Britain, Italy and Germany had any interest in this at all was laughable.

Seeing firsthand how an educated and respected member of society had been managed to be brainwashed into thinking that the Dalai Lama - a man who has seen his homeland invaded, his people's culture destroyed, around 1.2 million Tibetans killed and yet still continues to preach his one philosophy of kindness - was little more than a maniac bent on destruction was demoralising and by this time, having seen all I'd seen, I began to ask myself whether it was ethical for me to be in the country.

It was something I thought long and hard about and I realised that the ex-pats I had met in China could fall into two categories.

The first were those seeing culture; these are the tourists, the English teachers, the volunteers, those who come here to learn about another country, to see and interact with the foreign land and to see how life is in another place.

And then we have the second type: the businessmen. These people don't have time for culture, language or human rights issues, these people's eyes look at China, see 1.5 billion human beings and think 'There must be some money here, right?'.

In Kashgar, I met a couple from Holland who had been working as architects in Beijing for a year. By all accounts the job had gone well; they had furthered their careers and they'd made a lot of money. At the same time they'd learnt no Chinese and were all too happy to tell one of their anecdotes about how opposite their house there had been a building which, prior to the Olympics, housed around 2,000 people. One day the army went in, the next there was nothing remaining; the people's homes were gone and the building demolished as part of the tidy up for the Games. They had no idea where the people had gone and told the whole story with a big smile on their faces.

It is people like this who depressed me the most; they had gone to a country where people have been continually wronged, but in their eyes, they'd been, they'd made money and after all, what skin is it off their back if 2,000 people they've never met are homeless? At the end of the year they can go back to their Dutch friends, tell them how tickety-boo Beijing was, how much money they'd made, all the nice restaurants they'd been to and how, as foreigners, they felt at home in *modern* Beijing.

The companies and corporations were no better and during my time in the country Skype, Yahoo and Microsoft were the worst offenders, working with the government to provide transcripts of people's personal conversations and alerting the authorities whenever anything suspicious was being spoken about. Microsoft even encouraged bloggers to register with their real names so the moment they stepped out of line the government could pop right around. After all, so what if a few thousand people disappear off the radar for forming their own point of view? As long as your products are out in the global market and you're getting income that's all that matters, right?

The world's politicians are, of course, no better and as I cycled across the country my resentment to the situation grew; seeing televisions across the land broadcast pictures of Chinese president Hu Jintao meeting my own country's prime minister Gordon Brown pushed me over the edge. I felt thoroughly embarrassed to have had him in the UK.

My ride through China was a disturbing one, as I had

found a country whose leaders are there because of greed and violence. They are leaders who will stay there because of the greed of foreign politicians and businesses, combined with a culture of propaganda and ignorance.

Nothing will change in the short term; life will continue to get better within China as long as you're not an ethnic minority and know how to keep your mouth shut. Those who don't know how to keep their mouth shut will continue to disappear and the country's wealth will increase, whilst the Chinese government experiments with more misinformation exercises to convince the world China really is the happiest place on earth.

The biggest days will come when either the economic growth halts, or alternatively the Chinese military power catches up to that of the US.

Both of these days are some time away; in the meantime, I found the country to be one of the most depressing on earth.

10: Come Sing And Be Merry

China was behind me; just relaying that fact over and over to my brain felt inherently good and as I made my way to the port in Qingdao, I was definitely looking forward to leaving.

Boarding the overnight ferry to Incheon and feeling pretty smug at successfully managing to pass a fully loaded fifty-five kilo bicycle off as hand luggage, my plan was to simply get to my bed and sleep through the journey. It goes without saying that this didn't work out as planned, as when I found my way to the ship's large dormitory, I was approached by five Korean men in their sixties, four of whom introduced themselves as Chang. One of the Changs, asking that I call him Lee, explained that they were old high school friends who had been on a reunion, hiking the mountains of China. He had spent most of his life in the States, and it became apparent that not only he, but also his friends, all spoke perfect English. On hearing about my bike ride, he told me that he now saw it as his duty to give me a proper welcome to his country. I had to confess that whilst I had heard many positive things, I knew little about South Korea, other than that their capital was Seoul and that due to some suspicious refereeing decisions they'd somehow managed to make the 2002 World Cup Semi-finals. Lee reassured me that tonight he would give me a real introduction to Korean culture; this lesson started with Soju.

At 20% alcohol and sixty pence per half-litre, Soju, a rice-based whiskey, is the national drink of South Korea and despite the fact that it tastes like fire, the locals drink it like water. I would learn over the next few weeks that nothing in Korea gets done without a bottle of Soju.

Due to having barely drunk alcohol over the previous year my tolerance was low, so I paced myself, sat back and watched as five Korean men in their sixties drank more in the space of half of an hour than I could manage in a week. Thinking this was the Korean lessons over for the moment, I settled in my bunk for the night, thus was a little surprised when Lee came over and told me to go with him. I asked where we were going, and assumed his reply of 'to sing' was something that had been lost in translation. It wasn't, for if Soju is the national drink, then I was about to learn that accompanying it, karaoke is the national pastime.

The Weidong Ferry from China to Korea is an overnight service that can carry up to a couple of hundred passengers. It's a reasonably large number of people but it's not really that many, and with two large karaoke booths on board, both of which could easily contain twenty people *and* were also fully booked for the entire evening, I quickly realised that karaoke was serious business. We were rushed into the room, where we were joined by more of Lee's friends (several of whom also introduced themselves as Chang) and before we'd even sat down, due to having only booked an hour in the booth, the singing began.

My turn came after successfully hiding in the corner for twenty minutes, hoping they would forget about my presence. I bumbled my way through a slightly inebriated version of The Beatles – She Loves You, and returned to my corner in relief, thinking my duty for the evening was done. Not so. After a few more songs in Korean I was approached by another one of the Changs.

"Hey Max, (due to the Asian difficulty in pronouncing T's and L's I had been introducing myself as Max Black for the previous six months) come and sing Danny Boy."

Earlier in the evening, Chang had told me how much he loved this song and how he was going to sing it, but I had no idea it was expected to be a duet and this posed a couple of problems. First, after the opening two lines, I knew none of the words to Danny Boy, and secondly - perhaps more importantly - I couldn't hit any of the high notes.

A musical massacre followed; as we finished off to a room of confused gazes and sympathy applause, our time in the karaoke expired. I'm not sure how much of it was due to my singing, but the night died down pretty quickly after that.

Korea had made an excellent first impression and the following morning, with my singing debacle a distant memory, as we entered Incheon Lee gave me a parting gift of a road map, a Snickers and a sweet potato (the gifts were welcome but I had a feeling he was just giving me whatever he could find in his car), along with a warning about how dangerous the Korean roads were.

He needn't have worried as, despite a thirteen million population, Seoul proved easy to navigate and having spent three months with a constant headache at the noise and speed of life in both China and Vietnam, I was amazed at how such a big city could be as quiet and clean. Closing my eyes whilst on a main road and not being able to hear a single car horn, local calling me a foreigner or person spitting, I knew I was going to enjoy my time here - and this was before I was introduced to what I found to be the most remarkable aspect of life in Korea: the safety.

The Han River runs through Seoul and as I rode over it I noticed several tents by the waterside; I assumed they must have just been there for the day, as the river bank of downtown would be a far too dangerous place to camp, and carried on to my host's place in the city centre, whereupon I found a note to say that she'd had to go out, but had left her front door open for me and I should make myself feel at home. The amount of trust that had been placed - not only in me but also in other people in the block of flats - was huge and I was impressed, although when Lindsay returned, she began to educate me about Korean society and how something like theft from her apartment just wouldn't happen. She also told me that the tents I'd seen would have belonged to campers, as camping in the city centre was a popular thing to do.

I was finding it all a bit too good to be true and I was still sceptical when that night we went to a bar to celebrate the birthday of one of Lindsay's friends. The moment we arrived, Lindsay set her phone and purse down on a table and promptly walked off to speak another group of people she'd seen, leaving all her valuables at the mercy of anyone who wanted them. Having only just met her I was unsure if it was rude or not to point out that she'd just done something quite silly and that her stuff was about to be stolen, but I decided to gather her belongings and return them to her.

"You've not been here long, have you?" she laughed, "This is Korea, nobody will steal it in this place."

For the rest of the evening in every bar we went to she left her personal possessions wherever she felt like. And in every bar we went to her belongings remained exactly where she had left them.

She was right; nobody was going to steal them.

That afternoon, when I arrived in Seoul, I had let off steam in a big way. China had been the biggest mental test I had faced so far; not only had I beaten it, but I had by complete chance rocked up in a country which, despite having only been there for about four hours, I knew I was going to fall in love with.

Having the house to myself (a rarity I virtually never got to experience in that first year on the road), a computer with internet access and an iTunes library that contained many of my favourite songs, I spent a few hours in a state of euphoria: music loudly on the headphones, new episodes of my favourite TV shows downloaded to watch on the laptop and with no-one else around, the freedom to slob around in my underwear. It may have been for just a few hours, but this was exactly what I needed, although I made sure I was fully dressed for when my host arrived home and removed all signs of my slumbering afternoon.

Lindsay, accompanied by her other guest, Neil, a musician who had been given a $10,000 grant from the Canadian government to go on tour around the Far East, were excellent company and I would end up spending six days in Seoul. This in turn would be the story of my time in Korea, as despite the country only being 600 kilometres from top to bottom - a distance I could cover in five days - I ended up staying three and a half weeks.

After saying goodbye to Lindsay and Neil I made my way just thirty kilometres south to Louise and Hugh's. Louise was in my year at school and had grown up in the house opposite me back in England, so seeing someone who was one of my oldest friends meant another week off the bike, as she and her boyfriend shared with me their life as English teachers in Korea.

After a week spent visiting Louise's school, I finally pulled myself away, although it was only a further four days to Rob and Matt, friends of a friend from England who were also English teachers in Korea and who would host me in Ulsan.

Friendly people, quiet, safe roads and lots of easy places to camp: as I rode I confirmed in my mind that I had never been somewhere that was such an easy place to travel. Indeed, the only difficulty I faced in the entire duration of my time in the country was when coming down a hill and my rear rim popped, leaving the bike immovable. I'd had a lot of practice at having a broken bike by now, and stood by the side of the road to thumb a lift to the next town. The very first motorist that drove past stopped, picked me up, insisted on driving me twenty kilometres to the next town for a new rim and then took me back to their family home for the evening. A traditional meal of Bulgogi, a type of barbecued meat, followed before we all drank Soju and fell asleep in front of a televised baseball game. The bicycle had been broken for all of seven minutes before I had met these wonderful people.

There really would never be a place that was as easy to be as Korea.

There were two major changes to my life in South Korea and both signalled a shift in my own psyche as to how I viewed my bicycle journey.

The first was that I cut my hair. From the age of twelve I have never really had much hair as having to brush it each day was too much of a chore. Instead, every month or so, I would go to the barber's and get it all shaved off; when it grew back to a length where it began to need attention I would return to the barber's and repeat the process. It always looked OK and meant I had a generally acceptable appearance to members of the opposite sex during my teenage years, so I had been content. However, since leaving on the bike and with theoretically no females to impress I had instead chosen to grow it, merely to see what it looked like. The outcome was not pretty and despite an OK start, due to a receding hairline combined with a lack of hair care product usage, after fifteen months since my last chop I had begun to resemble a cross between Krusty the Clown and the Doctor on the *Weetos*' box. I had been mulling it over for a few weeks, so it didn't really come as a surprise when after a heavy night on the Soju with Rob and Matt in Ulsan I woke up to find that where before I'd had shoulder length hair I now had a shaved head, courtesy of Rob's trimmers.

This was the first change; the second was getting a new tent. I had left home with a Vango Helium F10, a great tent which had seen me safely through some terrible weather conditions. Whilst inside it felt like home, it had always been a one man tent and as such was tiny, without much space for spreading out and no porch in which to cook. I'd explained my predicament to a friend in England, who had

100

gone above and beyond and managed to get Vaude to sponsor me with a new tent, which arrived with me in South Korea. It was an absolute behemoth. Admittedly, it was a two man tent, which gave more room for sleeping, but it also had a porch that was bigger than the entire sleeping area of my Vango. Moving from one tent to the other was like moving from a box room into a castle and best of all, with the additional porch, I'd never have to struggle with cooking in bad weather again.

To me, the hair cut and the new tent signified one thing; that I still wanted to be on the road, but I also wanted to be a bit more comfortable whilst doing it. No more feeling paranoid about looking like a tramp, no more sleeping in uncomfortably small confines and no more struggling to cook outdoors in heavy winds and rain; I had done all of these things and I had discovered what my body was physically capable of, not just on a bicycle, but also in sleeping and when left to its own devices. I knew what my limits were and I was proud of what I had achieved in getting to this stage; but, in this respect I no longer needed to test myself. If I was going to go on with my bike ride, I was not going to do it to push myself, I was going to do it because I enjoyed it.

From then on life would be a lot more comfortable.

With so little stress, Korea often felt like an amusement park set in the adult world - be it walking into Tesco's to see the staff stop at the turn of the hour, every hour, to perform a dance as part of their exercise routine, or passing an amusement arcade where normally you would expect to see teddy bears as the prize to the 'claw' type game with the robotic arm, instead you saw live lobsters - there were so many times that I found myself muttering under my breath 'that's awesome'.

But if there was one thing I liked more than anything else, it was the affordability of everything. Korea is not a

101

poor country, yet the way services - particularly public services - are run is so that people can use them.

I thought back to England, where prices, such as those for public transport, cinema tickets or swimming in your local leisure centre continue to rise at an astronomical rate. In Korea I saw how things were cheaper and because of this, people did more together.

One example is the internet: despite people being able to afford domestic internet, Korea has 22,000 internet cafes, all of which offer internet use at very cheap rates. The result? Instead of sitting at home, young people spend their afternoons playing online together in the same environment. I'm not saying it's the healthiest lifestyle, but it's a hell of a lot more sociable than sitting at home playing online games on your own.

Another example is the Jimjilbang - the Korean public baths - which were cheap at around sixty pence for an entry. For the price of a Mars bar, people get an experience which amounts to a few hours in a spa, in the company of friends, and they do this on a regular basis.

Meanwhile in England our social and leisure facilities are on the whole run by businesses that have no interest in whether people actually use the amenities or not, as long as they're making money. In Korea these things are promoted at an affordable price in an effort to not only get people out there and be active, but also to encourage them to be sociable together. It was truly the most united and peaceful country I would ever visit.

Rob and Matt cycled the seventy kilometres from Ulsan to Busan with me and we shared our last night at a Jimjilbang. We had planned on camping somewhere near the city, but after we paid for our bath we were told that for a further £3 we could rent a set of a pyjamas, a roll mat and a blanket and sleep in the communal hall on the top floor of the building.

Busan is a city of 3.6 million and it was the Saturday night of a holiday weekend. It was past midnight when we entered the sleeping room, where we saw several hundred Korean families asleep on the floor in front of us, all having paid their £3, all having had their bath and all in the same set of pyjamas the Jimjilbang had given us. It was a sight to behold and as I woke up the next morning I realised just how much I was going to miss Korea.

I made my way to the port and after a slight delay, boarded a ferry to Japan two days later.

Japan is made up of four main islands: Hokkaido, Kyushu, Shikoku and the main island, Honshu. With time at a premium, I made the decision to cycle only the main island and boarded a ferry to a city located in the south-west called Shimonoseki. Whilst there were karaoke booths on board I successfully managed to avoid going anywhere near them and after a relaxing overnight ferry, we arrived the following morning in port, where I was promptly told that I couldn't bring my bicycle into Japan in its current condition. The reason?

It was too dirty.

My bike had been cleaned when I was in Seoul so it genuinely wasn't in bad order. Nonetheless, I was told that in its current state it was inadmissible and this left me in a bit of a quandary as to what to do. A solution proved just around the corner when one of the guards told me 'don't worry, we'll clean it for you'. Thinking this sounded too good to be true I watched on as one of the border workers took a hose and washed down my entire bike, as well as all of my bags; my bike was the cleanest it had been since leaving and I was at last free to roam into Japan.

In a similar way to how you would never tell an Englishman that England is a lot like Germany, you would never tell a Japanese person that Japan is a lot like South Korea. At the same time, there is no denying that England is most definitely very similar to Germany, and likewise, Japan is very similar to South Korea. The only real differentiating factor I found was in price; Japan was by some distance the most expensive country I had been to. This is unfortunate, as whilst it is a fascinating country, it is one of the few places on earth where trying to get by on £5 per day isn't really possible and this meant that I missed out on a lot of what I wanted to see in the country.

With no money and having arrived at the beginning of monsoon season, I decided to make a beeline for Lake Suwa, a small town up in the mountains and somewhere I had a place to stay. En route, I rode through Hiroshima and visited one of the most humbling places I would ever visit: The Hiroshima Peace Memorial Museum.

On the 6th of August 1945, the Enola Gay dropped an atomic bomb on Hiroshima, killing an estimated 70,000 people instantly. At least tens of thousands more would die over the following years and whilst the debate continues today as to whether dropping the bomb was the ethical way to end World War II, a trip to the Hiroshima Peace Memorial Museum can only confirm one thing; that these events took place and that the destruction was on an almost unfathomable scale. Filled with artefacts from the day of the blast, some - such as melted glass bottles - are there to make you realise the power of the bomb, whilst others - a pair of spectacles or the charred remains of a human hand - hammer home the human element. A walk around the museum left me feeling nauseous.

Going outside and wanting to find a way to visualise what had taken place, I walked to the exact location above which the bomb was dropped. The bomb itself was detonated whilst still 600 metres above ground level, and for a few minutes I stood there, looking up into the sky and wondering what it must have been like to have viewed that exact spot the moment the bomb had gone off.

There are things in life that you will always remember

and personally this experience will always be one of them; when you close your eyes and try to comprehend what went on it's impossible, even more so because when you open them again you are surrounded by such a tranquil place.

In the weeks after the bombing, a rumour spread among locals that the radiation was so severe that it would be seventy-five years before any vegetation could grow again in the land. Almost sixty-four years on, the area outside of the museum and the land below which the bomb was dropped is now a luscious park, with trees growing, birds chirping and children playing. Hiroshima saw a destruction the likes of which had never been seen on earth; its regeneration is an inspiring story. But the past is never forgotten and on display in the museum - in an effort to make sure these events are never repeated - is a collection of letters from various Mayors of Hiroshima: every time a Government anywhere in the world begins experimenting with nuclear weapons, the current Mayor of Hiroshima will personally write them a letter, reminding them of the destruction of their city and imploring the Government in question to stop development of these weapons.

It was a heavy day and I didn't feel much like riding, so I spent a serene evening in a public park just two kilometres from the epicentre, reflecting on what I had seen.

Tokyo was the end of my journey through Asia.

From there I would fly on to the US, but having already cycled 25,000 kilometres and with just a mere 1,000 more to my goal, I was desperate. Japan was a great place - a curious culture of East meets West, where you could spend your time watching Japanese girls in traditional kimono wolfing down McDonald's food - but after having spent so long in non-English speaking countries, more than anything I was looking forward to getting back to somewhere I could speak my own language.

I got my head down and rode.

The plan went well until, as I came out of Kyoto, a lorry pulled alongside me, began to overtake me and then, out of nowhere, cut in front of me to pull into a *7-11* rest stop, sending both my bicycle and me flying in the process.

This was the third time I had been knocked off in four months; this time was the most severe, as I bent both wrists back and scraped my knees. Much to the relief of the driver, I wasn't in any serious pain and he rather sheepishly forced the equivalent of £12.50 into my hand and drove off. At the time I thought this odd and would later learn that the way the systems work in Japan meant that if I had needed medical attention, as the cause of the accident he would have been liable for any doctor's fees. I was grateful, although I'm not sure £12.50 would have been enough.

Luckily for both of us, I didn't need medical attention but with sore knees and bruised wrists, and with my forearms controlling my handlebars, I pushed on to Lake Suwa, a small town where I knew a host and stayed for five days resting up.

The Japanese equivalent of the Jimjilbang is the Onsen - public baths which utilise Japan's natural hot-spring water - and these helped my body recover enough to get back on the bike. Alas, the problems didn't stop there, as when leaving Suwa my chain snapped.

I had resolved to not do any repairs on my bike until Tokyo, where it would get a full service and, despite another broken chain, I vowed to stick to this, replaced the broken link and carried onwards to the Japanese capital.

Then the punctures began. My rear tyre, a Schwalbe Marathon XR, now had approximately 20,000 kilometres on it, whilst my front tyre, a standard Bontrager I had managed to pick up in Cambodia, had done exceptionally well for what it was and had lasted a good 8,000 kilometres. They'd been brilliant but both desperately needed replacing and as I got closer to Tokyo, the punctures became more frequent.

Then, of course, there was the weather. It was still

tipping it down and I had barely seen a blue sky since arriving in the country; one of the iconic images people have of Japan is of Mount Fuji, snow-capped and standing proud. Having spent over a year cycling to get there, when the day came, I couldn't see more than fifty metres in front of me. If I hadn't had to cycle half way up it, I would never have known it was even there.

With soaking wet clothes and kit, a bike that was falling apart, a tired body with wrists aching, still not fully recovered from the accident, I edged ever closer, until eventually one Tuesday afternoon, after sleeping rough on a bench outside the Yokohama stadium that hosted the 2002 World Cup Final, the sun came out and I rolled into Tokyo in glorious weather.

I had left Banbury on the 29th of April 2008. 415 days later on the 24th of June 2009 I arrived in the Japanese capital.

I cycled down the famous Ginza and made my way to meet my host. Asia had been cycled.

11: Taking Stock

In Tokyo I was hosted by Phil, his wife Misuzu and their two sons Alex and Liam. I wasn't sure what I'd let myself in for, as after having cycled 16,000 miles to get there the first thing Phil did was take me for a twelve kilometre run around the city; yet, with boundless energy, a good sense of humour and a welcoming nature, he instantly made me feel at home.

Over the four years of my trip, I would stay with numerous hosts and whilst we would always get along, few would become genuine friends; Phil was someone who quickly became a genuine friend and I am indebted to him for his help - especially in organising my flight to America and the complete overhaul of my bike - all during the two weeks I stayed with him.

My flight was at 11.30 on the morning of Wednesday the 8th of July. With so much luggage and the prohibitive cost of the train, I decided to cycle the sixty-seven kilometres to the airport, but catching up with Phil meant I didn't leave until 7 p.m. the night before.

I left as it began to turn dark and rode through the night, stopping only for a couple of hours rest at 03:30 in a twenty-four hour internet cafe. I made Narita airport the next morning, taped several cardboard boxes together to form a crude bike box and passed through customs. With nothing else to do I used the last of my Yen to take a shower, before heading for the departure lounge to wait for my flight. As I sat, it seemed the perfect time to reflect on the previous fifteen months and evaluate everything that had happened on my journey so far.

I did this in two ways; first evaluating the places I had enjoyed the most and least, then proceeding to evaluate myself and the positive and negative effects that my journey was having on me as a person.

Deciding on my favourite places was easy, as two countries leapt quickly above the rest; I may have loved the hills of Laos, the kindness of the Georgians, the tranquillity of the people in Cambodia and the beauty of the women in Turkey, but the two places I had enjoyed more than the others were easily Kyrgyzstan and Korea. This is certainly not a slight on the other places I had been, as I could easily name many positive aspects of every one of the twenty-two countries I'd travelled through. But for me, if only for its rugged mountain scenery, the brutality of some of the climbs and the greasy-yet-delicious central Asian cuisine, Kyrgyzstan stood out in my mind. Meanwhile, for offering such a welcome environment, a ridiculous level of safety and a culture that was both respectful and united, riding through Korea had been a privilege I would never forget.

In contrast, whilst I didn't like to dwell too much on which countries I hadn't enjoyed, I knew deep down that I would be going back to neither China nor Vietnam. Perhaps if I did return on something that wasn't a bicycle, then maybe I could enjoy these places, but at this moment I had no desire to go back.

So that was easy enough; moving on to how the bike ride had changed my own personality, there were so many positive aspects and the biggest ones were obvious.

The most significant change was my own contentment with life: the time on the bike had been, to this date, undoubtedly the best days of my life, which left me feeling the happiest I had ever felt. Looking back to the year I had worked in order to save up for the trip, I thought about how I would spend forty hours a week in an office sat in front of a computer, often with very little to do. With no girlfriend, no career and - due to living with my parents - no independence, I had felt as though I was effectively treading water until the trip started, to the extent that during the first few months of work, particularly after a bad football injury had left me immobile, I had been utterly miserable. Since leaving, I had barely been able to stop smiling. Waking up each morning knowing something different was just around the corner, that I would soon be meeting new people and that each day I got to ride my bike, had left me feeling thoroughly alive.

Of course, not all the days had been happy, but I had gotten through the bad days and this showed another distinct change in my personality; I had overcome the tough times and taken challenges head on. Before the trip, when things had gone wrong I had always had someone by my side to either help me, or to apportion blame to, whereas on my bike I only had me. Every mistake I made was my own, everything that had gone wrong had been my fault and every time a problem reared its head it was me who had to deal with it. Be it a broken bicycle, adverse weather or a language barrier, to know that I had been able to take personal responsibility for overcoming the problem was an incredible feeling. Yes, there'd been the odd bit of cheating, such as the 200 kilometre bus ride in China, but I'd more than made up for that in Thailand and other parts of South East Asia and I felt proud of what I had achieved.

A side effect of all this responsibility was that I also found I had matured immeasurably and this was most noticeable in my attitude towards two of the main vices of men aged sixteen to twenty-five: drink and girls. At University, and also in the year leading up to my journey, I was part of the group that drank heavily, primarily but not exclusively due to being a member of sporting teams. True, I didn't drink any more than anyone else in this group and was certainly not an alcoholic or anything as serious as that, but at University in particular it was hard to think of a week outside of exam times when I hadn't been drunk at least once. Since leaving home on my bike all those months ago, I could count the number of times I'd become intoxicated

110

on one hand. I didn't miss that lifestyle one bit and was a bit ashamed by how much I had drunk beforehand. As for women, I had previously kept all women in my life at arm's length, wanting the carnal benefits of a relationship but often absolutely none of the responsibilities. At times, I had behaved in a shamefully selfish way and of the few previous 'Mrs. Blakes' there were, several no longer wished to speak to me. In contrast, on the road I had met Bella, someone with whom I'd stayed in contact with and developed genuine feelings for; since saying goodbye in Cambodia we had never been out of e-mail contact for more than three days at a time and were currently making tentative plans to see each other again in Canada.

Perhaps no longer getting drunk and chasing girls are things I shouldn't be shouting about, but having personally broken that cycle I realised not only how little I now missed these things, but also how the idea of them actually repulsed me. It was a sign I was growing up.

Finally in the positives column - something which no doubt helped my healthy brain and will have been abetted by the lack of drinking - was my own physical health; I was about two stones lighter than when I left, and had first noticed how big my lungs now were when up in the snowy altitude of China. In Japan I got to test my fitness for real, thanks to Phil.

Phil is a keen cyclist and on the weekend of my arrival, in nearby Matsumoto, there happened to be a bike race called the Tour de Utsukushigahara. One of Japan's main races, it is a hill climb, where competitors start on their bikes at 600 metres elevation and then ride twenty-two kilometres directly up a mountain to the summit, located at a whopping 2,034 metres above sea level. Phil had managed to get me both a bike and an entry to the race and before we left his comment that 'the hardest part is the first five kilometres which is an 18% gradient' had left me unsure as to what I'd let myself in for.

Feeling nervous enough, it didn't help that half an hour before the race was due to start disaster struck, when the cleat on the cycling shoes I'd borrowed broke. With such a short amount of time before the start, we only managed a botch repair job and when the cleat broke again five minutes into the 18% climb, it meant that for the entire ride I couldn't stand up on the bike, having to remain seated in my saddle and losing a lot of pedal power.

With a bike that I couldn't stand up on and with no comprehension of pacing myself, I still flew up the hill, finishing twenty-fourth in my category out of 254, with a time of one hour, twenty minutes and fifteen seconds. To qualify for the professional race that's held each year you need a time of one hour and twenty; even with all my problems and with never having ridden a road bike before, I had still only been fifteen seconds short.

That was the moment I realised just how fit I was.

Supplementing my riding was a balanced diet of rice, eggs, vegetables and fruits that left me feeling great and full of energy. So, in terms of the person who had left home, I was now happier, more responsible and ridiculously fit and healthy.

Alas, for all that I was satisfied with, not all of the changes in my personality were positive.

I had overcome so many challenges on the bike; yet there were others that I not only failed to overcome, but failed to even attempt, summed up in the fact that I was now at an airport. I had dreamed of crossing the Pacific in an ocean liner or cargo boat; however, my initial enquiries got me nowhere and my intention was to go to the port in Japan to speak to people running the cruise liners. Instead I cycled past a video game arcade and decided that playing Virtual Soccer III would be a more fun thing to do. My bike ride was easy in comparison - OK, it may not have worked out, but I was annoyed by the lack of effort I had put into getting a boat and knew that it was solely down to me; I had looked at something, decided it was too difficult and hadn't bothered. This wasn't a new discovery about myself, but it was something I had hoped to have changed by this point.

Another negative side effect was the loneliness I felt at times and also, on occasion, how I was reacting to it. I had met so many amazing people over the past year, and therefore had to say goodbye to them too. Even as I sat at the airport, I knew that despite having only just bid Phil farewell, the likelihood was that it would be a minimum of five years before I would see him again. Bella had been a blessing in keeping me company with her e-mails, as had my parents, but with no laptop and no phone I was barely online and this feeling of solitude had led to a dangerous habit of comfort eating. During my first time in China, in Chengdu I had eaten until I had thrown up and whilst I never did that again, there were times when I was sad or lonely that I would eat until I felt better. For instance, when I was knocked off my bike in Kyoto, I headed straight for a supermarket with the £12.50 the lorry driver gave me, bought a litre of milk and a large box of cereals, and sat in the car park chowing down the lot. I have always been one of those people who loves their food, but it was becoming apparent that sometimes I was walking a fine line between food appreciation and food reliance and it was something I needed to keep an eye on.

Much as the food was a problem to me, a harder thing to accept was a change in my own behaviour that was affecting others; put simply, I was becoming more selfish. Spending so much time on my own, I had become used to waking up first thing, thinking about what *I* wanted to do that day, what *I* wanted to eat and what *I* wanted to see. There wasn't much I could do to change any of this - on the bicycle everything revolved around me and as I looked back on some of the lower moments of the trip I realised that they were down to my own selfish behaviour. In Vietnam, when the man had threatened to chop up my tent with scissors - not a pleasant thing to do, but nonetheless - rather than accepting that he wanted me to leave, I had argued with him, so used to sleeping where I wanted and arrogant enough not to move along when asked. Another time in China, I had slept rough in a building site and had been asked to move along; with snow and sleet coming down outside and my feet soaked from the day's riding, I had asked locals where I could stay; they'd made it clear that they weren't going to help me and just wanted me gone. That night I'd retreated up the road until they'd all gone to bed, then snuck back into the building site and slept rough; it was a thoroughly selfish thing to do and rightly received some scornful looks the next morning. My sleeping arrangements had only caused problems a handful of times (certainly less than five), but I knew I was becoming more cocky and that I needed to change this.

There were times when I needed to remember that I was a guest in someone else's country and that I couldn't just do what I liked.

These were all things I vowed to resolve. As I sat in the airport I felt content with what I had achieved so far; I was happy doing what I was doing and proud of the person I was becoming. I also felt excited. Asia had been amazing, but the Americas would be something else. I couldn't wait to find out what lay ahead.

I had slept for an hour and a half in the previous thirty hours and was asleep before take off; the next time I awoke was as we touched down in Los Angeles.

Leg one: Banbury, England – Tokyo, Japan

Dates: 29th April 2008 – July 8th 2009

Countries visited: 22

England, France, Belgium, Luxembourg, Germany, Austria, Slovakia, Hungary, Serbia, Bulgaria, Turkey, Georgia, Azerbaijan, Kazakhstan, Kyrgyzstan, China, Laos, Thailand, Cambodia, Vietnam, South Korea and Japan.

Kilometres cycled: 25,998

116

12: The Benefit Of Going Backwards

My aim in the America's was a simple one: to cycle from the most northern road of North America to the most southern road of South America.

Given that I wanted to start my Americas ride in Alaska, it may seem strange that I chose to fly to Los Angeles, a city several parallels below even England. I followed this path for two reasons, both of which were financial: the first was that it worked out cheaper to fly to Los Angeles and take buses up to Alaska, and second, my purse strings could be aided further by the fact that I had been offered a job in Southern California.

I had met Scott, an American medical student, back in Laos on Christmas Day 2008. We had shared a few beers and I told him about the tight budget I was living on. He explained that his family owned a ranch and, if I ever wanted work in the States, then they would happily employ me. I'm not sure how serious he had been, but we stayed in contact and I e-mailed him from Japan, to see if his offer was genuine; true to his word, his family took me in and after landing in L.A. I cycled north along the ocean road for four days, to the sleepy coastal town of Cambria.

It took a few days to get used to speaking English again (I was still saying 'Arigato' in shops), but I gradually adjusted, and the next three weeks on the ranch were a wonderful way to spend the rest of July. Beth and George, the ranch's owners, were magnificent people who had lived all over the world and we would spend each day working out below the hot sun in the avocado fields, before relaxing with a fresh bowl of guacamole, whilst I listened to stories from my new friends. I made several other friends in this small town, which was somewhere I would be returning to on my ride south and even as I left, I was looking forward to coming back.

As for Scott - he was off to India to work as a medical student for the year, so I hung around to see him off, but with August approaching, I knew I needed to get up to Alaska in order to make it back south before the winter kicked in. With close to $1,000 earned - a massive amount to someone like me - I said goodbye to my new friends, promising to stop by again in a few months' time, and got a lift from Beth to the Greyhound Bus Station, from where I caught the first of my connections up to Whitehorse, a city on the Alaska Highway in the Yukon Territory of northern Canada.

My bus left Paso Robles, California, at 11 a.m. on the 29th of July and, after several changes, I arrived in Whitehorse, Canada, at 3:15 a.m. on the 2nd of August.

It was about as much fun as it sounds.

Arriving in Whitehorse - where the Greyhound Bus Line stops - I had a couple of days' rest, stocked up on supplies and checked the timetable: the next public bus to Fairbanks was at 11:00 on Sunday.

It was Tuesday.

Not exactly enthralled by this, I realised there was only one thing for it: hitchhiking. I'd never hitchhiked before and in truth it was something I didn't particularly want to do, as I never really felt comfortable asking complete strangers for lifts. That said, whilst I am a fairly patient person, I wasn't prepared to sit around for six days, so on the Tuesday morning I rode to a rest stop on the edge of town and started holding out my 'Haines Junction' sign in the hope that someone would pick me up.

Seven hours passed and nobody stopped.

I was five minutes from packing up for the day and heading back to Whitehorse, when a lady pulled in to offer a lift. The following hundred miles were quite an experience, as my driver told me how immigrants were destroying

Canada, blissfully ignoring the fact that she was one herself. But I kept my mouth shout; I was now officially on my way. I got one further ride that evening and spent my first night in Haines Junction with an Englishman who had, by sheer coincidence, been born in the same hospital as I was back in the UK. I eventually made it into Fairbanks, Alaska (with a lot of patience, a tired arm and having learned that if I turned the bike upside down it made it look broken, which in turn induced sympathy) three days later.

The Pan-American Highway unofficially starts at Deadhorse, a small town 500 miles north of Fairbanks, well within the Arctic Circle at the northern end of the Dalton Highway. With only two gas stations along the route which I'd been told would take a minimum of ten days to ride, I stocked up on food, making sure to get plenty of coffee and peanut butter, then rode out of town towards the highway in search of a lift north.

It soon became apparent there wasn't one coming (hitchhiking with a bike really isn't easy) and what's more, I discovered I didn't want one. I'd not ridden in over a month by this point, so just getting on the bike was more than enough for me and I began to think to myself 'what if I were to ride up *and* down the highway?'.

The Dalton Highway, a stretch of road built as recently as 1974 to aid the Trans-Alaska pipe system, doesn't begin until eighty-five miles outside of Fairbanks, and when I got there it hit me like a ton of bricks. Gone was the asphalt; in its place was a dirt road and an 18% gradient. The rain drove down and as I struggled along, the fact that I hadn't ridden in a month was obvious not just to me, but also to anyone who would have driven past, as I huffed and puffed red-faced up the hills. After turning onto the Dalton, and still with enough time to get a good couple of hours riding in that evening, I only managed six miles on the climbs before giving up for the night; I pulled over and cooked dinner.

As we'd driven north, I had seen several bears from the various bus and car windows, so that night, armed with my freshly purchased bear mace, I made sure to camp far away from where I'd cooked and equally as far away from where my remaining food was.

The next day was the same, although with intermittent asphalt, and in a sadistic way I began to enjoy getting back into the routine of systematically destroying my leg muscles. I enjoyed it all the more when, after crossing into the Arctic Circle, I met Alex and Finn, two English cyclists who were making a documentary about their ride from Alaska to Panama, as I found out that whilst I was being punished, Finn was putting his body through this pain for a second time.

The original documentary had been Finn along with a female presenter, but after cycling the Dalton once, they had had a massive falling out and the other rider had stormed off the show. Needing to still make a film, Finn had called Alex, an old friend of his, and had arranged for him to take the vacant spot. Unfortunately for Finn, this meant they needed to start from scratch, which involved lugging all the gear back up to the top of the Dalton and cycling one of the most punishing roads on earth. Again.

And it's no understatement to say that this is one of the most punishing roads, as by this point I knew what was tough on a bicycle, and yes, this was tough, to the extent that even truckers - a cyclist's mortal enemy - were stopping to see if I was OK.

With twenty hours a day of daylight sandwiching a couple of hours of dusk and the striking natural beauty of the barren lands, it was a great ride, but it didn't get any easier. In fact, I made life even harder for myself, as forty miles from Coldfoot - the last gas station for 240 miles - I ran out of cooking petrol.

The natural reaction to being in the wild without a cooker would be to conserve all the edible foods you have and get to the next available services as quickly as possible. Some good advice there.

In contrast, I ate everything I owned: the last of my bread, spoonfuls of peanut butter, the emergency Snickers bar and even the last of my birthday chocolate that Bella had sent and which I'd been saving for a special occasion. Coupled with a forty minute rest, this wasn't my finest hour, but as usual the guardian angel who had been looking over me on the ride struck again and I met Ralph.

From Anchorage, Ralph worked at Deadhorse and regularly drove new equipment up to the oil fields. He was one of those people who clearly couldn't stop smiling and after stopping, kindly offered me an orange. Upon seeing I had no fuel or food until Coldfoot, he instead insisted on giving me half a box of *Herschey* chocolate, along with his business card and an invitation to call him when I got to Deadhorse, where I could sleep in his company's office.

The chocolate saw me through to Coldfoot; I refilled my fuel bottle, ate a self-congratulatory bowl of ice cream and bought five chocolate bars - one for each day until I expected to arrive at Deadhorse. It was eight o'clock and I was all set to leave, when I was approached by a couple of young guys who were on a hunting trip. They told me they'd just flown their own plane from Fairbanks up to Coldfoot, and that evening, before the hunting started in the morning, they were going to have a couple of beers at their campsite about two miles down the road, and invited me to join them.

This sounded great, although after cycling a further six miles I couldn't find them, so gave up and camped for the night. I thought nothing of it, and had completely forgotten about them, until I saw them again the next morning when they drove past just as I was having my morning swim in a creek. They stopped their truck and one of them jumped out the back just as I covered myself with a towel.

"Aw hey man, sorry man. It was further than we thought last night man, but here. We're sorry you couldn't find us. Take this," he said. He put something in one of my hands, shook the other, then ran off and jumped back in the vehicle. With a toot of the horn, it promptly sped off.

The whole exchange took less than thirty seconds, and when I looked in my hand I found that what he'd given me was a joint.

Aside from the usual dabbling that most sixteen year olds go through, I had never really smoked pot. I was unsure what to do with it, so I put it in my barbag and rode on.

That night, camping at the foot of the Atigun Pass, with no one around and with me convincing myself that due to my tired legs it was for medicinal purposes, as I lay in bed I lit it and smoked the whole thing.

For a few minutes the sound of childish laughter was all that could be heard across the vastness.

The laughing stopped the next morning when I woke to find that the weed had caused a severe case of the munchies and that I'd eaten all of my chocolate. Emergency sugar supplies gone - the last three days into Deadhorse had just become a lot less appealing.

The Atigun Pass, the largest pass on the Dalton which takes you through the Brooks Mountain Range, proved something of an anti-climax as whilst it wasn't easy, it was nowhere near as steep as other sections of the road and by midday all that was left was a flat 160 miles into Deadhorse.

Whilst the riding was easier a strong cross wind made for slow progress in the day and also blew down the tent at night, but though I had my own perils I was not in as much trouble as some of the hunting parties that I met.

There are many benefits to living in Alaska: there's the natural beauty, the long summers and also the Alaska

Permanent Fund, a system which gives full-time residents of the State a share of the annual oil profits (in the year I was there all permanent citizens - including children - were given $1,305 for simply living in the State), but my favourite aspect of life in Alaska was their hunting rules. Due to the harsh winter climate, the cost of importing food and the large natural supply of wildlife, the majority of people go hunting each year for their annual meat. Most fish for salmon, although as someone who's allergic to fish, this didn't interest me. What intrigued me more were the moose and caribou: during hunting season each household is allowed to kill one animal per dependent.

So, for example, a family of Mom (we're in America now, hence the incorrect spelling), Pa and three kids would be allowed to kill five caribou.

Many families I met did just this and had industrial-sized freezers in their garages, so that after killing the animal and butchering it, they could then take the meat home and that would be their animal protein supply for the next twelve months.

As someone who eats meat but has never hunted his own dinner, I liked how in touch people were with their food, and whilst the sight of numerous trucks driving past with the carcass of a slain caribou atop their roofs was a little off-putting, I have to admit I thoroughly liked the idea of hunting all of your own meat.

Though whilst I might have been a fan, PETA, animal rights activists and celebrated morons weren't so keen, and as I rode north I met several hunting parties who'd had the tyres on their trucks slashed by members of the group. Stuck hundreds of miles from anywhere and having to wait at least a day for replacements, I felt empathy for the hunters. Realising that a lone guy on a bike could also look suspicious, I kept my head down and carried on into the wind.

The wind was joined by driving rain and I slogged on towards Deadhorse. The conditions were miserable, but what I was really struggling with was the food: I'd left Fairbanks with oats, 10lbs of rice, four loaves of bread, five cans of spaghetti, five cans of beans, a couple of kilos of peanut butter and, of course, a variety of chocolate. Losing the chocolate had been my own fault, but now everything else was being whittled down and by the end of the penultimate day all I had left was rice and an emergency tin of beans.

A diet of plain rice is foul, so with thirty miles to go I gave in and cracked open the beans. They were gone in seconds and not wanting to risk it, I was immediately back on the bike, finally arriving later that day in Deadhorse.

It had taken eight and half days. My entire body ached and I was soaked from head to toe, but I had made it. One of the most challenging rides I would ever do had been conquered and now here I was at the top of Alaska.

Looking out into the distance I could see the Arctic Ocean; it was the furthest north I would ever be.

I phoned Ralph who instantly came and met me. He had already become a hero of mine when he gave me the chocolates, but I could have kissed him when he took me in, set up a camp bed in his company's office, let me use their shower and then introduced me to something that would leave me weak at the knees.

The workers at Prudhoe Bay Oilfields generally spend six weeks at a time in what is a pretty depressing place. A small community, few leisure activities, few women, away from their families, no alcohol and, in the winter, no daylight, lead to a place that could easily get you down, and one of the ways the workers are kept happy is via food. Restaurant quality meals from top-end chefs are cooked four times a day and are free to all who work at the fields, whilst for when the chefs are off duty there's a soda machine and a twelve foot long 'wall of deserts' - a glass cabinet that holds every dessert you could imagine, all of which are free for the taking.

Ralph snuck me in and on the night I arrived, we dined on soup, followed by Hawaiian style roasted pork, topped off with double helpings of ice cream. After nearly nine days of suffering, it was the perfect antidote, and over the following day, whilst Ralph was at work, having left me in his room to rest, I made frequent trips to the snack bar, gorging on cookies, donuts, ice cream and Dr Pepper.

Surrounded by food, I realised that if my original plan to hitchhike up and cycle back down had worked then I never would have experienced the joy of a free desserts buffet.

I had made the right choice.

As I had begun cycling north, I had tried to convince myself that I would cycle the Dalton Highway both north and south. After around two days, I had realised this was a stupid idea, but not wanting to give in to the challenge, I told myself that I needed a legitimate reason for not doing it; I found the solution below my feet.

Back in Cambria, Tom Kennedy (a neighbour of the ranch and someone with the quite a fantastic claim to fame of being the first ever Frisbee Golf World Champion) had given me a new set of pedals to replace my beaten up old ones. As I'd arrived on the Dalton Highway, the right one of these had gradually become looser and looser, meaning that being cleated in was dangerous; the further I rode, and the looser it became, the less use me pedalling with my right leg had become.

So, the pedal was broken anyway but just to make sure, as I rolled into Deadhorse I stamped down on it several times.

Ho-hum, looks like I'll have to find another way to get back to Fairbanks.

After two nights in Ralph's office, and with a pannier

stuffed full of Danish pastries and donuts from the 'wall of desserts', I made my way to the offices of Carlile Transportation Systems, a name which had recently become famous after several of their staff had appeared on the TV show *Ice Road Truckers*. They were kind enough to offer me a lift back to Fairbanks (my driver even let me drive the truck round and round in circles at a pull-out when he'd stopped to have a rest) and as we moved away I looked back on the Oil Fields at Prudhoe Bay. This was the most northerly point I would ever go to; a barren town in the middle of nowhere that in the winter time won't see daylight for over two months and can get as cold as minus fifty degrees Celsius.

It hadn't been quite how I'd intended, and I may have cycled my first obstacle the 'wrong' way, but my journey in the Americas was well and truly underway. I liked it here.

13: Becoming A Machine

When you tell people that you are cycling around the world, one of the hardest things to convey is that for the majority of the time very little happens. Don't get me wrong, it's an amazing way to see our planet, but whilst it's great to be able to say that you never know what's around the next corner, the answer is usually the same: not much of interest. My favourite thing on the road was the people I got to meet, and with only one town of over 10,000 people en route from Fairbanks to Prince George, I knew not too much exciting was going to occur, so over the following twenty-eight days I knuckled down and rode 2,700 kilometres.

Having gone from someone who had never previously cycled to someone for whom four weeks of near continuous riding was relatively easy, it occurred to me that I had never really taken into account what I was putting my body through. During this time, I took a step back and worked out both exactly what my daily routine on the bicycle was and also what food I was putting into my body to achieve this. There was one word, and one world only, for it.

Repetitive.

Wake up, put on smelly cycling clothes, eat, pack the tent away and be on the road for nine; ride for around two and a half hours, followed by a half hour break and some sandwiches, before another two hours on the bike. With the odd toilet stop this usually means a lunch hour somewhere between two and half past, where the day's middle meal is washed down with a cup of coffee and a chapter of whatever book I'm reading, then it's three-thirty and time to get back on the bike for another two hours or so, during which I'll have a couple more sandwiches to keep me going. Six-thirty onwards is time to keep an eye out for a creek or river to get water to cook and wash with, and once that's on board, it's a simple case of guessing when the sun will set. Just when I think I've got about an hour's daylight left, I'll pull off to the side of the road, set up camp and cook dinner. When that's all done, the light will just be about to go, so the final aspect of the day is boiling up a litre of water, taking off my smelly clothes and having an improvised shower by the side of the tent, before collapsing into bed usually around 9 p.m.. Due to the physical nature of the ride, I need about ten hours sleep a night. Then the following morning I'll wake up and do it all again. And again. And again. And again.

And that is it: the exciting life of a cyclist.

But what about the diet?

I'd gotten used to simply eating when hungry, and whilst I knew it was a lot, I'd never really thought about just how much I was eating, so on the ride down from Alaska, I kept a food diary. The results were as follows:

Breakfast: Four peanut butter and/or jam sandwiches and a cup of coffee.

Lunch: Saucepan full of oats mixed with either peanut butter or jam and a cup of coffee.

Dinner: Rice, usually with fried vegetables on top, (although in Alaska and Canada I was forced to resort to tins of beans).

Between meals: More peanut butter sandwiches.

There was also the odd chocolate bar thrown in, but this was my core diet. To determine just how much food this was, I also took the time to count the calories:

1 loaf bread (2,400 calories)
250g peanut butter/jam (1,900 calories)
200g oats (800 calories)
250g white rice (350 calories)

1 tin baked beans (500 calories)
2 large cups black coffee (8 calories - they all count)

It all amounted to near enough 6,000 calories per day and my body needed them all.

The scenery would change; I would usually get my water from taps rather than rivers, and the cycling hours would vary according to the daylight, but for the most part, this routine, along with the diet of bread, jam, peanut butter, rice and fried vegetables, would remain constant throughout my four years on the road.

And there you have it. That's pretty much what the majority of days on the road were like. It's a good life; just don't think it's always exciting.

Meanwhile, back on the road...

Every year, millions of children in the US write their annual Christmas letters to Santa. Using their best handwriting and offering falsified reassurances that they've been well-behaved, thousands of these kids go on to post their letters to the following address:

Father Christmas
North Pole

Riding away from Fairbanks, thirteen miles to the east of the city, I passed through the place where these letters end up.

North Pole, Alaska - some 1,700 miles south of the actual North Pole - will receive as many as 12,000 letters per day during the holiday season, and in the true spirit of Christmas, local volunteers who dub themselves 'elves' will come together and try to reply to as many of them as possible. Given that the average winter daytime temperature is minus twenty-five degrees, thinking about what goes on here at that time of year is quite incredible; people leave their homes on St. Nicholas Drive or Snowman Lane (both real places), go past the forty-two foot tall fibreglass statue of Santa - the largest statue of Santa in the world - and brave the conditions to get to a community centre, where they'll reply to letters from all over North America out of sheer kindness.

It's one of the truly heart-warming stories out there; however, as I rode past what is called 'The Santa Claus House' in the burning sun of a warm August day, I had two main thoughts:

1) For those few weeks of the holiday season it must be a real pleasure to live up here and be part of such a great project, and;

2) For the other eleven months of the year, a forty-two foot fibreglass Santa is something that looks ridiculously out of place.

The August sun beamed down. RVs and buses of tourists stopped to have their pictures taken next to giant candy canes, and after a quick chuckle to myself, my bicycle and I rode on to the Alaska Highway in the direction of Canada.

Alaska was an interesting place to visit and in terms of the people, whilst I found there were lots of seasonal workers, of the people who were permanent residents, I noticed a couple of trends. The first was that from speaking to these guys (and girls), you could instantly tell that they knew how to survive on their own. With essentially three months of summer, with long hours of day light and warm temperatures, balanced against three months of darkness and temperatures that won't get out of the minuses, the people up here are toughened up to the environment and know exactly what's needed to get through winter. Spending summer hunting the year's meat supply, getting wood for their fires and just generally stocking up for the winter, particularly in rural areas, you could see how independent many of the people were.

Accompanying this independence was a detachment from the outside world, and when some of the people talked about places other than Alaska, they either showed no interest, or exerted a fear hinting at the 'outside world' as a very dangerous place. There were others who chose not to talk about the outside world, and I found a common story among the people I met - that the person in question had been born somewhere in 'the Lower forty-eight' (the colloquial name for the US mainland) and had been in some form of trouble, so had moved to Alaska for a fresh start. Whilst I never raised the issue, nor asked what they'd done, the number of people who freely told me they'd spent time in prison was high, and I got the impression that many of the people didn't want to talk about the outside world because there were things in their past that they didn't want to remember.

I have little doubt that the natives who showed fear towards the outside world did so because of the American media. 'Live in fear' was the constant message, with scaremongering and sensationalism the methods in which it was delivered. With terrorists, serial killers and deadly viruses clogging up the news, if a television is your only source of information, you could be forgiven for being scared to pass your own front door. Of course, I'd come across sensationalist news before, yet I was still surprised at the number of people who told me that I should be carrying a handgun for my own safety. Indeed, I was completely taken aback when someone in Fairbanks told me his daughter was moving to Dublin and asked if it was likely that she would be the target of sectarian violence.

So that was Alaska - one of the most naturally beautiful places, with people, who if not a little detached from reality, were highly welcoming.

But now I was off to Canada.

A great ride and some miserable weather later, I arrived in Whitehorse, where after a couple of days I moved on south, accompanied by a Japanese cyclist called Koko. Currently in the fourth year of a round the world trip, Koko was a quiet man, but made for excellent company, and we rode off and on together for a week, at the end of which he carried on along the Alaska Highway towards the Rocky Mountains, whereas I made a right turn towards Prince George and, a few kilometres down the line, Vancouver.

During the four weeks from Fairbanks to Prince George, I began to suffer from genuine loneliness for the first time on the trip.

I had felt lonely on the road before, but now I was feeling it for sustained periods and rather than waking up eager to get on, I was staying in bed for longer each morning and had less enthusiasm to be on the bike.

Throughout my time in Asia, when I had struggled with being alone, I had been able to point to the fact that I couldn't speak the language and had thought to myself that when back in English-speaking territory I would find it easier to be happy. Now that I was here, I still had the same sorrow at repeatedly having to say goodbye to the friends I made almost instantly. This, coupled with spending eight hours of each day on the bike, talking to myself, meant that I was becoming unhealthy.

As a result I found that a lot of the time I just wanted to be left alone; I could get along with people just fine, but if forced to be around those I didn't want to be with, I would get wound up unbelievably fast, as one night in northern Canada showed.

I was staying with a host called Terry: a guy in his fifties who worked all day and in the evenings would kick back with a big meal and a bottle of gin, and fall asleep in front of a movie. Terry was a really easy guy to get along with and I liked being his guest; however, on one of the evenings we were joined by a young girl with a big ideology and little common sense. Wherever I go, I always like to do something for my host, and on the night this young lady arrived, it happened to coincide with my offer to do some DIY Terry needed around his house. As I was hanging some pictures in his office, Terry slept on the couch and the young lady chose to join me. During the following conversation she told me a) that in her vision for the world she wanted to create there would be no such thing as money, people would all live in communal caravans, that all transport would be free and there would no longer be such a thing as class, and b) the trip she was on currently had cost around £15,000, she'd been very privileged in what she'd done in life so far and of the money she'd spent on this trip, several thousand pounds of it had been on a 'food detox', where for a lot of money you go to a special place where for six weeks you don't eat a single item of food, living on only water.

She seemed like a nice girl, but having spent so much time on my own, having broken into tears due to loneliness on the ride out of Fairbanks, and with a lot of confusion as to what was going on in my own mind at the time, hearing someone who led a privileged life promote hippy virtues, despite having no intention of living that life, was something that pushed me close to the edge.

As we did the DIY and she went on and on about how the whole world would be happier if money didn't exist, I looked at the hammer I was using and had the urge to end the conversation the only way I knew how; by using the claw end to gouge out my own ear drums.

With no means of escape, I went to bed incredibly frustrated that night, but developing a short fuse wasn't the only outcome of so much time alone. Since arriving in the Americas, I had begun to notice every single semi-attractive female, to the point of sexual desperation. It had been over two months since my last encounter with a woman, when a trip to a baseball game in Tokyo had led to a drunken smooch with a Japanese lady. Despite the warning I'd been given, that when it came to the women of the north, 'the odds are good, but the goods are odd', now that I could communicate I wanted to speak to every girl I met. Of course, dirty clothes and a lack of smoothness meant I never got very far, but in Whitehorse I spent the day with Anna, a Czech girl whom I had met on the way into town. We spent the afternoon hiking and at some point had decided to go for a swim in the Yukon River. Whilst there was very little sexual attraction, just spending some time with a girl and seeing a female body relatively close up had left me yearning and I realised just how much I missed having a woman in my life.

And finally, to compound my lonely side of life, I had spent the week with Koko. Koko and I had got on well; we'd both been on the road long enough to be in the same boat, so had developed that sixth sense that told the other when one of us needed some space, or when one of us wanted to talk about something. One night, Koko had been quiet and confided in me that it was his ex-girlfriend's birthday. They had been together in Japan but he had had to make a choice between cycling and her; he had chosen cycling and whilst he stood by his decision, he couldn't help but think about where he would have been, had he not been with me in the Yukon right now.

To make sacrifices for a life alone: it was both something I could relate to and something that made me think about where I would have been if I hadn't been cycling.

My solutions to these problems had, until this point, been either targeting something to look forward to in the future, such as a border crossing or my flight to America, or simply comfort eating.

Now, as I arrived in Prince George, I bought something that would change my trip permanently, as with the remaining $350 I had from my work in California, I went to a local department store and bought a laptop.

When I left England, I had purged myself of all forms of communication: I had travelled with no mobile phone and no computer, relying on internet cafés as my only means of communicating with areas outside of the one I was in. For the first nine months this had been a glorious freedom, but after nearly eighteen months on the road, I couldn't take the solitude any longer and needed to be able to Skype with people when I wanted.

It may sound so simple, but that one piece of equipment changed my life immeasurably, and over the next few days I rode from public library to public library - all of which had their own wifi - with the feeling of a massive weight being lifted off my back at finally having independence in my communication.

Thanks to the built-in video, for the first time since the day I'd arrived in America, I was able to video chat with people at home. Seeing their faces made me instantly happier.

When entering British Columbia, one of the first things you'll notice is the Province's slogan, which is brandished down the side of every road sign: 'Welcome to British Columbia - The best place on earth'.

Whilst not exactly humble, there is at least some truth in it and, as I made my way through the Province - with my head back up after the laptop purchase - for the first time I found a place that I could truly see myself living in permanently. The people were warm and welcoming, the small towns were quaint and the ride itself was amazing, with the hundred kilometres from Lillooet to Pemberton being one of the most beautiful stretches of road I would ever have the privilege to ride.

Vancouver proved no exception to BC's greatness, and with a population of over 600,000, it was the biggest city

I'd been in since landing in L.A. three months previously. Having spent so much time in rural areas, devoid of noise and - for a large part - too much activity, arriving in Vancouver proved something of a shock. Young people played street hockey; 'yummy mummies' roller-bladed past me pushing prams in front of them. The diverse, yet friendly nature of the people left me feeling welcome in a city with a vibe like no other I'd ever been too.

Arriving over the iconic Lions Gate Bridge, through the famous Stanley Park, and on to my hosts' house in Kitsilano, I would spend the next three days with Mike and Jenna, a Canadian couple who met whilst on their own separate bike tours and had just returned from a honeymoon which had seen them cycle from Canada to Ushuaia, at the bottom of Argentina.

Staying with cyclists is always more fun, as they know exactly what a rider wants upon arrival (usually little more than a meal and a warm shower) and we enjoyed our time together. At the end of these days though, I wasn't quite ready to cross the border to the States just yet.

It was now time for another one of those dates in my diary that I had been using to motivate myself to stay on the bike: when I left home, I had set myself the target of getting to Istanbul in time to watch some of the football; in Asia it was getting across China as quickly as possible; and in Japan my flight to the States had kept me riding.

Since arriving in North America, my motivation had been to get to Vancouver for this specific week of October, as on the Friday night, eight months after we'd said goodbye back in Cambodia, Bella flew into town.

14: Bella

"I'm so in love with you I just don't know what I should do,
So I'll do nothing and I'll just dream,
I never seem to get it right,
It seems that I,
I don't know how to say goodbye
and if I did I'd surely cry,
I lie, if it's a choice between you and me I'd go for I
And here's why, I never really thought
that you liked me anyway."

The Pigeon Detectives - Don't know how to say goodbye.

Bella and I hardly knew each other.

This much became clear when, on the way to the airport to pick her up, her friend that we were staying with in Vancouver pointed out that my pronunciation of her name was so bad that if I were to ask one of her fellow Quebecoise about the person I thought I was talking about, given my accent they would think I was speaking about a man.

Pronunciation problems aside though, apart from my parents, it had been Bella with whom I had been closest over the previous months. We had e-mailed constantly, had managed to get birthday presents to each other, despite being a minimum of 3,000 miles apart, and we had shared in all that had gone on over the time since we'd said goodbye.

As I approached the airport I felt nerves building inside; we had spent so much time talking, but physically we had barely been around each other and it began to dawn on me that whilst I thought I knew her and she knew me, in many respects we were little more than strangers.

What would I feel when I saw her?

Taking a deep breath, I stepped into the airport.

At first sight she looked different to how I remembered: back in Asia I'd thought she was attractive; standing before me now... she looked stunning, with shoulder length red hair and bright blue eyes. In comparison, I was wearing the same clothes that I'd been wearing when we'd said goodbye eight months ago and to top it off my glasses had broken and were currently held together by *Sellotape*.

Beauty aside, I had only ever known her when she had been travelling with her father and now that she was alone she was an entirely different person: far more confident and outgoing. There were so many things I didn't know about her, but as we hastily caught up, all that I was learning I really liked.

Bella stayed in Vancouver for ten days and brought her bike with her, so after a weekend in the city we caught a ferry to Vancouver Island and spent five days touring the small towns and inlets of the Pacific Coast. The weather was miserable, but Bella joined me on the road in the day time and kept me warm in the tent at night; these were fast becoming some of the happiest days I could remember. We were getting to know each other so well and it was obvious a bond was forming, but towards the end of the week there were times that I would drift off and become more distant, as inside of me a battle was beginning to rage.

I had set myself the challenge of riding my bike around the world. I was going to do that, of that I had no doubt, but I had always assumed it would be a solo trip. Now, in Bella, I had met someone for whom I had genuine feelings and who I knew would be interested in doing the trip with me.

But was I prepared to ask someone I had only spent ten days with to give up everything and come and cycle with me? *No, that would be crazy.* But then why had I arranged to meet up with her here in the first place? What did I hope to get out this week? *I have no idea, I just knew I really* *wanted to see her again.* Well, she's going home again in a couple of days, what are you going to do then? *I have no idea.* You do realise that if you don't say something to her before she leaves then the chances are you won't see her again? *I know, but I don't know if I could ask her to give up everything to ride with me.* Well why don't you stop your ride? *I set myself the challenge to ride around the world, every single bit of effort for the past three and a half years of my life has gone into this trip. I can't just give it all up now.* Well then you've either got to ask her or say goodbye? *Sticks fingers in ears* LA-LA-LA-LA-LA.*

I had no idea what to do.

Gradually time passed and it was the morning of Bella's departure. We told each other that we loved one another, but out of nowhere and with me unsure why, I told her that when she went home she 'shouldn't wait for me'.

That morning, still in a daze, I found solace in the one thing that had kept me going for so long: comfort food. Since leaving Alaska I had somehow developed a love of baking and as a result had promised Bella I would make her a batch of cookies to take back to Quebec. And so it came to pass that as someone I loved was upstairs packing away her things, preparing to depart from my life forever, I was downstairs, hiding from my emotions and baking cookies.

We made the journey to the airport almost in silence. As we said goodbye and she passed out of sight, a rush of panic took over me; I had just watched her walk away.

Being on a bicycle on your own you become a control freak, for you get to make the decisions on every aspect of your life. You decide where you go, where you'll sleep, what time you'll wake up, what you'll eat and all that goes along with it. The only person you ever have to think about is yourself.

In the space of a week, the feelings I had developed for Bella should have forced me to face up to the fact that I needed to take other people into account, but when up against emotions that I had no control over, rather than square up to them, I had run away. I wanted to cry. I looked at the food outlets around me and none of them were appealing. I was at a new stage of loneliness that not even comfort eating could solve; I had never been here before.

I didn't feel hungry. I felt devastated, ashamed and alone.

I went back to Bella's friend's house, gathered my possessions and left immediately, returning to the first couple I'd stayed with in Vancouver, Mike and Jenna. It would be another two days before my replacement glasses were ready and, as childish as it was, I wanted to be far away from anything that was connected to Bella, as for the first time I faced a real emotional battle.

It wasn't just Bella; it was Vancouver too. I had been to many places I liked, but nowhere near as much as B.C. I'd often found myself thinking 'I'd like to live here someday', but here not only was it true, it was also a possibility: having met a few Brits who lived in the city, I discovered it wouldn't take much effort to turn my tourist visa into a year-long working visa. And I began to wonder. I could live here, in Vancouver. I could live in Quebec. I'd be happy here. I could get a job. I could raise money for the rest of my ride. And see Bella again.

I successfully managed to ignore all of those things and instead listened to the voice that said: "*You're attempting to cycle around the world. You can have all of those things in the future. For now just turn off your feelings and get back on the bike.*"

My first attempt at leaving was on the Tuesday, but halfway between Mike and Jenna's and the US border, I got a puncture. As I fixed it I realised I wasn't ready to say goodbye to Canada just yet and so turned around and went back to the city. *Just one more night.*

The following day, I got back on the bike and even though I successfully made it to the border, I was praying that they would reject my entry and send me back to Canada. I'd met three separate people who had all been refused entry to the US over the previous months without any real reason and, thanks to the nonsensical system the US has, I knew it could go one way or the other. *Maybe luck will be on my side?*

I showed my papers to the border guard, who'd clearly had an encounter with a charisma Dementor, and after twenty minutes of questioning about who I was, why I had an unused Pakistan visa in my passport and just how I came to have the money I did my answer was given: I was allowed into the country. With a three month stay secured, I was once again off in the U.S. of A.; The Canada vision was gone.

I had begun in Alaska around two months after what an ideal start date would have been; as a result, the weather had been pretty miserable for the majority of the 2,500 mile journey down. Crossing the border into Washington State, the rain continued and an air of melancholy set over me that night, as deep down I knew I had just left something major behind.

I was pretty miserable the next day as well and as I arrived in the town of Stanwood, I'd stopped paying attention and managed to get lost. With no idea where I was, I pulled into a cul-de-sac where I could see a man working in his garage and called out asking for help.

The man introduced himself as Mark and I told him that I was lost, to which he pointed out that it was getting dark. Within five minutes, I'd been ushered into his house, fed, told I could stay the night and introduced to his family. As well as Mark, there was his wife, her sons Kyle and Eric, and finally young Matthew, a four year old Chinese boy whom the family had adopted from a Beijing Orphanage.

Their kindness was continual, as after inviting me in and hearing how I wanted to know more about American culture, Kyle gave me his old Seattle Seahawks NFL Jersey (as well as a detailed history of the team) and also a silver Dollar coin, before the night continued with another American pastime: playing the game show Jeopardy. The evening finished off with a couple of beers and the next morning Mark and Kyle rode the first few miles of the road to Seattle with me.

This was exactly the type of positive experience I needed to give me the enthusiasm to get back on the bike, but what made it all the more special was that the previous evening Mark confided in me that he and his family shouldn't have been there to meet me at all. They had planned to go on a cruise with several groups of friends that week and just a few days before they had been due to leave, the organiser (a long-time friend of theirs) had done a runner with Mark's (and everyone else's) money. To know that even after having what must have been several thousand dollars stolen from them by a close friend, both Mark and his family were still so willing to bring a complete stranger into their house and show true hospitality lit a spark inside. I had enthusiasm for being on the road again.

I spent a weekend in Seattle and a couple of days in Tacoma, then, just under a hundred miles from Portland, I met Nick and Alex on the road. Both in their mid-twenties, Alex had spent the summer in Alaska working on a fishing boat, whilst Nick was a bike mechanic, and they were spending their autumn cycling from Seattle down to San Francisco.

The day we met happened to coincide with my eighteen month anniversary on the road and we cycled into Portland together to stay with friends of theirs. They were staying for a couple of days, whereas I was moving on to Salem, so we arranged to meet up again the following week and carry on riding south together.

The next morning as I rolled towards Salem, my odometer passing 20,000 miles in the process, there was an air of excitement within me. This was for two reasons: the first was that I would stay with Tara Simpson (a friend I'd met in South Korea) and her family, so I was looking forward to seeing a familiar face *and* staying with an American family called 'The Simpsons'; the second was that the date of my arrival was October 30th, the day before Halloween.

I had studied the Salem Witch Trials in school and for the uninitiated, these were a series of trials which took place in and around Salem Town between 1692-93, whereby, in a state of mass hysteria, people accused one another of witchcraft. Over 200 people were arrested on these charges, twenty were executed, including one by the painful torture of having large stones placed atop him until he was crushed to death, and nowadays the trials are considered a cautionary tale about the dangers of mass hysteria (a tale large sections of the US media would do well to heed).

The whole story is remarkable, but the aspect that made me so happy to be arriving in Salem was what goes on now to commemorate the witch trials: every Halloween the town of Salem hosts the annual 'Witches Ball', a street party where people from all over America come to Salem, put on their scariest costume and celebrate big time.

It was something I had been looking forward to for several months, so when I arrived and told my hosts of my plan, I ended up feeling just a little stupid. It turns out that the town of Salem I'd read about in school, and the street party I'd been looking forward to, were not in the Salem, Oregon, but were actually taking place over 3,000 miles away in Salem, Massachusetts.

Despite making a fool of myself and not getting my street party, I did get an insight into American Halloween and all I can say is 'wow'. I thought we had Halloween in the UK, but having been to an America version, a place where seemingly everyone was dressed up and where trick or treaters lined every street, I was amazed at just how into it people were. Tara and I spent the night at one of her friend's houses in neighbouring Eugene and on arrival home the next day her father Dave told us that the previous evening had seen 237 children knocking on their door.

"It was a bit quiet compared to last year," I heard Dave muse to his wife.

I spent a couple more days with the Simpsons and when I left Dave gave me several carrier bags full of leftover Halloween sweets and chocolate, thanks to this year's 'quiet' Halloween.

Armed to the teeth with sugar, I made my way to Pacific Coast where I met up with Alex and Nick, who had quite excellently chosen for us to meet at a brewery and we continued our group ride south. As we camped on our first night back together, raccoons got into my panniers and took every single bit of food they could find: my oats, my bread, my peanut butter and of course, worst of all, a few carrier bags of candy.

For someone who was surviving mentally on comfort eating, I was gutted. Nick and Alex, on the other hand, found it hilarious.

For the next two weeks Nick, Alex and I rode together, joined for a few days by David, a Wisconsin native cycling from New York to Los Angeles. Down the West Coast many of the State Parks offered a 'Hiker-Biker' rate of $5 a night to camp and thanks to finding a chain supermarket which sold five litre boxes of wine for $12, the happy times flowed and we became good friends. This continued until a day short of San Francisco we said goodbye; Nick and Alex went on to the city and I turned left to Vallejo to stay with Becky, an American friend who had lived next door to me five years previously in university halls.

By the time I left Becky's I found myself in a weird state of limbo. Four weeks previously I had had to say goodbye to Bella, now I had just said goodbye not only to Becky, but also to Nick and Alex, who had been by quite some distance my favourite riding partners, and once again I was on my own. In one week's time in Los Angeles I would meet a friend from England and three days later my parents would fly out to see me for two weeks. Having had such a great six weeks with the people I was with I had thought about home a lot and how I missed being in one place; I thought seeing people from England would clarify things in my own mind about how determined I was mentally to carry on with the ride.

In the meantime, I just wanted to be around these people and this meant getting on my bike and riding. I barely spoke to anyone on the ride south and slept rough the first two nights back on the road, first on the beach in San Francisco, then in a ditch on the outskirts of Aptos, before crossing Big Sur and arriving back in Cambria.

Pulling off of Highway One into the sleepy town, my desire to be around people I knew was satisfied early as a car pulled up alongside me and I heard a voice shouting at me from inside; it was Aaron, a cyclist I'd met during the previous summer and someone who had offered me a job at his restaurant over the upcoming Christmas holidays. We had a quick chat and I moved on to the ranch - before I'd even gotten to say hello to Beth and George, I'd been greeted by a more than happy creature who welcomed me back - it was Bodie, the farm dog, who recognised me from my last visit. It was wonderful just being somewhere where people knew me and I didn't have to retell my story and I enjoyed catching up with my old friends. When I'd previously been on the farm, their dog had killed a deer and we'd butchered the meat. The night I arrived back in town we dined on deer meat sausages and shared stories of what had been going on in our lives over the past few months.

Beth and George had become my second family the last time I had stayed; returning to their ranch was the closest I had to feeling at home throughout my time on the road.

My plan for the next few weeks was simple; in a couple of days' time I would leave the majority of things in Cambria and take the train to Los Angeles, where I would meet first Claire and then, three days later, my parents.

Los Angeles is a disgusting dump of a city where the car is king, public transport non-existent, pollution rife and the people seem in constant need of attention; it was somewhere I had no real desire to be, but seeing Claire again was definitely worth it. Claire and I had met through work and she had been my best friend during the year prior to my departure, the wise head who had offered me advice when I needed it and who had guided me through difficult times during my injury. Wondering what it'd be like to see someone from home again, I showed up at her hotel with a big hug and a bottle of horrendously bad $4 red wine and after a few hours of talking she happily pointed out to me that 'you haven't changed'.

Claire came and went and on the day she left my parents flew into town. It felt strange to see them again; so much had changed in my life over the last nineteen months that I thought there would also be major changes in our relationship, although I realised how silly this was when I saw them again. We had spoken constantly throughout the time I'd been away, with the only difference to our normal relationship being that I hadn't been at home. Now that I was with them, of course, nothing had changed. I enjoyed the two weeks we spent as a family, but what did strike me was that whilst I'd been off on my own journey, little had happened at home; my sister had moved out, Mum still loved to gossip about the neighbours and Dad still had delusions that QPR were actually quite good at football.

It was great to see them again, not least because having seen that I was OK I knew Mum wouldn't worry quite so much about me being on the road anymore. However, I began to realise that being part of a family didn't necessarily mean being in a certain place, but more who you spoke to most and who you cared about.

I thought of Bella.

After they'd gone I made my way back to Cambria, where for the rest of 2009 I would work in the day time as a handyman for the numerous contacts I'd made around town and in the evenings as a bus boy at Linn's Fruit Bin Restaurant, owned by Aaron and his family.

As the days passed in the run up to Christmas I looked back contentedly on the year; it had begun in Laos, and twelve months and 10,000 miles later, via the Arctic Circle, it was now going to end in Southern California. I had made friends, I had seen old friends and I had got to spend some time with my parents.

And on top of all of this, there was Bella. We still spoke; it had sometimes been not as often, but on a daily basis she was becoming more and more important to me. Every evening coming down the west coast the pictures of us together had been the last thing I'd look at before going to sleep and when I needed someone to make me feel better, it had been her I'd turned to.

But I still didn't know what she meant to me or what our future was.

On my way out of Salem I'd seen a mailbox with her surname on it and had asked the owner in the driveway if I could take a picture of it. When they'd asked why I wanted to take a photo of something as obscure as a mailbox I'd involuntarily replied "because you have the same last name as my girlfriend." She wasn't my girlfriend, but I needed to sort out what she was because at the back of my mind I knew things couldn't stay this way forever.

Added to this there was the lesson that the time with my parents had taught me; that family wasn't a place. I had no idea if I wanted a long distance relationship or to settle down somewhere that wasn't near home, but I now knew that I could do it.

But these were all problems that would sort themselves out later.

For now, I just wanted to be happy and enjoy my settled life in Cambria for the holidays. The serious stuff could wait.

Just as I started to make plans for the new year, on the day before New Year's Eve, Bella said she had something to tell me. After a brief conversation it became apparent she'd met somebody else.

In the blink of an eye, my world fell apart.

15: Acceptance

The fallout lasted two and a half months. We tried staying in contact. We tried not staying in contact. We tried many things. None of them ever really looked like working and by mid-March, when I had arrived in Veracruz in the east of Mexico, it was Bella who - being the mature one - told me we were better off not in contact.

Whilst I was desperate for that not to happen, I knew she was right and so it came to pass that the hardest thing I would ever have to do was look at someone I cared for more than I'd ever cared for anyone else and know that they were better off without me.

By the time we said our final goodbye I was a broken man.

Since finding out Bella was with someone else, the days that followed were some of the darkest of my life. At first I'd lost all appetite and found it impossible to sleep. Thinking this would be temporary, when two weeks later I was still neither eating nor sleeping, I realised I couldn't go on like this and had resorted to sleeping pills. I would use them every day for two months before I was able to wean myself off. I became things I'd never been before: jealous, bitter, angry. I did selfish things that I never even imagined possible of myself and, realising these things didn't help, I would more often than not end up with a far simpler coping strategy: crying.

I couldn't remember a day during this period where I didn't cry at least once.

These were by quite some distance the darkest days of my life and whilst there were many frustrations, the simple fact remained that no matter which way I looked at it, through whichever angle I tried to view things from, however I tried to twist facts in my own mind to suit my own thoughts, the truth remained; it had been all my fault.

It had now been four years since the dream of cycling around the world had been formed and it was approaching two years since I had left the UK. Thinking back to the person who had set off on his bike, I wasn't sure why, but one of the main aims I had for the trip was to become a *better* person. I had no idea how I was going to achieve this and looking back, it seems a laughable target; how does someone become a *better* person simply by riding a bicycle? What would I do to achieve this? But I knew there were things about myself that I wanted to change and I had hoped travel and cycling would do this. Instead, what happened with Bella had highlighted every aspect of myself that I despised and it was sickening to see that whilst my failings were my own, I could make a distinct link from them to the bike.

I had always had a cocky side to my personality, but I now began to realise that through cycling this had turned to arrogance. 'What you're doing is amazing'. 'I'm going to be living vicariously through you while you're on the road'. 'I am in awe of what you're achieving'. All sentences I had heard countless times and whilst I had always tried to keep my ego in check, as Bella slipped away, I realised I had started to believe it. When people are constantly saying positive things to you, there is no-one there to keep you in line and point out your failings. I had started to believe I had none, so despite the warning signs and my pushing her away, I had told myself that Bella would always be there for me. I knew she loved me, and in my eyes, well, I thought I was fantastic too, so it stood to reason she'd never find anyone else as great as me.

My own arrogance was breathtaking and equally as stupid was how I had continued to run away from my feelings. I had done this prior to the trip and I'd thought I had changed, but now I realised how untrue this was, through telling her not to wait for me - I had also tried to transfer my feelings from her to other women, ignoring the voices in my own mind.

If you can't be true to yourself, then you're in big trouble.

But what cut the deepest was the realisation that it had been my obsession with doing my bike trip and doing it solo that had prevented me from being honest with Bella. After finding out about her new love, I contemplated several things; I contemplated telling her how I felt, I contemplated cringeworthy romantic gifts, I even contemplated showing up on her door step in Quebec to break down in tears to tell her that I loved her.

The one thing I never contemplated doing was abandoning my bike trip.

Every bit of effort for the previous four years had gone into riding a bicycle around the world on my own. Now I was two years in. I had done it all by myself. I had had no help from anyone. I was entirely self-sufficient. The fact that these last three sentences weren't true was irrelevant; in my own mind it was gospel and so when I'd met Bella, instead of embracing someone whom I loved and who could change the way I saw the world I had shut her out, pushed her away and continually told myself I didn't need her.

No, I was Matthew Blake, I could cycle around the world on my own. I can do everything all by myself.

In a strange way I was quite correct; I didn't *need* her. But I loved her, I would miss her always and now I was alone. I had lost her due to my own selfishness.

Over the coming months I made a conscious point of trying to lose my arrogance, putting others first and also going out of my way to change the self-centred person I was becoming. But the fact remained: in Vancouver I'd had to make a choice between Bella and the bike ride. At every corner I'd chosen the bike ride. Until this point on the journey I had felt nothing but pride in who I was, what I was doing and the mature young man I was becoming. Bella hammered it out to me; it was all bullshit. All the self-congratulation, all the believing I'd changed; it wasn't true. I'd been running away from feelings all my life and had just found out that not even 20,000 miles on a bike was enough to get me away from them.

As far as I was concerned, in terms of changing who I was, whatever happened now the trip would always be a failure.

For the rest of the journey, whenever I felt alone, all I had to do was look in a mirror. Looking back at me was the person whose fault it was.

I would miss her a lot.

16: From A Farm To A Ranch

Having chosen a bike ride over a girl, this meant, of course, that I had a bike ride to be on and I was still in Cambria. 2009 became 2010 and as the first week of January rolled around it was time to head south before my visa expired. With all the emotional upheaval that was going on around me, it felt particularly hard to leave George and Beth. I had met their son Scott in a bar a little over a year before and whilst I had been fairly sure his comment of 'if you ever need a job then give me a call' had been a throwaway one, I had now spent the best part of three months with the family. I wasn't looking forward to saying goodbye.

Trying to make the best of a bad situation, there was aid from their neighbours. Tom, the Frisbee golf world champion and keen cyclist, had become both an employer and close friend over my time on the ranch and his wife Michelle arranged for me to stay with first her daughter, then her grandson and finally, her mother on my route south.

The ride was beautiful, interspersed with glorious beaches which invited breaks during the day time, and as I arrived in San Diego I realised that if it weren't for the cesspool of humanity that was Los Angeles, then California would just about be the perfect place.

I was accompanied on this section of the ride by Anna, the Czech girl I had met in Whitehorse who had a few days to kill before her flight back home and who had become a good friend. As we arrived to stay with the fourth generation of the same family, whilst we should have known better, I don't think either of us were prepared for the lady who was about to greet us.

Well into her eighties, Julane was a delightful old lady

who, despite her years, still had the energy of a teenager and voiced her opinions strongly. She welcomed us both to her home - an apartment in central San Diego - saying she hoped we'd enjoyed our ride through the US, before going on to apologise vehemently for the state the last Republican government had left the country in. I immediately liked her and it was just as well, because as we arrived in San Diego clouds began to gather. Usually one of the drier places on earth, roughly once every three-to-seven years a storm cycle known as *El Nino* moves in and batters the Pacific coast with rain. Whilst *El Nino* can technically last much longer, the storms themselves only usually last about a week and given that these occur once every five years, with odds of 260-1 and excellent weather for the majority of the rest of the time, I hadn't really taken too much consideration of whether we would see rain in San Diego; waking up to our second morning, the rain came, and for the next six days it didn't stop. High winds, lashing storms and thunder and lightning meant that leaving the house was fairly pointless and for a week all we could do was wait patiently for the bad weather to disappear before we could finally get back on the road and head for the border into Mexico.

During this week off I looked back at my journey through the USA and thought about what I had learned about the most powerful country on earth.

I smiled at the thought of how the one thing that connected all Americans was the kindness that they had shown towards me as a foreigner in their country and was warmed by just how many good people I'd met. It was hard not to be amused at the fact that whilst they were all linked in their goodwill, just how different some of the American citizens I'd met were meant I was now fairly sure that I could place where someone came from on a first meeting. So, they like to talk about guns, hunting or how dangerous the world can be? They're probably from Alaska. Someone who likes surfing, looks stoned at eleven in the morning and doesn't seem to have a place to be? They were probably part of the group of surfers who went to southern California thirty years ago on a surfing holiday and had never gotten around to doing anything else. Leaning to the left politically, riding a fixed gear to work and making a point of how open-minded you are? Then Oregon is probably where you're from.

The stereotypes could go on, but I found it amazing just how so many of the different people I met conformed to being from a certain place.

Of course, I had experienced the good side of the country and whilst I could unite the people I had met through their hospitality and the Star Spangled Banner, on a broader scale these people themselves were becoming far less united.

It was now a year since President Obama had taken office and the big issue of the day was Health Care Reform; it was driving the country apart. Coming from a country with universal health care I couldn't really understand the arguments against it being implemented in America; The US was a predominantly Christian country so the idea that you wouldn't look after your fellow man was in stark contrast to your most basic ideology: all studies were showing that the American system cost the average person $5,000 per year more than the British counterpart and several high profile reports were being made public into how insurance companies were exploring avenue after avenue in efforts to not have to pay for treatment, even when people had coverage.

Yet despite this, I met numerous people who were severely against the Health Care Bill and it was always for the same reason. They could all identify someone they knew who was lazy and who, in their eyes, they didn't want to have to pay for healthcare.

It didn't matter that this system would be cheaper and -

for the overwhelming majority of people - better. What mattered was that through personifying the system, the most important thing to these people was not letting someone they knew have something they didn't pay for.

This all linked backed to one of the key points that lures people to America and that citizens take pride in: The American dream; the idea that anybody can come to America and, through sheer hard work, achieve prosperity.

The basis of the American dream was still so ingrained in citizens that when it came to Healthcare it became apparent that the opposition to it was based on the notion that if you give people something for free then somehow, somewhere, someone will get something that they don't deserve.

The debate raged long after the Bill was passed several months later, but how I saw it was clear: for those who opposed the Bill, it was better to let a large number of unfortunate people be worse off than to let a small minority have a free ride.

That was what the American dream would have wanted and now Americans themselves were at a crossroads. Meanwhile, partisan politics was taking over, the media - which more often than not contained little more than fear-mongering and outright lies - stoked the fire and with several states, including California, essentially broke, there was no sign that the good times would come back any time soon.

From the outside looking in it was sad to see; I had met so many Americans that I liked on the road; however one thing they were not anymore was united.

Thinking we had sat out the storm, we were proved wrong as when we got on our bikes and moved towards the Tijuana border the heavens opened again and the rain came down, so much so that as we arrived at the frontier we found the road to be under a foot of water. The border guard at the head of the line, adorned in a bright yellow Macintosh that was about three sizes too big for him, waved us straight through. '*Vamos! Vamos!*' was the shout at everything that passed as he desperately tried to be heard over the rolls of thunder. We were waved straight into Mexico without so much as having our passports checked and we carried on, assuming that Customs must have been further down the road. Having gone nearly a kilometre into Tijuana, it became apparent that there wasn't any further post and realising it was probably best to get our documents in order, we returned to the border, only to spend forty minutes hunting down the appropriate officer who had been away from his office smoking at the time; given how strict gaining entry to the US had been, finding anyone at the Mexican border to even look at our passports had proved extremely difficult.

But we were here, freshly documented and carrying on south into Baja. We rode through Tijuana, stopping at numerous road side taco stands, and made our way to Ensenada to stay with Isaac, the cousin of a Mexican cyclist we had met coming through San Diego. With the surname of Amadoor (it's hard not to doff your cap to anyone whose initials are I. Amadoor) Isaac welcomed us in from the rain and warned us about what was ahead; reports had it that this year's *El Nino* had been one of the worst on record and that three bridges had been washed away downstream. Furthermore, word on the street was that nothing was getting through.

That night, after several tequilas, we slept and the following morning awoke to bright sunshine. We did come across a small bit of road that had been washed away, leaving a four foot by four foot hole in the ground, but for the most part we encountered no problems and set up camp that night wondering what all the fuss was about. We found out several hours and a mere 800 metres later, when we descended to the bottom of the hill and found a large bridge had been completely washed away.

Whilst not particularly deep, the river was around twenty metres wide and despite the flood waters having subsided a little, it was still dangerous. Contrary to the reports of how nothing was crossing, we were pleased to find a local farmer had spotted a good business opportunity and was using his tractor to tow people's cars across, which at the deepest point was about three or four feet with a strong current. Local truck owners were also finding it easy to get through. This meant that all we had to do was sit there and wait for a truck willing to put us in the back, and in the meantime we were free to watch the entertainment. Entertainment being the correct word, as whilst the farmer had no problem crossing in his tractor and the truck owners found it relatively easy, there is always one idiot who thinks their vehicle can get across. Or in this case, there were two.

The first was a White Ford Transit van. I wasn't sure what was inside, but given that luggage was piled on top of the roof as well I dread to think how much weight he was carrying, and regardless of people telling him not to cross he went for it, trying to drive through the water. To absolutely nobody's surprise he got stuck in the deepest part of the river and with water leaking into the van, the people on our side of the river offered little sympathy. After it became clear he was going nowhere, he was eventually pulled out by a somewhat angry looking farmer and his tractor.

So it became obvious which vehicles were capable of making it over and which were not, but this was Mexico and that wouldn't stop some people. For those that remember *Scooby Doo*, please picture the *Mystery Machine*. Then imagine that, made in the seventies and loaded down with a large supply of carpets and rugs. Then grasp the idea of that trying to drive through a flowing river.

The driver wasn't going to wait for anyone (or common sense) to get in the way and, despite what he'd just witnessed, was the next to try the gauntlet. Unsurprisingly, his failure was even more spectacular than that of the Transit and he was in genuine danger of being washed away. With black smoke billowing out of his engine and the water loading up his vehicle, he owed one hell of a lot to the now even angrier farmer who, after an almighty struggle, pulled him and his vehicle out of the water to safety.

We crossed about thirty minutes later in the back of a truck belonging to two Canadian Fisherman and as we reached the other side the *Mystery Machine* was still sat there smoking, as the owner set about angrily drying out the inside of his vehicle.

We had little sympathy.

Carrying on our journey, a few hours later we came to the second collapsed bridge, which this time crossed a river that was far wider. Using one of the few Spanish phrases we had - '*No hay Puente? (there is no bridge?)*' - we were told that we could cross the river in the scoop of a JCB. This was travelling in style and we were soon on our way again.

After these two, the third bridge proved something of an anti-climax, as by the time we arrived the flood waters had drained and we were able to just walk straight through the now dry river bed, and carry on our journey south.

The following weeks were quiet, although still fun. A few days' south of the broken bridges we bumped into Koko, the Japanese cyclist I had met back in the Yukon, as well as Josh and Greg, two cyclists from Washington heading south. We spent a good couple of weeks riding together, but one by one though our group got smaller; first Koko left, then Anna went to catch her flight, before finally I got a boat over to the Mexican mainland and headed across to Veracruz alone. The previous weeks had been tough on the soul and I was looking forward to my next stop: a rural ranch in Mexico.

Back in California one of the four generations of

Michelle's family I had stayed with had been her daughter Monique in Santa Barbara. In turn, Monique was married to Antonio, a former professional footballer (proper football, where you use your feet, for any American readers) for several Premier League clubs in Mexico, the largest of which was Pueblas. For someone who had led a life as amazing as his, which included playing and winning at the famous Azteca stadium in Mexico City, Antonio was a kind, humble man and upon realising my need for Spanish in order to be able to travel in Latin America, suggested I go to work on his family's farm in the state of Veracruz and in return they would teach me some of the language.

His family were as welcoming as he was: his mother, Maria, his father, Salomon and his niece and nephew, Ximena and Chema, would look after me throughout my time with them, and I quickly settled in, finding much excitement on the ranch. On my first weekend, Chema showed me Dino, a seven foot long crocodile that a neighbouring family had rescued from a nearby river and who now lived as a pet; afterwards the same family hosted a meal which consisted of an unusual main dish.

That afternoon, several of the young men had been off into the nearby jungle with a catapult. Using rocks as ammo, they'd knock iguanas out of the trees, pin down the injured animal and hammer a nail through its head. They were then bought back to the house, skinned and deep fried. For dinner that night we dined on fried iguana, served with an array of salsa sauces.

It was quite an introduction.

I spent four weeks in Veracruz; on the weekends we would either watch football or go to Mexican horse racing - a bizarre event which only ever consisted of a two horse race over a non-marked 100 metre track and without a proper finish line - whilst in the week I would keep myself busy in and around the city.

My arrival had coincided with saying goodbye to Bella,

and I was indebted to the support the family gave, not to mention how much Spanish they taught me. As my time to leave drew near, an acceptance settled over me. I had lost someone, but life was still throwing up some amazing experiences. I looked forward to what lay ahead in Central America.

17: Philosophical In The Face Of Stupidity

After the stint on the ranch I would stay a further two weeks in Veracruz, visiting local schools with some students I had met. It's not often I got to make friends with people that are both my own age *and* who I'm going to see more than once. So, having formed new friendships, established a daily routine that didn't involve a bicycle and a long distance, and even having something resembling a fixed social life, it was hard, even if only having these things for two weeks, to let them go when the time came. Drinking one last Michelada - beer mixed with tomato juice, squeezed lime and Worcestershire sauce, served in a salt-rimmed glass - on my last night in the city, I prepared and left.

Within a few hours on the road, the stark realisation that I now had a new challenge facing me sank in: in the time since I'd stopped riding, the heat had changed dramatically. The students had warned me that April and May - the period prior to the rainy season - were the hottest months, however the problem was that whilst they'd been telling me this we'd been sat in an air conditioned apartment with fans in every room, so it had been hard to take them seriously.

Three days back on the road and it was pretty clear they'd been right.

The days were hard, hot, and very, very sweaty. The temperature was constantly well into the forties, and with it being a sticky heat as opposed to a dry heat - which my time in the deserts had taught me can actually be a pleasure to ride in - I had to drink a lot and give up even trying to ride between the hours of twelve and three.

But the heat comes from the sun, the sun goes down at night, and therefore the nights should be cool and easy to sleep in, right?

Oh so very, very wrong, and herein lies the issue that would be the cause of all my problems for the next few weeks.

The first night I was lucky: I managed to find a nice part of deserted beach about fifty kilometres out of Veracruz with a strong wind whipping in off the ocean and cooling down the air. This meant not only could I sleep, but I could do so inside the comfort of my tent away from the attention of the numerous mosquitoes.

It was the next evening, after a day's riding that can be best summed up with the word 'slog', when the fun and games began.

I tried sleeping out under the stars; this didn't work, as the mosquitoes wouldn't leave me alone. I tried putting up the mosquito net and sleeping under that on the ground; this didn't work, as the ants attacked me from below. I tried putting up the tent and sleeping in there; it took all of thirty seconds for the inside of the tent to become like a sauna.

No matter what I tried it became obvious I would not be able to sleep and after deciding that the ants were the lesser of three evils, I lay under the mosquito net, but even then out in the open, lying in just a silk sleeping bag liner, it still remained too hot to drift off, with sweat dripping all over.

At what must have been about 04.30, I finally fell asleep. The sun rose at 6 a.m. By 06.30 the temperature was such that lying in an open field was simply unbearable.

I got up, rode another long, sticky day and by 7p.m. the time had come for the same routine. Again I tried the tent: it was too hot. Again I tried outside: the mozzies got me. Again I tried the mosquito net: the ants got me.

Again, more importantly, even outside, it was too hot.

For the second night in a row I got a little under two hours' sleep.

By this stage I was pretty cranky; the lack of sleep meant I was tired, the heat meant I was grumpy and the fact that the Mexican tap water had turned my urine a healthy shade of dark red meant I was becoming slightly worried about my health; it was obvious something needed to change.

I stopped at around six o'clock for a swim in a lake I'd found just off the highway, which left me feeling far more refreshed; I came up with a new idea. As I'd been riding along the highway, I began to notice that all of the bridges had something in common: underneath and to the side of every bridge was a ledge about a metre wide and around two and a half metres long - easily flat enough for me to sleep on - away from the mugginess of ground level and with a solid concrete base, which meant there would be no ants.

This seemed like a brilliant idea to me and just after it had got dark I found the first bridge I could, pulled over, left my bike at the bottom and took my roll-mat up to the ledge to see if, as I hoped I would, I could sleep there.

I lay out the mat and had a test 'lie down' to see if it was comfortable; it was better than expected. There were no ants, the twenty foot elevation took me far enough from the ground to catch a breeze and the cool air brushing against me was heavenly. Better yet, the breeze meant no mosquitoes.

This. Is. Perfect.

I lay on the ledge, which I'm fairly sure was more comfortable than any bed I'd ever slept in and looked down at my bike.

OK boy, now you need to go down there, move the bike further out of sight, bring back up the silk liner, also your bar bag containing your valuables, brush your teeth, make sure the jam is away from the rest of the food so when the ants attack it again they don't spoil everything, have a wash, write the... zzzzzzzzzzzzzzzzzzzzzz.

I didn't make it down to the bike again. I didn't even take my boots off. The next thing I knew it was 6.30 a.m. and after a beautiful, ten hour sleep, the sun had given me a rather rude awakening.

I looked down at the bike in panic, but the bar bag was still there; it looked like I'd got away with not looking after my valuables, if only for one night. I clambered down to the bike, happy to see that both my wallet and my camera were still there and set to making breakfast.

Hang on, I had a loaf of bread and a kilo of bananas. Where have they gone?

I've had food disappear before and every single time it's been animals, so I figured that this is what was happening here and it worried me, as since the age of fourteen I've suffered from migraines if I do too much exercise without eating enough.

I rarely get them anymore (I'd only had one on the ride, back in China when it had been caused by sickness anyway) but when I do the procedure is as follows: I get blinding lights in my eyes for around three or four hours, where I won't be able to see more than ten feet in front of me. This is just the build-up and, it is followed by the most painful, splitting headache you will ever feel; we're talking two to three hours of moaning and groaning, waiting for the pain to end, begging for mercy. The relief comes in the form of vomiting. Lots of vomiting, until whatever was in my stomach is purged and boy does it feel good, going from hellish pain to peaceful tranquillity in the space of a few heaves. After the vomiting is over, with nothing left in my body, it's time to sleep. I won't be out of bed for at least another twenty-four hours, as the body and head recover, and I'll usually be back to somewhere near full strength around forty-eight hours after the original 'lights' begin.

A beautiful cycle.

This is not to say I am complaining; I get migraines, this is what happens when I get them, this is a fact and I know how to stop them. But the reason this is relevant is that in 90% of the migraines I've ever had, the cause was a failure to eat breakfast: if I don't eat something, at least a sandwich or a bowl of cereal within an hour or so of waking up, I know the chances are, especially if I am exercising, then I am running a high risk of getting a migraine. So, upon waking to find my raw food supply vanished, being in the middle of nowhere, God knows how far from the nearest town, and with the knowledge I'd have to cycle to get any food, I was more than a touch anxious to get something to eat for two reasons:

1. To avoid getting a migraine;
2. In case I did get a migraine, I needed to eat so my body had something to throw up.

This second point I had learned around my third or fourth migraine when I was younger: you get a migraine because you don't eat enough? The pain only stops when you throw up? You have nothing in your body to throw up? The pain doesn't stop. And as such, when the blinding lights begin I'll start eating anything I can get my hands: rice, sandwiches, pizzas, cakes. Doughy stuff is the best, as it fills your stomach and comes back up without too much of a fight.

So yes, I needed food. I wolfed down the remaining half pot of jam I had and went to strap my roll-mat to the back of my bike when I realised something else was missing.

WHERE THE F*CK IS MY F*CKING TENT!?!

You'll have to excuse the language but it's only fair to give an honest representation of what went through my mind. Someone had stolen it.

I panicked; why would someone nick the tent? It was of no value, three of the poles were broken and the zips on the two doors hadn't worked properly in months. So why would they take it? It didn't dawn on me until much later that the thief probably didn't know the uselessness of what they were stealing. And it wasn't just the tent either. I checked my valuables: camera - still there, wallet - still there. These had both been in the bar bag, around three feet from where the tent had been, so this really was a bit weird. And then I realised what else was missing.

Why the f*cking f*ck, when my wallet and camera are right here, would someone steal my tent, a kilo of bananas, a loaf of bread and my sodding cycle helmet? No-one in Mexico wears a f*cking cycle helmet.

I was now left to face up to the fact that, in spite of all the *hilarious* e-mails I'd had from friends and family over the last two years laughing at the hobo lifestyle I led, this time it wasn't funny: I was now officially homeless. I tried to think of who the culprit could have been. I hadn't seen so much as a farm in the previous thirty kilometres, and from the top of the bridge I could see nobody for miles around.

I could have looked harder, but I knew deep down I wouldn't see the stuff again.

And besides, I had other priorities. It had now been forty-five minutes since I'd woken up; the migraine clock was ticking and I had to get on the move. Losing the tent was stressful, but it'd be nothing compared to the pain I'd go through if I didn't eat soon.

I pulled the bike out onto the road.

FOR F*CK'S SAKE. ARE YOU F*CKING KIDDING ME?

A puncture.

Another fifteen minutes lost (two minutes to take the old tube out, one minute to find the cause of the puncture, two minutes to put the new tube in and ten minutes to really throw my toys out of the pram, scream, shout, kick my panniers about, curse God, the sun, the bicycle and pretty much everything else to do with this trip) and then it was off on the road.

I got lucky: five kilometres on I found a small café about 400 metres off the highway. The café was on a separate road and I would have to leave my bike unattended. I was still pouting and, knowing that my bicycle would be out of view, I left it unlocked, cynically hoping that someone - perhaps the same person who took the tent - would steal it. Then, with no bike, I would have to fly home and stop this

167

stupid idea of trying to sleep under bridges and cycle in the forty degree heat each day.

This childish thought didn't last very long: I placed my order and as soon as I'd drunk two cans of ice cold *Coke* (for some vital sugar), I remembered that I actually quite liked my life on the bicycle and I really didn't want to lose everything I had, so attempting to throw it all away in a highly petulant manner probably wasn't a good idea.

I ran back to the bike, elated to see that in the ten minutes of my absence she hadn't been stolen. I gave her a passionate hug and secured her with a chain, before rushing back to the café to wolf down my breakfast.

With food inside of me, and having bought enough biscuits to stave off the risk of a migraine for the rest of the day, my head became a bit clearer, the benefits of a good night's rest also kicking in.

Losing the tent was not a good thing. But at the same time the door on the damned thing didn't work and in the previous year I had broken no fewer than ten different poles belonging to it (the tent is comprised of four poles - I was on my fourth set when it was stolen, two of which had already broken) so I'd been trying to get a new tent for a while now; here was a kick up the backside to actually organise getting one.

Furthermore, would I miss the tent in the immediate future? I'd tried to sleep in it for three of the previous four nights and it had been impossible, so I was hardly going to be using it much over the next few weeks anyway and as such its loss really wouldn't disrupt any of the immediate plans.

These thoughts cheered me up a bit and I decided to treat myself to something I rarely get; a hotel room for the night.

I arrived in the town of Cardenas, only stopping as I'd seen a hotel with rooms offered at what looked a ridiculously cheap rate. It turned out that these prices were 'by the hour' and also came with the services of the female employee of my choice. Whilst I wasn't exactly in a cheerful mood, a night in a brothel probably wasn't the answer, so I moved further into town, found a cheap place where I wouldn't need to change the bed sheets, and spent the evening sat on the internet, where I put out a post about the predicament I was now in.

The response was overwhelming. One of the first replies I got was from Stephen Lord, the author of The Adventure Cycle-Touring Handbook, a book which without I never would have made it past Calais. Stephen was always one of my heroes and since leaving home, he and I had spoken every now and then, with him checking up to see how I was doing. As soon as he heard what had happened, Stephen immediately offered one of his spare tents and we arranged for it to be posted out to Guatemala City. I was so grateful for this, but even more humbling was the response from the internet forum that I was a member of. This was the place where the idea of cycling began and since that day I had kept the members of it informed of how I was doing, developing quite a following; and so it was that various members clubbed together and raised over £400 to keep me on my journey. Meanwhile, another cyclist who had contacted me for cycle touring advice and who was planning to ride back to the UK from his Dubai home, sent me money, as did my grandmother. Even Anna insisted on sending me £100, as by cycle touring with me to Mexico instead of backpacking from city to city in the US, she'd saved what she thought to be well over half a grand and thought it was only fair I got some of this.

Within a few hours of my things being stolen, I had a new tent on its way to Guatemala City and had over £900 being sent to my bank account, the majority of which was from people I had never met. It remains one of the most humbling experiences I would ever have.

The next day, after I had thanked everyone (and relishing the fact I had a new tent on its way), I was back on the road with something other than a new home to look forward to on the horizon.

The tent was stolen on the 25th of April; the 29th of April marked the two year anniversary of leaving England.

Of course I had to get to that date first, and this meant more painful riding, but I was now in quite a good routine: I would get up at first light, cycle until about 10 a.m., sit in a bus shelter and read or sleep until about three or four in the afternoon, then ride until total darkness, at which point I would sleep under a mosquito net in another bus shelter, of which, for some reason, there now seemed to be many along the highway, even in the middle of nowhere.

The best example I have to sum up how hot it was occurred three days after the tent had been stolen. I'd stopped at a river for a swim with some locals, thinking it'd cool me down. Stepping into that water was like being back in the Japanese Onsens: it was boiling. The only coolness I could get out of the entire river was in my feet when I was treading water; I'm 5'11", so you had to go down about five and a half feet to get anything resembling cold water. It was not pleasant and gives an idea of just how hot it was during this period.

The 29th came and went. I celebrated by cooking myself a steak, topped off with boiled potatoes, fried onions and gravy. Better still, I found an abandoned petrol station with running water and working toilets in which to spend the night. Under a mosquito net on a flat surface, it was pure luxury.

I was now at the point where I simply wanted to get out of Mexico and after two more days of riding, I was just 200 kilometres from my goal, the Belize border, with the added motivation being that I'd spent all but ten of my Pesos. With the heat still steaming me over, I made a decision to do something I love doing, but due to safety issues I hadn't done in a while: night riding.

A long, flat road with a healthy shoulder and virtually no

traffic, coupled with a clear night sky, meant riding through the night was easy, even if the headwind slowed me down.

167 kilometres later, which had taken eleven and a quarter hours to ride, and it was 5 a.m.: I was just thirty kilometres from the border. I stopped in another bus stop for a quick, two hour nap and then at twelve o'clock, I crossed into the twenty-sixth country of the ride.

Belize, it's fair to say, I liked instantly. The thirteen kilometre ride from the border to the town of Corazol ran parallel to a crystal blue lake, with parrots squawking and iguanas looking down on me from the treetops as I rode past. Everything was good.

However, I am, and always will be, thoroughly embarrassed about what followed.

At around six o'clock, I'd stopped in a net café, having earlier e-mailed a Couchsurfer in Orange Walk, a town about thirty miles down the road, to ask if I could spend a couple of nights at their place to catch up on some much needed sleep. They hadn't been online unfortunately, which was no big deal, as I could just mosey on out of town and find a place further down the road, but instead of doing this I got chatting to a friend I hadn't spoken to in a while on Skype - it was only supposed to be a quick two minute chat, but that's the way it goes sometimes - and before I knew it, we'd spent four hours catching up, the net café was closing and the fact that I'd ridden a little over 200km (or fourteen hours, depending on how you wanted to look at it) in the last thirty-six hours on only two hours' sleep started to catch up with me.

I'd met a local earlier who'd told me that in the summer lots of people love to camp on the beach, so this is where I headed. I went a few kilometres out of the town centre, found a quiet spot where I couldn't be seen from the road, and where I was fairly sure that no-one would ever find me.

This was not the stupid thing.

The stupid (really stupid) thing was that in my bar bag,

having had to get them out to cross the border were: my passport, my wallet, my back-up wallet containing credit cards and emergency money and my digital camera.

All of my valuables in one place is a silly enough thing to do, but it had only been since crossing the border and I was going to put these things back in their respective homes before I fell asleep, wasn't I?

Wasn't I?

I found the spot where I'd be happy to sleep and sat down next to the bike.

OK boy, now you need put the valuables away, get out the silk liner, brush your te… zzzzzzzzzzzzzzzzzzzzzz.

I count having a broken tent stolen from the back of my bike in the middle of nowhere as unlucky.

I count having all of my valuable possessions stolen when I've left them nicely bundled together in my bar bag for anyone to take as something thoroughly undeserving of sympathy.

I had been asleep for roughly two hours when I woke up in a panic. I sat up in a bolt, and looked to see if I'd been robbed.

My bar bag was open, and next to the bike on the floor were the three items the thief had deemed not worthy of stealing: my diary, my Lonely Planet Central America and my passport. Somewhat bizarrely, the thief had kindly placed them in a pile and put a rock on top to stop them blowing away in the wind. (I would later be told that the passport was only left as it was something too dangerous for them to steal. With no easily accessible monetary value and a police force happy to use force, Belizean thieves are far safer stealing material things they can move on quickly).

So that's what they'd left; what had they taken? In no particular order: my wallet, my back-up wallet containing credit cards, my digital camera, my head-torch, my prescription sunglasses, my bike lights and even my odometer.

172

I really didn't learn much from this experience; I already knew all the lessons I would have learnt from this and all I got out of it is that, despite having survived on my own for over two years, when I put my mind to it I can still take stupidity to new levels.

The next morning, after a quick talk with a couple of police officers, who were saying the same things to me as I'd already said to myself, I evaluated the situation.

The first priority was money, as without that I'd soon have no food, and when I had no food, well... you get the idea.

I managed to get online and e-mailed home asking for my dad to *Western Union* me some cash. God bless the world we live in, where in the space of five minutes my father could wire me money without even leaving his computer, which I could then collect from a local bank within an hour and a half of the first e-mail being sent.

Now with the equivalent of £100 in cash and having cancelled my credit cards I took stock of the situation.

No, things were not ideal, but the world hadn't ended. I had a spare head-torch, I hardly wore my sunglasses and I could be thankful I still had a passport. The things I was going to miss most were my odometer, which had clocked every single kilometre of the journey, and my camera. But even these I could live without until Guatemala City, where, as well as my new tent, I would now pick up my replacement credit cards.

Rather than being angry at having had stuff stolen, I was more just firmly embarrassed at the way I'd set myself up for it and felt as though I had let down the people who had helped me at home.

I rode to Orange Walk that day, where I'd since had an e-mail from the Couchsurfer there saying I could stay, and I spent three nights in the town, during which my self-hatred subsided and I began to appreciate what an awesome place Belize is. A range of cultures make up the people; among

173

them were natives, Creoles, a few Koreans, a reasonable ex-pat population and, bizarrely, a significant proportion of Chinese people. The place has a vibrant feel, especially when the sun goes down, and the fact that everyone speaks English makes it easy to get by on the language front. (A quick side point: Creole is both the local language and a form of English, and the people who speak it do appreciate you trying to talk it as well, however it is technically impossible for a white guy to talk in a Caribbean accent and not look like a complete idiot. In my case, I didn't even try.)

OK, so it isn't the perfect place: the food isn't the best (although the Chinese restaurants all offer cheap chicken fried rice), the national beer, *Belikin*, won't go down as one of history's greatest inventions and yes, it was still hot (my host had a thermometer attached to his roof - the temperature had hit forty-two degrees by 8 a.m. every day of my stay) but as for the country Belize itself? Beautiful. Clear lakes and rivers give a real relaxed feel to the place and I also found out some utterly useless trivia when I discovered that 40% of the UK's sugar comes from the country.

I remained in Orange Walk for three nights, before moving onto San Ignacio, close to the Guatemalan Border, where I stayed with Skip, a retired American who had moved down here a few months before to enjoy the easy life of Belize. Skip finished every meal with ice cream and tequila, so it was hard to leave, but I was down to the last £35 of the money I'd been sent, £13 of which I needed to cross the border, and I had six days of riding to do to get to Guatemala City.

I crossed into Guatemala, towards Tikal: another world-famous tourist spot attracting people from all over the globe and another place I wouldn't be stopping. I rode on, sleeping in abandoned buildings each night.

Guatemala is both mountainous and beautiful, with steep climbs meaning I rarely left gear twenty-seven on the hills.

174

The country has a large indigenous population, many of whom still lead 'The Good Life' and wear traditional Mayan clothing; I was amazed at what I saw and sad that without my camera I had no way to preserve my memories and as I rolled into Guatemala City I became philosophical.

Over the previous weeks I had been reading *Robinson Crusoe* and whilst I could in no way compare my own journey to a fictional story about being ship-wrecked on an island alone for twenty-eight years, there is a reflection made by the main character in which I took solace:

"I learned to look more upon the bright side of my condition and less upon the dark side and to consider what I enjoyed rather than what I wanted; and this gave me sometimes such secret comforts that I cannot express them; and which I take notice of here, to put those discontented people in mind of it who cannot enjoy comfortable what God had given them because they see and covet something that He has not given them. All our discontents about what we want appeared to me to spring from the want of thankfulness for what we have...

...These reflections made me very sensible of the goodness of Providence to me and very thankful for my present condition, with all its hardships and misfortunes. And this part also I cannot but recommend the reflection of those who are apt in their misery to say, 'Is any affliction like mine?' Let them consider how much worse the cases of some people are and their case might have been, if Providence had thought fit."

Yep. I did something stupid. Yep, I had a bad few weeks. But at the same time they didn't get my passport, they didn't take the bike, and whilst I had no photos, they couldn't take my memories. Most importantly, I was safe.

I vowed to learn from my mistakes, but never to complain about them.

18: Spare A Thought For The Old Girl

I would end up staying for ten days in Guatemala City, waiting for my new tent and bank cards to arrive. Accompanied by Dietmar, my half-Guatemalan, half-German host (who had a love for the board game *Stratego*), I found the time passed relatively quickly and when I did finally receive my gear, I rode out of the city a short forty kilometres to Antigua. The reason for this was that Dietmar and I had gone on a day trip here and I had spotted the camera I wanted to buy: the excellent *Olympus Tough*. Now that I had access to money again, my plan was to ride into town, spend the night with a friend of John Honney's (he who I stayed with back in Cambodia) and then ride on south the following morning.

I had become accustomed to my plans never working out as expected, but what happened next was a new one, even for me: a volcano erupted.

With the eruption occurring about fifty kilometres down the road, we were in no immediate danger. But landslides were reported, clouds of ash filled the sky and if this weren't enough, that evening, tropical storm Agatha swept into the area, adding flash floods to the list of problems.

I was staying with Rocio, a Spanish teacher who had taught John the language when he had travelled in Latin America several years previously, and she told me that all roads were closed and all travel was suspended. I phoned Dietmar to see how he was and he told me that at the time of my call he had just come down from sweeping several inches of ash off his roof, but that he was fine. For the time being, I was just going to have to sit it out.

On the third day of waiting, still with no end to the storm in sight, the Guatemalan President went on TV, appealing for calm whilst in the same breath telling us that the country was expecting an earthquake in the next day or two.

The earthquake never came, but just as I was finally beginning to think about leaving, yet another problem became apparent: the front rack on my bike (which holds a reasonably heavy pannier) had begun to crack the front fork apart and it was only a matter of time before the whole thing snapped off.

My poor old bike had taken one hell of a beating over the last couple of years, but one of the main reasons I had bought it was for its Chromoly steel frame, which means, when needed, that it can simply be welded back together. So, another day was lost doing just this, although for the price of £1.60 I couldn't really complain, and it looked like my trusty companion was back to full strength.

As such, after five nights in Antigua, and with all volcanoes, flooding, earthquakes and bike failings out of the way, it was back on the road: a big descent down from 5,000 feet to sea level to begin with, before heading on towards the El Salvador border. I thought my journey was finally back on track; at the bottom of the descent I came to a bridge over a river...

Well, I came to half a bridge over a river.

I had seen broken bridges before in Mexico, but this one was on another level; around twelve metres above the water, the previous week's storm had ripped apart most of the foundations and left a fifty metre gap between the two remaining parts of road. Below, the flooded river still rampaged and looking down from the edge, I could see several tons of the bridges stanchion that had been washed away downstream.

The thought of how powerful the water must have been to do this was frightening.

This lack of bridge left with me a conundrum; I was a good sixty kilometres from the nearest alternative route, getting there would mean re-climbing the 5,000 feet I'd just descended and even then there was no guarantee that the

177

other bridge was functional. But it wasn't just I who needed to cross the river, local people did too and I was about to be reminded of two of the great truths of our humble planet. The first is that if people have a problem, no matter where in the world they are they will find a way to fix it. The second is that when they've found a solution, someone will then find a way to make money from it.

And so it proved on this occasion. As I sat on the safe part of the broken bridge, eyeing the destruction below, a local pointed to a crowd of people down by the river. Venturing down, what I found was quite ingenious; with the river far too dangerous for any boats to cross, three locals had instead set up a highly sturdy zipwire and were charging forty pence a ride across.

With little other option I watched nervously as first my bicycle was placed on the line and pulled across the river, then as the empty hook was sent back, my bags were placed on and pulled over, before finally the rope was sent back, a harness attached and I was hoisted across the divide.

Whilst it all seemed perfectly safe, given the speed and size of the river below, touching down on dry land was an almighty relief, and for a mere £1.20. I employed a couple of shrewd children-come-businessman to help me carry my bags and bike back up to the road and began to think that maybe now I was at the point where I could carry on my journey. I camped that night just short of the El Salvadorian border and crossed the next morning, only to find that the border was marked by a river and that this bridge had been washed away as well, although fortunately in this instance the flood water had receded and it was possible to cross the section of broken bridge via climbing down one ladder and back up another. Five trips up and down and I was now into El Salvador, and wondering whether more people would travel if other international borders consisted of giant obstacle courses.

By this point I had come to accept that in terms of crime, Central America was the least safe place I'd been too. I'd been stolen from in southern Mexico and Belize and I had felt unsafe in areas of Guatemala City. As I arrived in the town of Santa Ana the reality of the situation was spelled out in absolutely clear terms: in the city centre, there were numerous circular signs making clear that hand guns were not permitted in that particular area of town.

I hadn't thought too much about guns before, but I knew that Honduras, where I was about to head to, had the highest murder rate in the world. With my brain finally making the connection between guns and murder, I wasn't looking forward to going.

After the last night in El Salvador, I woke to find that my chain-whip - the tool which removes the rear cassette - and the replacement bike helmet I'd bought in Guatemala, had both been stolen and with an ominous feeling I made my way into Honduras; we didn't get off on the right foot.

I had been run over three times between February and June of the previous year, and I was fast approaching the year anniversary since my last traffic accident; unfortunately a Honduran man with a truck and particularly low I.Q. were about to change all that.

The previous times I'd been hit, whilst it was someone else's fault, it was also easy to see how the accident had happened. In Vietnam, I'd been hit by a motorbike after I'd had to swerve to avoid a little girl who'd nearly fallen off her bike in front of me; in China, a man had been reversing round a blind corner into a cycle path (something that isn't as unusual as it sounds out there) and in Japan, I'd ended up in the blind spot of a lorry. So I'd never been worked up about them, because I knew the person hadn't meant it and that it, as the name suggests, was an accident.

This time around, whilst I don't believe the person wanted to kill me, I genuinely believe he tried to knock me off. We were both travelling along the same road and there was a petrol station coming up that he wanted to get to. I was already a quarter of the way across where the turn opening was, as the driver pulled alongside, then slightly in front of me and then just swerved into me, the back end of his truck sending me sprawling across the street.

His reaction?

To stop? No. To see if I was ok? No.

He just drove up to the pumps and started filling up, as if nothing had happened.

Meanwhile, my bike - which was thankfully unscathed - was on its side, the contents of my bar bag were all over the street and whilst I was OK, I did had a nice new set of scratches.

Those who know me will testify I'm not someone who gets particularly angry, and when I do I'm far more likely to avoid confrontation, choosing rather to go off on my own and sulk. On this occasion though, whilst I was still laid out on the ground, seeing that the guy wasn't going to come back to see if I was OK and was choosing instead to refuel his car, I really lost it.

I marched up to his car, fighting the urge to kick off his wing mirror. I was effing and blinding, making hand signals, screaming in his face, banging on his windows; all things that are highly out of character for me, but that I confess to doing on this occasion. I was livid.

In return, he and his friend laughed in my face, started making jokes in Spanish and the only person who was upset by my outburst was the guy's young son, who became pretty distressed at the foreigner screaming up close at his dad in a language he didn't understand.

Running people over was obviously just one hilarious joke to these guys, and I dragged myself away, picked up my bike, packed up my things and rode off. I couldn't claim even a moral victory on this one and it wasn't until much later that I realised instead of the rant I should have simply taken his car keys whilst he was filling up the truck and thrown them into a nearby river.

So Honduras and I hadn't started well and the following few days were a strange experience; the Honduran countryside is divine, with thirty kilometre climb after thirty kilometre climb, offering cracking views of the mountains, but the majority of the towns I passed through were not pleasant: littered, polluted and with a local macho population constantly hissing sentences along the lines of "Hey man? Where you going man? What you doing man? You riding a bicycle man?" at me, whilst verbally sexually harassing any western women they saw.

But this was nothing compared to Tegucigalpa, which became the first place that I had truly felt unsafe in - even during daylight hours.

I had ventured into town to try and watch a World Cup game, as the tournament being hosted in South Africa had just begun. As I did so, I found myself drawing many more stares than usual, and barely any of them friendly. There was something in the air, the looks I was getting were not welcoming and by the time I found a café in which I could see both a TV and my bicycle, the Germans had already crushed the Australian team and I decided to just get out of town. I left on the ring road - a dual carriageway that had been reduced to a single lane up ahead - and as I rode past, I came across a motorcycle crash, where a body lay dead under a white sheet whilst traffic filtered through. Wanting to respect the situation, I kept my head down and tried to move slowly past. As I did so, the police photographer who had been taking images of the scene turned and, completely against the mood, his face lit up and he began taking pictures of me and my bike.

I would later find out that the following day one of these pictures appeared in a National Honduran Newspaper with the caption 'This citizen carries all his belongings with him, a really heavy bicycle indeed'.

So it appears Honduras really is a strange place and I

was happy to have got out of the country with all my belongings intact. Or so I thought.

As I rode out of Tegucigalpa I looked down between my legs and noticed something was missing: it was my fuel bottle, containing my stove pump. It had been stolen from my bottle cage, presumably whilst I'd been watching the football. With its loss, I could no longer cook on the road.

This was a breaking point for me; I'd had enough not only of the crime I was experiencing, but also of the fact that what was being stolen was completely useless to the thieves who were taking it. Fair enough, in Belize the crooks had done well, but since then, well, my bike helmets were useless in the sense that nobody wore them in Central America, the tools that had been stolen were of no use, as the majority of cycle mechanics I'd met out here had no idea what a chain-whip was, and now the stove bottle - something that was so vital for me - was absolutely no use to anyone else without the stove itself. And of course, replacing all of these things meant spending more money that I didn't have.

That night, for the first time in months, I comfort ate and dined on a twelve-pack of raw meringues, before pushing for the Nicaraguan border the following day.

If there was one thing that consistently made me feel better when I was down on the road, then it was human kindness and having become surly to the outside world, I was once again knocked firmly back into line by the local population.

It was my last night in Honduras, and I was skulking towards the border, foolishly riding into the night, secretly wanting something bad to happen to me so I could blame Honduras for something new. I stopped at a roadside kiosk and began speaking to the women who ran it. A rushed conversation followed and the worry in one of the women's eyes was obvious as she said to me "What are you doing? Don't you know how dangerous these roads are at this

182

time?" She ran inside to her husband and they promptly insisted I stay in their spare hammock for the evening on the basis that I never ride at night time in Honduras again. I was taken in, showered and fed, before their twin sons, aged seven, brought out their guitars (both minus several strings) and spent the rest of the night singing songs to me, playing football with me and even correcting my ever expanding Spanish vocabulary.

As I lay dozing in the hammock I realised that whilst I had complained about both Honduras and Central America, and the crime rates were certainly higher here, in my own ignorance I had ignored just how kind and generous so much of its population were and how they saw it as their duty to take care of me. I had stayed with several families across the region and it suddenly twigged that as a guest in their country, they saw my safety as their responsibility.

The next morning I crossed the border to Nicaragua, not sad to be leaving Honduras, but glad that I'd visited. I found Nicaragua to have similar levels of hospitality, but also a far more relaxed vibe. My last night in Nicaragua was spent sleeping on the porch of a retired police officer, who told me stories of how, when he was younger, he had been in the same football team as Paulo Wanchope's father (Paulo Wanchope being a Costa Rican footballer who had scored in the opening game of the 2008 World Cup) and then tried to arrange a marriage between myself and one of his daughters.

Whilst my own crossing of the Nicaragua/Costa Rica border was routine, the border itself would become famous in the coming months for a story that went on to be one of my favourites during my travels.

To set the scene: Costa Rica doesn't have an army, as after World War Two, the government disbanded it and pumped all of the freed up money into education - a policy which has resulted in the country having the lowest illiteracy rates in Central America. That said, the fact remains that whilst Costa Rica doesn't have an army, Nicaragua certainly does and one day, in October 2010, said army, rather than using their traditional borders, the maps they already possessed or indeed the simple concept of common sense, decided instead to look at *Google Maps* and noticed that, according to the online map, the Costa Ricans were seemingly occupying a small piece of Nicaraguan land. Choosing not to double check any of the facts, the Nicaraguan army invaded the 'occupied' area and subsequently took control of it for several weeks. Word quickly spread of what had happened; the official maps were checked and lo and behold, it turned out that *Google Maps* had been slightly incorrect; an embarrassed army retreated and for their part *Google* released a statement saying:

"Google maps are of very high quality and Google works constantly to improve and update existing information, but by no means should they be used as a reference to decide military actions between two countries."

Quite simply brilliant, but also a harrowing warning for what happens when advanced technology meets collective stupidity.

I may have avoided this 'war' by a few months, but my own ride through Costa Rica was still not particularly successful. First of all, on the date of England's decisive group match with Slovenia, I found that throughout the country only the USA v Algeria game was being shown, leaving me somewhat frustrated as I was forced to miss England's lone victory in the tournament. Things didn't improve on the football front either, as after missing that game I was then able to watch the 4-1 spanking we received from a useful German team four days later, which goes to show that you can be halfway round the world and following England is still a blow-out.

The second reason for struggling with Costa Rica was that whilst it had its moments, I was sad to discover that this was probably the first place I'd come to which was best explored via another form of transport than the bike. I'd recently arranged a boat to take me from Panama to Colombia and I needed to arrive in time to catch it, so whilst the back roads may have had their charm, I had to stick to the highway, and with its narrow lanes and big trucks I didn't feel safe (especially as I'd not replaced my second stolen helmet). Thus, I was very much relieved to get to Panama.

I didn't have the best time in Costa Rica, although I did have one notable success: in San Jose, I had stayed with Roxana, Andrea and Montserat, a family who knew the Pezzoli-Kennedys back in Cambria. This was the sixth place of accommodation I'd received through the contacts of this one family and the success I achieved during this time was that I replaced my cooking stove, but not via conventional methods. I spoke to the company that made the fuel bottle and pump and they told me that I would be able to get a replacement, but not until I reached Bogota, Colombia. This left me with at least a month of travel to fill with no stove. I needed a replacement, and after searching online I found my solution: instructions on how to make a *Coke* can stove.

As per the instructions, I took two empty *Coke* cans, cut them in half and inserted one of the bottom halves into the other bottom half, before stabbing in some air holes, adding a strand of mop string as a wick and filling it with pure alcohol to create a mini methylated spirits burner. Success wasn't instant, but with a bit of tinkering I had a new stove, complete with a grill fashioned from some spare spokes. I was able to cook again and the *Coke* can stove would see me through to Bogota, not to mention leaving me feeling pretty chuffed with myself at successfully having solved the problem.

I soon arrived in Panama City; a city which, like so many other places, had something that I'd never seen before. Throughout the world there are rich people and there are poor people. There is poverty and there is wealth. There are 'the haves' and 'the have nots'. But never before had I seen the two groups in such close proximity to each other, and never to such extremes as I saw in Panama City.

The city's rich leave their brand new apartments, which are located in the brand new twenty storey building complexes; they talk to each other on their *Blackberries*, shop in the expensive boutique stores, get into their Mercedes or BMW and drive home, straight past some of the poorest people I've seen in any of the places I've been to - people who struggle to make ends meet, who live in areas with high pollution, high crime and obvious drug problems.

The only other place I've been to where the divide between rich and poor is so ridiculously noticeable is China, but out there it is segregated: the well-off live in the cities, the poorest of the poor live in the countryside. In Panama City, they are right on top of each other; unsurprisingly a talk with the locals let me know about some of the social problems this causes.

I did like Panama City though and arriving on the 4th of July, with my boat to Colombia scheduled a couple of days later, it meant I was free to enjoy the 5th of July, which just happened to be my twenty-fourth birthday. The first birthday on the road had been in Trabson, the second in Tokyo and my third passed in Panama City in a haze of liquor.

It felt strange to know that having left at twenty-one, I was now twenty-four. Not only that, but as I rolled out of Panama City, it dawned on me that I had finished North

186

America; it was the first continent that I had visited that I wouldn't be going back to on the ride. Alas, my celebration proved premature, as the three days to the San Blas Islands were tough, with the final forty-five kilometres being the hardest road in the world I would ever cycle, with several of the gradients so steep that I couldn't even push my bike up, instead having to remove all of my bags, carry them up to the top of the hills one by one and then drag the bike up after them.

Battered, bruised and absolutely knackered, I arrived at the desert islands and knew I had made it; almost a year to the day since arriving in North America, I was now about to leave. Thinking back, I felt as though I was the still the same person who had arrived, delighted and enthusiastic for what lay ahead. But when I looked at what I'd been through over the previous year, how low I'd been with everything that had gone on with Bella and - feeling sick inside at the thought - the realisation that for over two months I'd cried daily and hadn't been able to sleep without sleeping pills, it dawned on me that I was over the worst of it and enjoying my life again. I felt good about myself, yet despite the emotional turmoil of the last year, and the fact that over the previous weeks I'd been repeatedly stolen from, hit by a truck, and held up by a volcano, there was someone far closer to me who deserved my sympathy: my bicycle.

In Nicaragua, the front fork had snapped off completely and had to be welded back on again; on top of this, she'd been hoisted across rivers by zipwires, dragged up ladders to cross a border, hit by a truck, been pulled up dirt roads on gradients of over 35% and the whole time had to carry my fifty kilos of luggage and seventy five kilos of body weight.

I deserved no sympathy for the problems I faced on my escapades, but it was hard not to spare a thought for the old girl as she was bundled into a sail boat bound for Cartagena.

She would need to stay strong, for in front of us lay the Andes.

19: Happy Place

I spent five days on the San Blas Islands, patiently waiting for my sailboat and its worrying Argentinian captain to depart. During this time, I decided that I needed to make some significant changes to my lifestyle. My mental health had improved steadily and I was relising the new challenges that lay ahead. However, it was apparent that if the rest of my ride was to succeed (both in South American and in general) then there were two things above all else that I needed to address: language and money.

The former was something that I had been working on anyway, but now vowed to take more seriously. So far, my Spanish had consisted of what I had learnt on the farm back in Mexico, supplemented by a GCSE Revision Guide Workbook sent out by my parents, which I had studied intermittently; now, with five days to spare and no distractions, I was able to immerse myself in study and was amazed by how much I learnt in such a short space of time.

I promised myself that from then on, I would do a minimum of half an hour's work each night in the tent and by and large this was something I would stick to. OK, I never became perfect, but several months down the line, when the time came for me to leave the Latin countries, my studies and time with the people there had left me able to converse competently in a language that, a few months previously, had been entirely alien, and I could always link this success back to my time on the island.

Whilst learning another language certainly made the trip more enjoyable, without money the rest of the trip would simply not be possible. I'd always been careful over what I was spending but in Central America I'd lost track and had been spending far too much on restaurant food, primarily as a result of wanting to watch the World Cup. I did some maths and came to the conclusion that for the trip to be viable (and leaving a little bit extra for emergencies and kit replacement), I needed to live off about £5 per day. I created a grid in the back of my diary and wrote the dates out for the next six months so that I could write down exactly how much I'd spent at the end of each day. Of course, there was the odd day when I'd spend more, and the odd day when I'd spend less, but for the most part I stuck to my budget religiously. Indeed, I became neurotic when it came to recording it, to the extent that nearly two years later, when I returned home, I possessed diaries containing several pages of self-written finances, from which I knew exactly how much money I had spent on any given day.

It may not have been much fun, but my time on the islands was a perfect opportunity to reflect and make these very necessary changes.

As for The San Blas Islands themselves: they lie just off the northern coast of Panama and it was from here that I would travel by sailboat south to Cartagena. It sounds glamorous, doesn't it? Sailboats on the open seas, desert islands, golden beaches, seafood straight from the ocean and all topped off with beautiful sunsets...

With this image in mind, it proved something of a disappointment that the first thing I witnessed on my arrival was an islander crapping off an end-of-pier toilet into the water, while less than five metres away children swam and fishermen cast their nets, and things didn't get any more romantic after we left.

I was fine for the twenty minute motorboat ride to the island where our sailboat was moored; the moment our vessel actually started to move in the direction of Colombia though, that was it. I spent the next three days either being sick or hiding below deck, lying as still and as horizontally as possible, eating nothing but the occasional salt-cracker and doing my utmost to avoid further vomiting.

Whilst for some this is the exotic trip of a lifetime, for me the overriding memory of crossing the Darien Gap was the relief I felt at finally arriving in Cartagena to touch foot on what was the thirty-third country and fourth continent of the trip.

My first impression of Colombia was that the whole place (including many tall buildings) needed to stop swaying up and down, and someone needed to do something about the fact the pavements were constantly moving beneath my feet, giving me the sensation that I was walking on a bed of marshmallows. It soon dawned on me that the buildings weren't moving, neither was the pavement and it was actually me that was the problem; I'd never found my sea-legs, but in the five days on water it became apparent I'd definitely lost my land ones.

The plan had been to leave Cartagena on the day of arrival and head on towards the mountains: I didn't need to even attempt to ride the bike to know that this wouldn't be a good idea. Instead I went to a hostel with some of the other guys who'd travelled on the boat and spent the evening letting my body catch up, whilst finally eating something that wasn't a salt-cracker.

A night's rest was the perfect antidote and the following morning my plan for Colombia became clear; back in Panama, literally 100 metres from the port, the digital camera I'd bought in Guatemala had packed in. It's a waterproof camera, so seeing liquid inside the lens had not been a good start, but thankfully it did have a warranty and a quick 'Google' of where the dealers were in Colombia determined my route for me: I would leave Cartagena and head south to Medellin, from where I would then come off the Pan-American Highway to Bogota to get the camera fixed, before heading back down to Cali and on to the equator and Ecuador.

Medellin was the first stop on this route and it was an

infamous destination.

When setting off on long overland journeys, many of the people I'd read about commented on the inspirational books they'd chosen to read themselves as they set out on their own adventures. Sometimes these were serious reads, such as an autobiography by one of their heroes, sometimes it was a story with an inspirational message such as 'The Alchemist', or perhaps a more light-hearted tale, such as 'Around the World in Eighty Days'. Whatever it was, the thing that linked them all was their travel theme and positive tone.

In contrast, the first book I read when leaving England had been 'Killing Pablo', an excellent account about the life of Colombia's most famous criminal, Pablo Escobar, and the subsequent attempts by the US Government to kill him, which would eventually succeed with an assassination in 1993.

Whilst not a pleasant story, his tale of small time crook to international drug kingpin is most definitely a fascinating one and by the end of his life, his rise had led him to being the seventh richest man in the world, whilst also being responsible for the deaths of over an estimated 4,000 police officers.

Given the excessive wealth of the guy and his record of murder - in the early nineties, Medellin was widely considered the most dangerous city on the planet - you may think he would have been hated. Part true, but at the same time Escobar used his wealth to fund many social programmes, such as building floodlit football pitches for the local working classes to play on, and as a result Escobar had a popular following in Medellin until the day he died.

Whatever you think of the man himself, the story is a fascinating one and it was for this reason I wanted to stop in Medellin: to try and see something to do with Escobar.

Pablo's grave is one of the most visited tourist

attractions in the city, although it didn't seem right to want to visit the grave of a mass-murderer; nor does visiting a flower-covered grave give any sense of the events that actually happened during Escobar's life and to be blunt, it sounded very boring. So, armed with a map, my bicycle and a street address, I went off in search of something else.

In December 1993, the Americans were so desperate for Escobar to be dead that one of the tactics of finding him involved using a surveillance technique that tracked people talking on mobile phones. The technology wasn't great, but it did give a general idea of where he would be. The Americans drove around Medellin and would have driven right past, as the house looked the same as all the others, but through sheer luck, someone was looking the right way at the right time, saw their target standing in an upstairs window and ordered an attack on the building. Within minutes Escobar was dead.

It would be one of the major turning points in Colombian history: I spent my time in Medellin by going off to find the house where all of this took place.

It was surprisingly easy to do; the house was still there, it was relatively close to where I was staying, I'd found directions online and I was outside the front door within half an hour. With no camera, I wanted to just stand outside and stare at where the final moments had taken place.

It was hard to comprehend; rich beyond belief, politically powerful and a violent murderer, his last days had been spent hiding in a derelict dump of a house.

After a while the woman who now occupied the house - it hadn't occurred to me that people may be living there - came out and seemed suspicious of why I was staring at the building, so I left, but I was glad I'd managed to visit for a simple reason: it's people such as Mr. Escobar (whilst the most famous, he's certainly not the only one) who give Colombia such a bad name.

Friends had warned me about how dangerous the place

was, not just because of the historical violence, but also the FARC kidnappings and other bits of bad news they'd heard. I visited the house to know in my own mind: whilst the place wasn't perfect, the most dangerous people were now dead. The violence was very much in the past and in its place a land of power and pride was emerging.

I would end up staying for two months, and not only found the country to be safe, but also the most beautiful I would ever visit. There were three aspects that made Colombia stand out above all others.

The first was the scenery: leaving Cartagena I had been a bit underwhelmed by the first couple of days riding, but this changed the moment I hit the mountains. Seemingly from nowhere, the Andes hit me and a drawn-out climb took me from sea level up to around 3,000 metres elevation in a day. The views were spectacular and at the right time of day, Bogota, viewed from Montserrat (the mountain which overlooks the city) has one of the most picturesque skylines of anywhere in the world. And whilst in other countries, some days would feel like a *Scooby Doo* cartoon, where you were moving, but the backgrounds repeated themselves over and over, this was not so in the Colombian mountains. Every day was different. Every view was new and I couldn't wait to wake up each morning.

Aside from the great ride and wonderful scenery, the second factor I fell in love with was the climate. Not many people realise that the equator runs through Colombia, but it does and this obviously leads to hot days. But then factor into this the 2,600 metre altitude of Bogota and what you're left with is a country with twenty-eight degree days, but cool nights, meaning that when the sun goes down, unlike many of the other places in warmer climates, there are no mosquitoes. Warm climates, cool nights and crisp clean air: perfect.

And of course all of this was supplemented by my most

beloved aspect of travelling: food. My favourite thing was the bread; *Panaderias* (bakeries in English) were literally on every corner and served the best bread I've ever had, with my particular favourite being *Pan-con-queso*, a freshly baked bread served with molten cheese inside. This was washed down *Agua de Panella*, a hot drink that is made of concentrated sugar cane - something which offered high energy to cyclists and a guilty treat for those with a sweet tooth - and then for special occasions there was *Lechona*. A celebratory dish, *Lechona* amounted to a pig stuffed with rice and vegetables and then spit-roasted. It was served directly from the pig and was a particular extravagance.

I met many fellow travellers who avoided Colombia because of the rumours of how unsafe it was; during my two months, I found a country that had unparalleled beauty, a welcoming people and a diet that could even fill up a cyclist. These people had missed out.

It was not often I got to show off about how far I could ride in a day, but on the journey into Bogota I rode 147 kilometres in a little over twelve and a half hours, with a cumulative altitude gain of a little over 4,000 metres.

It was something I had never done before, but in truth it was fuelled by spite. In Medellin, after two months of no contact, Bella and I had spoken, speculating to see if we were capable of being friends. We weren't. Both of us said things we regretted and things were left worse than they were before. I'd had a positive few months, but now the loneliness and anger welled once more; I was back to being a shell of a man.

My guardian angel would arrive in the form of Caro. She was one of the first people I met when arriving in the city and we were not an obvious match; from different walks of life with different interests. On the face of it we had little in common. But circumstance moved us closer together, our friendship turned to romance and our relationship led to me

194

staying several days longer than I should have in Bogota.

Caro remains one of the strongest women I have ever met, with beauty and intelligence to match. It didn't sink in for several months just how heavily indebted I was to her for the time we spent together. Since losing Bella, the closest I'd come to romance was spending the day with an American girl in Guatemala, only for my amorous plans to be scuppered by the discovery that my new friend had a girlfriend of her own waiting at home. Spending time with Caro gave me someone to care about and showed me that I could be happy again. Over the coming years, whenever I would feel lonely on the road, it would be the memories of the time we shared that I would think of: she was my new happy place.

I could've been through in a couple of weeks; instead I left Colombia on day sixty of my sixty day visa. That night, I camped high up in the mountains a few miles from the equator, woke up to a frost and rode on into the Southern Hemisphere. Quito beckoned.

20: Shit Outta Luck

In Quito I stayed with Luis, a guy who dubbed himself 'The Monkey on a bicycle'. Obsessed with all things cycling, Luis had arranged for me to be interviewed by Ecuadorian radio and by sheer chance, as I bumbled my way incoherently through questions about my ride, the radio station received a phone call from the local SOS Children's Village, who'd heard that I was raising money for them and invited me to come and stay.

I had passed several SOS Villages previously, but had never interacted with the children. The following night, I visited a village containing 140 orphaned, abandoned or temporarily displaced children and was asked to talk to them about my bike ride. I was nervous at first, but the welcome they gave me was something truly special and after my presentation and lots of questions about my bike and what all the equipment did, I played football with the kids until the sun went down. I had been apprehensive about visiting at first; I wasn't sure what I or they would get out of it. Witnessing how happy the children were in an environment that seemed entirely normal to them, as I left I tried to keep one thought in mind: *just think about where those kids would be if it weren't for SOS.*

I felt a great pride that day to be associated with them and vowed to kick on with my fundraising.

I was once asked, given all of the places that I've been to, where would the perfect location for a geography school trip be? The answer is Ecuador.

If you cut Ecuador into three vertical columns, on the west you have the ocean and all that goes along with it, in the middle you have the Andes Mountains, and in the east there is the Amazon Rainforest. Driving from the beach to

196

the jungle can be done in a little over 200 miles and for a country roughly the size of the UK to have such diversity is astounding.

Wanting to see some of this variety, I decided to head from the capital down into the rainforest. I had seen plenty of coast before and would no doubt see plenty more in the future, so taking the only chance I would get to see some of the Amazon seemed a 'no brainer'.

Leaving Quito, I made a brief stop in the town of Banos, famed for its natural hot springs. It was a far cry from the Onsens and Jimjilbangs of East Asia and instead consisted of a couple of industrial-sized swimming pools in which I have no doubt the water was kept warm by the large amount of urine peed into it by local children. The baths were a blowout and I avoided them, although one thing I did manage was adding another tick to the list of bizarre animals I'd eaten. In Kazakhstan I'd had tinned horse meat, in China chicken feet soup, in Mexico I'd had the fried iguanas and now as I walked around the town's main square I found something I'd heard much about but never seen. Cuyo. AKA Guinea pig.

Slightly larger than the guinea pigs we keep as pets, the poor animals had been killed, skinned, disembowelled and their remaining carcass had been stretched over a wooden device that looked identical to a boat paddle, before being placed on an open top barbecue. If you walk past that and can resist even the mildest curiosity as to what it tastes like, well, you're not human, are you?

For $3 I was given a part of the guinea-pig I'm assuming was its leg and after thirty seconds of chewing I realised you weren't supposed to eat the outer-layer of fat, so instead turned my attention to the actual meat part of the rodent. It tasted good. Really good. Similar but not too similar to stewed beef, but far softer.

Happy at the discovery, whilst lamenting the fact that when as a five year old I'd been given a pet guinea-pig, nobody had told me that if I'd killed him and barbecued him he'd have tasted great with rice, I carried on my journey, descending fully out of the mountains to Puyo in the Amazon.

It was a little disappointing to find that it was nowhere near as exciting as it sounds, but even so, I was happily riding along, and I hit a mini-descent, where I got my speed up to around 40kph, then suddenly came around a corner, onto a road that appeared to be... ice?

Of course, I knew it couldn't be ice, but whatever it was, I was slipping on it. When I'd been preparing for this part of the route, Luis had told me that large sections of the road here were now asphalt, but he didn't know about the first part and I'd just found out the answer. They were paving it now and one of the first stages of asphalting a road is putting down a layer of wet tar. When this is done the road becomes slippy, with the added fun that the wet tar also sticks to anything it touches. If people are going to be doing this work you could argue that it might be a good idea to cone off the section of the road they're doing it on. If they're not going to do that it would be an equally good idea to put up a sign saying 'men at work'. And if they're not going to do that, then perhaps it would be a good idea to have one worker where the slippery section begins to guide traffic round the wet tar.

They'd done none of these.

I came round the corner at speed, hit the wet tar and not knowing what was going on, I panicked and hit the brake. The next thing I knew, I was flat out on the floor and had taken a heavy crash, with the impact pretty much solely on my left arm. Better yet, the left hand side of my face, my left leg and arm, my panniers and my clothes were all now covered in sticky hot tar.

I lay on the road in pain for no more than twenty seconds before one of the Ecuadorian road workers came over. I thought he might be offering assistance with the crumpled heap I was in, but instead he told me I was in the way, that they needed to carry on laying the road and therefore me and my bike needed to move.

Despite the blood coming out of my knee and the fact I was visibly struggling with the use of my left arm, not a single person bothered to help me drag the bike off the road. I was grateful when finally one of the workers (the only one who stopped in anyway what he was doing on the road) came over and offered me some warm diesel to rinse the tar off my skin and clothes.

Needless to say, I didn't want to hang around and rode off as quickly as possible, irritated at both what had happened and that despite my best efforts at cleaning, both me and my possessions were now covered in hot sticky tar. An explosion at a nearby pillow factory and my image would be complete.

The next two days were quiet and uneventful. The ride was flat and whilst I was in what was technically the Amazon, I was on a tarmacced road and was most certainly not in the jungle. So, apart from a large black snake (I couldn't tell you the species, but he was about six foot long) whizzing across the road in front of me, the days weren't exciting and were mostly spent in the saddle, continuing the journey.

That said, the two nights were notable, for two encounters.

The first was on the same day as the crash, an hour or two after it. I'd come through a small village and asked if I could camp there. I'd been directed to the local school where I was told I could set my tent up and after doing this and beginning to cook I was joined by a local man who greeted me in English. The Amazon side of Ecuador is very sparsely populated; farms span the roadside, but there aren't many towns along the way and the population in these areas is small, so meeting someone who spoke perfect English was surprising. After he'd come over and offered me a place to stay (my tent was up and my dinner was cooking, so I thanked him but declined) we began to talk and he told me how he'd been born here but in the early nineties had wanted to go to live in the States. Through legal means this was impossible, so he told of how he had hitchhiked from the Amazon to Quito before going up to Cartagena in Colombia. Managing to get on a cargo ship over the Darien Gap, he had made his way overland on buses through Central America to Mexico, where after hopping the US border he'd lived in New York City for the next sixteen years.

He didn't go into great detail, but from the time I'd spent working in California I'd known the lengths some Mexicans had gone to in order to get into the US, so to have travelled what is well over 5,000 miles just to get to the US border was incredible. *And I thought I'd been on an impressive journey.*

We chatted for a bit, but soon the conversation turned to something I've found that all people who've worked illegally in the States are always overly keen to talk about: money. *'How much money did you make in England?' 'How much did you get paid in California?' 'How much does your bike cost?'* It's sad in a way, but I've found that money is always the preferred topic of conversation when meeting people who have lived or worked in the States, and when he saw I had no interest in answering these questions, he lost interest and we both went off to sleep.

The following day was followed by an encounter of a different kind. At the end of the day, I'd not found anywhere to camp and with the light rapidly disappearing, I pulled off to a side track which I thought led to nowhere. Like every night, I set up camp and started cooking. Again, someone came to speak to me, only this time instead of friendly chit-chat, she wanted to tell me that I was actually on her front driveway and that my tent was blocking the only way in and out of her house.

Now take a step back for a moment and ask yourself what would have been the reaction if I'd done this in England? If, for example, a Brit had come home one night and found that a smelly cyclist had just put his tent up in the entrance to their house, what would they do? Would they be happy? Well thankfully I wasn't in England, I was in Ecuador and instead of being told to leave as I might expect, I was told it was no problem for me to stay where I was, but I would have to leave early the next morning so she could get to work, that it was great I was there and if I wanted to, I was more than welcome to join her and her family indoors for a cup of coffee.

Certainly not what I was expecting when she had come over, but a most welcome conversation.

These two events had certainly cheered me up a bit after the crash, but I still wasn't in the best of spirits. My arm was recovering but still hurt, I was on a road I thought would be flat but wasn't, I found myself thinking often of the people I'd left in Bogota and most frustratingly of all, the tar on my panniers still hadn't dried after forty-eight hours. I knew my luck was out that night when I dropped my iPod, a birthday gift I'd been given in Panama City, and of the roughly metre squared area it could have landed in, it dropped square into a freshly brewed cup of *Panella*. The iPod had saved my sanity at various times over the last few months. When things were bad it gave me a place to hide; somewhere I could listen to a podcast, shut my eyes and forget about who and where I was.

This escape was now gone.

Childishly, when things don't go my way I often want to leave whatever country I'm in and choose to blame places for my bad luck. It was no different this time and my frustrations were completed the next morning when I woke to find that an overnight storm had turned a section of road

201

into what I call 'quick mud' - mud where the moment you step on it, your legs disappear. The stretch was about fifteen metres and was also the only possible route, so I had little choice but to continue. I stepped into it and immediately my feet were about a foot below ground level. The bike sank, with mud coming up over the wheel hubs and the only way through was to physically drag it, using all the strength I had.

It took thirty minutes to get the bike through, another twenty minutes to take off my shoes, socks and shorts to wash in a nearby river and further twenty to wash away all the wet mud from the hubs, gears, derailleurs and brakes. Ecuador was an undoubted place of beauty, but now I just wanted out. Crossing the Andes via the town of Loja, I made my way to the border and into the coastal desert road of Peru.

I chose the desert road of Peru in order to visit Lucho's Casa De Ciclista.

Casa De Ciclista's, translating literally as *House of Cyclists*, are places all over Latin America run by local people, where touring riders are welcome to come and stay free of charge. There is a renowned network of them all over the Hispanic world but the most famous was Lucho's. Located in Peru's third largest city of Trujillo, Lucho is a bit of legend and it's thought that since starting to host over thirty years ago, he has since had over 10,000 cyclists through his door.

It was an opportunity not to be missed, but there was an obstacle in the way: Paijan was a city fifty kilometres to the north of Trujillo and came with a well-deserved reputation for mugging cyclists.

There are quite a few blogs of people who have been mugged in this town and the way it works is thus: in Peruvian small towns, there are guys in rickshaws that drive around, usually providing a taxi service. In Paijan though, they'll see a cyclist, inform their friends and follow said cyclist out of town. When a little way out of town, they'll run the cyclist off the road, one or two of them will pin the cyclist down and while this is going on, the rest of the bandits will run to the bike and grab whatever they can, usually ripping off a pannier or two, or basically anything they can get their hands on.

Still feeling my sore arm from the fall, looking at my tar covered clothes and noticing the distinct lack of headphones in my ears, I knew that with my luck down, riding through this town would be tempting fate. As it was, the advice I'd been given for passing through was a) take a bus or b) ask the police for an escort.

I'm too stubborn to take a bus and in terms of a police escort? Well, Paijan is a town of no more than possibly 2,000, whilst the amount of cyclists who have been mugged over the last couple of years is in the hundreds. As I saw it, for a town that size to have such a large problem, there is no way on earth the police don't know who the bandits are and as such I wasn't going to trust them.

So I came up with my own plan: I would ride to about ten kilometres before the town in the afternoon - it's a desert so no-one lives out there - and then get up at five in the morning to whizz through while the bad guys were still asleep. And if something did happen or someone did follow me, I would ride through with my bear mace - which I still had from my time in Alaska and Yukon - on my handlebars and anyone who did try to attack me would have that to deal with.

It seemed a workable plan, and as all of the robberies I'd read about were a case of people just grabbing what they could off the bike and making a sharp exit, I made some additional adjustments to my bike, just in case of a worst case scenario: the rear panniers were locked to the bike anyway so they were safe, so I moved anything valuable from the front panniers to the rear. Also to be on the safe side, using my spare lock I secured one front pannier to the bike frame and using bits of rope, lashed the other pannier to its adjacent frame. I removed everything from the bar bag and stored it safely in the rear panniers. As a final touch I put on my rain jacket, as it was the only item of clothing I owned that had zip pockets, and in these I put my wallet, passport and digital camera.

It was now physically impossible to rip anything off of the bike and if any bandits did manage to get a hold of my gear, it would be through yanking off a front pannier or my bar bag, neither of which now had anything valuable in. And if all else failed, I was ready to pepper spray the bad guy.

The more I thought about this silly, silly idea, the more I realised I didn't even know if the bear mace worked. I had purchased it in Canada, but frustratingly had not so much as seen a wild bear up north and had certainly never even been close to using the spray. How could I be sure it wouldn't let me down?

I needed to test it.

I took the safety lock off the can, pointed it into the ground away from me and pushed down on the 'spray' button. Nothing. I turned to look at what was going wrong. I couldn't make out any obvious flaw so again I pointed the can at the ground but this time I kept looking at the can as I pushed down on the button: this time it worked. The spray came out with far greater power than I'd anticipated, flew into the ground and bounced back up directly into my eyes.

I've felt pain before: I've torn ligaments, pulled muscles, taken a hell of a lot of football knocks and have, of course, fallen off a bike numerous times. None of these pains compared to what I was now going through.

My eyes were on fire and rubbing them made it worse. I couldn't see a thing and the only relief I could get was from blindly fumbling around in my bag to get out a towel, pouring cold water over it and leaving this to soak on my face. The only positive was that in the middle of the desert, nobody was there to see me do all this.

The pain lasted what must have been fifteen minutes, although it was a further fifteen before I could start to open my eyes again. I'd spent the last few days cursing the headwinds: now I was thankful for them, as the cold blowing across my face cooled down the burning sensation in my eyes and I was eventually able to get back on the bike with, thankfully, nothing more than my pride in serious pain.

In a moment of intense pain I'd managed to keep a clear enough head to take a picture of my maced face and eyes. I vowed that from that moment on, whenever I was about to do something that I thought might be a bit stupid, I would look at that image and at least think things through before I proceeded.

With tears still in my eyes, I was at least comforted by the knowledge that the mace both worked and was certainly powerful enough to take down a rickshaw full of people. I camped twenty-five kilometres from town; in the morning, I would find out if I needed it.

I was out of bed by 04.30 (the wind had wonderfully disappeared), on the road for 05:00 and in and out the other side of Paijan by 06.30.

I hardly saw anyone in town and even then the police followed me for twenty kilometres out the other side. I had done it: a place known for stealing from cyclists and I'd got through with no problems at all.

A rush of adrenaline coursed through me.

It wasn't just getting through Paijan that was the cause; over the last fourteen days, I'd crashed into wet tar, broken my iPod beyond repair, pushed the bike through foot-deep wet mud, fought terrible roads, repaired numerous punctures and cycled against vicious headwinds. Hell, I'd even bear-maced myself in the face.

But I had done it, I'd made it through and now I was in Trujillo, about 200 metres from Lucho's. I had earned the three days rest I was about to have and maybe, just maybe, things were going to start going my way.

I was in the city centre and pulled to the side of the road to ask directions; I was on one side of a market, Lucho's was on the other side. I could see the iconic mural painted on the building of two cyclists holding up the entire world.

I was straddling my bike and was about to set off again when I felt a pulling at my shorts' pocket. I turned around to find a kid, who couldn't have been much older than fourteen, grabbing my camera out of my pocket. Before I knew it, he had it and had run off.

I chased him; I was gaining on him and I would have caught him, but he ran down an alley and I knew I couldn't leave the bike on its own. I screamed out, but not one of the fifty or so people present even so much as batted an eye-lid.

This was, without doubt, the most depressing moment of the trip.

I'd been stolen from before, but each time I'd had stuff stolen it had been my fault. In Kazakhstan I'd had my lights stolen when I'd left the bike somewhere I shouldn't have; the solution was to take more care of where I leave the bike. In Laos I'd had a bag stolen from a bus because at the time I'd been hallucinating from the anti-malarials I was on; the solution was to stop taking the pills. In Belize I'd had the contents of my bar bag stolen because I'd stupidly fallen asleep on a beach having left my valuables in my bar bag; the solution was to remember that my IQ is higher than sixty.

When things are my fault, I'm more than happy to blame myself.

But this was different.

I'd been so prepared for Paijan. Everything on my bike was theft-proof. All my valuables were all in my zip pockets for when I'd crossed through; there was no way my

206

stuff could have been stolen as I'd been as cautious as I could possibly be.

But as I'd entered Trujillo I'd taken pictures and instead of putting the camera back in the zip pockets, I'd put it back in my shorts' pocket. Even then it should have been invisible, but from the way it was stolen I knew exactly what had happened: The string on the wrist-strap had dangled out of the pocket, this kid had seen it, was smart enough to know what it was, knew that it would have value and because of this, it was enough to lose the camera.

Before I could learn my lessons, but what were the lessons here? Don't ever carry your stuff in pockets? Don't ever expect to feel safe again? Don't take pictures in the inner city?

I'd never felt so vulnerable. I'd never felt so far from home.

Having spent the entire trip delighted by how great the people of the world had been to me, I now felt naked, exposed. Having strode so confidently before, I now found myself viewing the people around me with suspicion. I didn't feel safe.

It was a new emotion. I hated it.

Over the days that followed, I gradually began to feel better. Lucho proved as much of a gentleman as I expected and reassured me that what had happened was extremely rare. As the week progressed I also gradually began to feel safe walking around the markets, although it must be said I kept a closer eye on my possessions.

I began to feel OK about what had happened, but whilst I was willing to forgive, what I missed the most was my camera. When all you have of a solo trip is memories, losing the photos you have is devastating. The camera contained all of my photos from Ecuador and Peru - the wonderful mountains, the snaps of my bike up to the hubs in mud and, of course, the photo of my bear-mace burnt

207

retinas.

Now without these pictures I would have only what I could remember.

My mood did improve over the next few days via several avenues: Inca Cola, the bubble gum flavoured national drink which ensures that Peru is one of only two countries in the world where the regular type of cola isn't the highest selling drink, gave a spectacular sugar high and enough energy to return a smile to my face, whilst meeting Simon, an English cyclist also staying with Lucho who had been mugged in Paijan and had lost far more expensive equipment than I did gave a sense of perspective that my own endeavours could have been far worse.

But what made me feel best was thinking of the kids back at SOS in Ecuador. I knew what I was doing for SOS wasn't going to save the world, but to know how happy they were in the village in Quito, and that this was being replicated around the world, made me realise that even if only in a small way, I was helping and I was proud to be a part of it.

Throughout the journey, I had seen a side of poverty I had never witnessed before and now accepted that both in what I was doing and in the background I had in life, I'd had it extremely easy compared to large portions of the world.

I was sad to lose the camera; I was sad to lose the pictures, but whilst I'd had a rough few weeks with things going wrong, regardless of what I wanted to tell myself, I was a very lucky man.

21: A Side Trip To Remember

The ride along the Peruvian coast was miserable. I liked the desert, I liked the Inca Cola and I liked watching the sun set over the Pacific each night. What I hated was the wind; it was the strongest headwind I had ever come across. Getting up at six each morning I was able to get some miles in, but from 10a.m. onwards the gales would begin and remain until sunset: strong, unrelenting and always in my face. If I had been coming from south to north it would have been the ride of a lifetime. Instead, after two weeks of riding through dust storms and with wind-burnt lips, I turned inland. Over the following week I climbed to altitudes of over 5,000 metres on terrible roads, but it was a doddle compared to the coast.

Many people question how difficult cycling at altitude is. The truth is 'not very', as the lack of oxygen only really affects your recovery time and so long as I rode at a pace where I didn't get out of breath it was rare that I'd notice it. Conversely, if I ran up a flight of stairs, I'd be out of breath and would need to sit down for a few minutes to recover. So there you have it: at altitude cycling was easy, but running was hard.

The only other slight issue I had was sleeping, as on the one night I camped above 4,500 metres I suffered from insomnia. It was no big deal though and, easily catching up on rest, I navigated through the mountains and salt flats, under the watchful eyes of a thousand llamas, making my way to the world's highest navigable lake, Titicaca, and then onwards across the border to Bolivia.

Peru was another country I wasn't particularly sad to leave; I appreciate that the theft had soured my time there, but I'd also found some places to not be as friendly as others. It was in Peru that for first time I found myself being refused service in restaurants and in one case, had a Peruvian customer request that I be removed from the eatery entirely. Of course, I also met many welcoming people, but as I crossed the barren back roads of the mountains, my request for directions being ignored by several drivers (something you can take incredibly personally when 5,000 metres above sea level, thirty miles from the nearest village and with a low water supply), the time felt right for a change and I looked forward to the next challenge.

Formerly a much larger nation with a Pacific coastline, Bolivia successfully lost large amounts of territory to Chile, Brazil and then Paraguay through various wars, to be left as the diverse, if slightly less grandiose nation that they are today. As I crossed the border, my knowledge of the country amounted to three things:

1. the existence of the *Camino de la Muerte* - The Road of Death - which is a sixty-nine kilometre descent from La Paz to the town of Coroico and famed around the world for its danger;
2. the capital La Paz had the honour of being the highest capital city in the world;
3. their nation's footballers had played Germany in the opening game of the 1994 World Cup, during which their star striker Marco Etchevvery was sent off for kicking Lothar Matthaus.

I rode the 'Death Road' and found that it was only as famous as it was for the fact that it was entirely downhill, thus an easy sell for the guides in town selling bike tours. That was a bit of a disappointment, but La Paz was far more impressive.

At 3,600 metres above sea-level, and with its notoriety for being so high up, I somehow expected the city to be on top of a hill; instead, coming through the town of El Alto which overlooks the city, I saw in front of me a wavy valley covered in as many houses as it seemed the citizens could fit in. With buildings spanning the hillsides and barely anything else in sight, it looked as if someone had just picked up a city and thrown it against the side of a hill. The effect was stunning.

Five nights in a hostel, resting my body and dining on llama steaks - I did little else and my two main memories of La Paz both involve money in some way.

The first occurred on the shoulder of the highway coming through El Alto, when I spotted a 5 Boliviano coin (worth roughly 45p) on the road in front of me. Not thinking too much of it, I pulled up to the coin and was about to pick it up when from the pavement a guy of about sixty ran out into the road, stuck his hand literally under my front wheel and grabbed the coin, when my hand was about twenty centimetres away. After he'd picked it up, he stood right in front of the bike and shoved the coin in my face in celebration, to make the point that this was five Bolivianos that the Gringo would not be getting. A strange experience but all I can say is good luck to the guy.

The second incident took place a couple of days later: I'd ridden to the other side of town to a specialist bike shop to get a new tyre and as I was approaching a roundabout on the way back, I realised my wallet had disappeared. I'd had it about 300 metres beforehand so I knew that it must have fallen out of my pocket and I frantically retraced my steps to and from the roundabout. After twenty minutes of looking and no success, I found myself once again back at the roundabout. It was then that I was approached by a local lady who told me she had seen it fall out of my pocket. She pointed at another lady - a street vendor - who, she told me, had picked it up, given it to her eight year old child and told him to run off with it. The lady in question denied everything, the police got involved, her story changed, she confessed she had it and I was told to come back in two hours when I could get it back. I came back two hours later and apart from a couple of small value coins everything was there. However, the police asked me to give a 100 Boliviano (£9) 'reward' to the lady who had got her kid to run off with it in the first place, on the basis that she'd been honest enough to give it back. I felt more than slightly ripped off!

It's amazing how being somewhere you like enables you to forgive these things, so my time in La Paz wasn't soured and I enjoyed myself until the fourth day, when I took a look at my finances. I was still keeping the diary of how much my daily spend was and a pattern was emerging: when I was on the road I didn't use too much money, but when I was off the bike I would spend a lot. Even without the £9 thief tax, I had massively overspent in La Paz.

Christmas was now six weeks away and knowing I had a place to stay in Mendoza, Argentina for the holidays, I decided to save money and spend as much time on the bike as possible. A quick play around with Google Maps and I sent the following e-mail to Graham, another QPR fan and the man who had generously offered to host me in Mendoza.

'Hello mate, how's it going? Just a quick e-mail to let you know the plan - I've looked at the maps and I've decided to make a side trip to Paraguay for no other reason than to say I've been to Paraguay. From there I'll be heading down to Mendoza and if all goes to plan I should be with you the day before Christmas Eve. Matt'

This route seemed perfect. If I could average 100 kilometres a day (something which was never usually a problem), for the next month, it meant I would be able to get through Bolivia to the Paraguay border. From there it was an entirely flat 800 kilometres ride, on what was apparently brand new asphalt, to Asuncion, where I could send off my Christmas cards and have a day or two off the bike, before heading on into Argentina and arriving in Mendoza just in time for a well-earned break over

Christmas.

There was nothing in Paraguay I had any desire to see, but the idea of bagging another country appealed and by being on the bike I knew this would be the cheapest option. Perfect.

I left La Paz and whizzed along to the next major city, Oruro, helped along by the flat roads of the alti-plano and a strong tailwind, before turning off of the highway and exiting the paved roads at the town of Llallagua. From here it was five days' riding to Sucre, the alternative capital of Bolivia, and even with the high passes, cold nights and poor road conditions, things went smoothly. That is, until my rear rim cracked a day and a half short of Sucre.

I had bought the entire back wheel secondhand in San Diego 10,000 miles ago in January, so the fact it had got this far was nothing short of a miracle. But the bump-bump-bump of flying down unpaved mountain roads had finally taken its toll and it had split at the sidewall, leaving a hole through which I could fit my little finger.

This left a conundrum: did I try to see what I could do with the broken rim, try to make it rideable and hope that despite the fact it was beyond repair it would possibly get me to Sucre? Or did I hitch a ride to Sucre knowing I wouldn't come back, and as such 'cheat' for this leg of the journey? The rim had cracked at around midday and I decided to see how far I could get with it, a choice vindicated by the fact I wouldn't see another vehicle until the next day.

When the rim cracked it had punctured the tube, but whilst there was the hole in the rim, the wheel itself would still go round, so in theory all I needed to do was sort out the sharp metal around the hole and stop more punctures from happening. The first attempt consisted of plastering several layers of electrical tape onto the shards of metal, which worked for all of twenty minutes, before the hole in

213

the rim grew a couple of inches longer and ripped the tape away.

The next plan was to use bits of old inner tube to cover up the hole. This didn't work either and as I was mending what was the fourth puncture of the day, the sun went down. I was still seventy kilometres from Sucre and resigned myself to the fact that when/if I saw a vehicle, I would be hitching there.

Inspiration came the next morning, as I put what was left of the wheel back on the bike and noticed that the piece of cut-up tube I'd put in to stop punctures had slipped inside the rim. I realised that if I put it half over the rim and half inside the rim, cushioning the inner tube, it might just work.

After seven hours and seventy kilometres of painfully slow and careful riding, both my bicycle and I arrived in Sucre, amazed at the fact we'd made it.

With time being tight, the last thing I wanted was to be hanging around trying to get a new wheel, so it was just my luck that I arrived on a Saturday night, when any half decent shop would be closed the following day (hardly anything is open on a Sunday in Bolivia).

The next morning I ventured out and at the back of a canvas market found a rim that would fit my bike. It was at this moment that I made an important decision: when I left England, as several people can vouch for, I could barely fix a puncture. Since leaving though, my confidence had grown; I'd replaced cables, adjusted mechanisms, aligned brakes and even trued the odd wheel to the point where I'd even felt safe to throw away my cycle maintenance book that had been teaching me as I went. Having seen it done before, I was now sure I could do it; in Sucre I decided to try building my own wheel.

It wasn't plain sailing. It took a while of threading and unthreading and several times the spokes were in the wrong holes, but after four hours I had built a new wheel and boy did I feel chuffed with myself for it.

I placed the wheel on my bike, fixed all the punctured tubes from the week's excursion, and double-checked my Lonely Planet map and Google Maps for the right road to Paraguay. I even managed to meet someone who was headed there too, although not by bike, and they confirmed to me that the road to the border was unpaved on the Bolivian side, but paved entirely in Paraguay. I finally felt ready to go.

The road from Sucre down towards Paraguay was frustrating. The climbs were tough and the downhills were on roads so bad that I could never amass any speed; having worked so hard to get there I got no pleasure from descending over 3,000 metres. When I did finally get to the bottom, the roads were covered in inches of sand, which meant that for much of a sixty kilometre stretch, I had to push the loaded bicycle through beachlike conditions.

All of this was a proper test for the wheel I'd built and at the end of the third day's riding a spoke snapped. This in itself was no big deal and, given the conditions, was not particularly surprising. Unfortunately though, it was at this moment that I found the spare spokes I'd bought for the original wheel several months before were not the right size and couldn't be used.

All I could do was true-up the wheel as best as I could and hope to find a bike shop soon. Two days later I hit asphalt for the first time in five days and rolled problem-free into Camiri, the last town before Boyuibe, which was where, according to my maps, I would be turning off to go to Paraguay. In the twenty kilometres after Camiri, my bike suffered eight punctures.

Some were from thorns, some were from me not having repaired the old ones properly and some were caused by broken *Presta* valves and as such could not be repaired. Whichever way they broke, in the space of two hours I went from having four spare tubes to having none and I was out of patches too.

As I felt the air leak for the ninth puncture of the day, it became apparent the bike and I were stranded with no other option but to hitchhike.

Camiri was twenty kilometres behind us, Boyuibe forty in front and again I had the same debate with myself: could I justify to myself getting a ride to Boyuibe and cheating for this forty kilometre section? And if I got to Boyuibe, would I then be carrying on from there, or should I cycle back to where I'd broken down? If I didn't, would that not be cheating?

For four hours I had this debate with myself; for four hours every single car, truck, lorry and bus drove straight past me.

The sun disappeared, I was out of food, out of water, tired and my patience was wearing thin. I eventually decided that if I had to hitch back to Camiri then that is what I would have to do and I changed my tactics, from only trying to thumb-down Boyuibe-bound traffic, to waving my arms at any car going either direction. The very first Camiri-bound car stopped, told me I was stupid to be out on the road this late at night, put the bike in the back of their car and drove me to my destination. The irony wasn't lost on me that thirty seconds into our journey, we had to stop the car so my driver could put more air in his tyres.

The next morning I went straight to the local bike shop - I knew where it was because I'd tried to buy spare spokes the previous day - and found that they didn't have any inner tubes with *Presta* valves. My front rim is *Presta*, my back rim (the new wheel) would take *Schrader* so I bought two *Schrader* tubes, put one on the bike and prayed I could repair anything bad that happened to the front tube.

For the second time I left Camiri and this time successfully made it to Boyuibe, seeing my odometer tick over 50,000 kilometres in the process.

In planning for the side trip to Paraguay, I had checked both Google Maps and the Lonely Planet. Google Maps is programmed to take you the quickest possible way (and this means asphalt if there is any) and the Lonely Planet mentioned that there were two border posts from Bolivia to Paraguay, one here and one in a town called Idibobe, which was on a road apparently so small it didn't even bother to include on its map of Bolivia. So arriving in Boyuibe I tried to find the place to get my passport an exit-stamp only to find that no-one would tell me where Customs was. I asked several people but they couldn't help and the soldiers I saw seemed to be intimidated when speaking to me as despite the fact they all had guns, with me being foreign and at least five years older (I was a mere twenty-four myself) than all of them they appeared nervous and did their utmost not to help me. So after an hour's attempt I gave up, decided that the road must run into the Customs post at some point and that it was best just to get moving; I'd lost enough time with the broken rim and terrible roads over the last few weeks, so I was keen to get to the flat asphalt and looked forward to making up some ground to Asuncion. I'd arrived at the turn off at about 5p.m. and managed fifteen kilometres that night before camping. The road, despite being dirt, was in a reasonable condition. The next day started well, I had fifty kilometres in by lunch and then I started to hit the first of many hitches over the next couple of days when I came across dirt that had recently been rained upon, causing it to turn to thick mud.

For four kilometres, I pushed the bike through the tar-like sludge until I got to better ground. It took about an hour and a half and having lost more time I was keen now to just get to Paraguay. A further forty-five kilometres passed, leaving me just twenty from the border, and this is where the deep sand started.

The sand was patchy and for the most part was rideable, although it was a sign of things to come and after five kilometres of riding/pushing the bike, I arrived at a Bolivian Army checkpoint.

They were very polite, they told me any stamps I needed I would get in Paraguay and that the border was fifteen kilometres away. As the time was just coming up to 5p.m., they offered me a place to stay for the night, but I was desperate to get to Paraguay, so I thanked them and went on my way.

Up until this point I had no doubt that I was on the right road: I had been told by people headed this way that the road on the Bolivian side was unpaved, so this had been no surprise and it was in a better condition than most other dirt roads I'd ridden in Bolivia. So even with the lack of traffic, I'd not questioned my research, as from the tracks on the road it was clear that it was in use. This changed 100% after getting past the first Bolivian Army checkpoint.

The moment I left, the road turned to deep sand; there were no more tracks to the border and it was pretty obvious that nothing apart from me had been down there in a while. The border was fifteen kilometres away; in the afternoon I left the checkpoint I managed an hour of pushing the bike through the sand, covering three further kilometres.

Getting up early to avoid the thirty-five degree day heat, I pushed (literally) on to the border and on arriving looked at the odometer: from the first checkpoint to the second – such a short distance - had taken four and a half hours. Added to this, two more spokes had broken, so my back wheel was now down from thirty-six to thirty-one and looking very wobbly.

"It'll be fine. We'll just get to the border and then there's asphalt in Paraguay. We can play about with the wheel there and then next week is paved so the bike will last to Asuncion. Everything is going to be OK."

This is what I was telling myself, but I didn't believe my own words. I crossed the border and the hallowed asphalt I'd been pining for didn't exist. After two kilometres of what was now even deeper sand I came to the Paraguayan Customs, which consisted of three guys out of uniform, who looked shocked to see an idiot approaching with a bike. I explained to them what I was doing and why I'd come this way.

"No, there's no asphalt here, you've taken the wrong road," one of the men said, proceeding to get out a map. "See, here's the road you wanted, you needed to go 100 kilometres further down in Bolivia."

I asked where the nearest asphalt was.

"370 kilometres away. The road is sand until there, but there's a village in fifty kilometres in which you can pick up some food."

Out of curiosity, I couldn't resist asking. "When was the last person to come through this border? Not on a bike, but in a car, or in a truck?"

"We had a truck come through about two weeks ago, I can't remember before that."

Shocked and annoyed at myself for not doing enough research, I also transferred much of the blame to The Lonely Planet and Google for having sent me this way. Nevertheless I was here now, resilient and determined to carry on. The guards filled up my water bottle, gave me a couple of loaves of bread, a tin of sardines and watched as I pushed the bike off into the sand.

If the road had been bad on the Bolivian side, this was nothing compared to how deep the sand was on the Paraguayan side and in the following two hours I would manage to cover a further five kilometres, with two more spokes going. Exhausted, I collapsed in a heap by the bike.

After I'd let out a scream of frustration and calmed down, I took stock: I was on a road on which I was travelling at an average of 2.5kph, the nearest town was fifty kilometres away, I simply could not ride because of how deep the sand was, so I would be pushing the whole way, my one spare *Schrader* tube had broken at the valve as I'd crossed the last Bolivian checkpoint, my back wheel was falling apart, I had no spare spokes, I was low on both food and water and even if I were to somehow make the 370 kilometres to the town where the asphalt began, without an exit stamp in my passport there was every chance they would send me all the way back to Bolivia.

In retrospect it seems odd, but my thought wasn't '*If I go this way I'll die*' or anything like that. Instead all I could think about was Christmas. I'd never met 'Graham in Mendoza'; he'd been another of Dad's QPR message board friends, but I knew I wanted to be at his for Christmas. Christmas and birthdays are the times of year that it's hardest to be away, and the idea of a Christmas with a place to stay, some proper food, an internet connection so I'd be able to call home and well, just having some good company, had been such a motivating factor. Now here I was, in the middle of the Chaco, having lost so much time that I'd be lucky to make it there for New Year.

And why?

I thought back to the e-mail I'd sent Graham upon leaving La Paz: '*I've decided to make a side trip to Paraguay for no other reason than to say I've been to Paraguay.*'

Me and my fucking ego.

I sat in the thirty-five degree sun, pouting and repeatedly insulting myself for about ten minutes, before something clicked and a voice inside of my head, which for some reason spoke in the style of an nineteenth century Dickens character, exclaimed 'But my dear boy, you've gone this way to say that you've been to Paraguay, well please answer me this; where are you now?'

I'M IN PARAGUAY!

I may only be seven kilometres into Paraguay; I may have only met three Paraguayans and I may have absorbed none of the culture but who the hell cares?! I had no desire to go Asuncion for the place itself, the chances of meeting the two Paraguayans I'd like to meet - Jose Luis Chilavert and the model with the massive personalities who had become famous during the World Cup - was unlikely and you know what?

I WAS IN PARAGUAY!

The best part of this plan was that in the rules I'd set myself for the ride I'm excused from having to ride the same road twice, meaning if I get lost or take a wrong road I can hitch a ride back to my starting point, so now all I had to do was get back to Bolivia and from there hitch a ride back to Boyuibe, where I could sort out the wheel and get on my merry way.

It took another two hours to get back to the border. The Paraguayan guards found it hilarious that I'd got as far as I had and after another three and a half hours I was back with my friends at the first Bolivian checkpoint. Again, I was invited to stay the night and this time I accepted, was fed, watered and given my own bed. They *loved* that I knew who Marco Etchevvery was.

Spirits firmly on the up, I left my army friends at 6.30a.m. and whilst I knew there wouldn't be much traffic from the border, I didn't mind too much, as I knew that all I had to do was cycle as close to Boyuibe as possible and the closer I got the more likely I was to be able to hitch a ride.

Given all that had happened already, what could go wrong?

The first thirty kilometres were fairly smooth sailing and the only incident of note was having a fully grown wild boar run alongside the bike for twenty metres, and as I crawled closer to Boyuibe I finally heard noise from behind of a vehicle approaching. Unfortunately it was a car already fully loaded with passengers and luggage, so even if they'd wanted to take me they wouldn't have been able to, but it was a sign I was back near civilization and that things were all going my way.

They waved, the car went past and as it cruised off into the distance I went to push off, looked down at my back tyre and saw an all too predictable sight: a puncture.

Not just a puncture, a valve puncture on my last *Schrader* tube; it was now useless. From having been in total control, to abandoned in the middle of nowhere in roughly 4.2 seconds.

I tried, for no other reason than to at least justify it to myself that I had tried, to fix it - but I knew it was a waste of time. Boyuibe was eighty-five kilometres away, I was still at the unpopulated end of the road and I knew I wouldn't be seeing anything likely to pick me up for at least twenty-four hours. Standing still was not an option, but I had no tubes. What could I do? The only solution I could come up with was a feeble one. I stuffed all my socks, tea towels, underwear and towels into the tyre and padded it out with sand, surmising that it must be better than nothing.

It wasn't one of mankind's greatest ideas, but the clothes protected both the rim and the tyre, whilst offering enough 'pressure' for me be able to ride very slowly to Boyuibe.

Three hours and twenty-two kilometres later a truck drove past in the opposite direction and told me I was two kilometres from the nearest, and only, village on this road and that from there I'd be able to get a lift back to Boyuibe. It wasn't two kilometres, it was five, and I walked the bike (which was now losing spokes more rapidly and was down to twenty-six) the whole way, but seeing that village was one of the biggest reliefs I've ever had.

The locals fed me, gave me water and that night I was put in the back of a truck with the bike and driven back to Boyuibe.

I had made it.

The following morning I went to a different bike shop in town, built another wheel (one that would last me to Ushuaia), found some inner tubes, bought some extra spokes that fit and rolled on down to Villamontes, the town where the road to Paraguay actually is.

But I wouldn't be taking it because, well, Paraguay? I'd been there and done that.

Cycle touring is not in any way dangerous and I'd now been on the road for nearly three years without ever once feeling in danger of my life, but I do honestly believe if I'd carried on trying to push the bike through the sand for 370 kilometres there's a very good chance I might not have made it. It took a lot for me to do it, but turning around had been the correct decision. Was it worth it?

Well, hands up everyone who's been to Paraguay.

22: Rushing Down

"I'm not being funny, but I have to say that on the whole the people here do seem pretty lazy."

"You can't say that, it's their culture."

"Exactly, it's a lazy culture."

It was Boxing Day 2010 and I was at a bar in Mendoza, Argentina's fourth biggest city, located among the wine fields at the foot of the Andes. Accompanying me were over twenty CouchSurfers, who, all away from their homes for Christmas, had arranged to meet and share a few festive drinks. With the group were Anna and Kris, a Polish cycling couple I had met back in Ecuador and Simon, the guy I'd met in Peru who'd been the victim of the Paijan robbers. Si had been a little downbeat when we met first time round which was understandable, as a week into his trip he'd been mugged of several hundred pounds worth of possessions. Now, over two months down the line, he was sky high, as not only was he enjoying his trip, on this night he was accompanied by Adrienne, a Canadian lady who was riding a motorcycle from Colombia to Ushuaia. The two had encountered each other a week after I'd last seen him and it was clear they'd hit it off in a major way, as by all accounts they'd barely been away from each other since they'd met. We sat together, talking about what we'd been up to since we'd last seen each other.

We had all been heading north to south, had all entered from Bolivia and with most of the Argentinean land being little more than a barren desert, had all endured the same drawn out ride along the largely dull Ruta 40 to Mendoza. The temperatures had hit forty degrees each day and aside from the odd town or city along the route, it had mostly just been the bike and the sun for company. With little else en route, the subject had turned to the people of Argentina.

"You can't just call an entire culture lazy."

"They have a five hour lunch break every day, explain to me how that *isn't* lazy."

Whilst I was enjoying winding Simon up (who for some reason saw it as his duty to defend the Argentineans), I also felt that, though exaggerated, there was some truth to my comments, as the main cause of any stress I'd had on the bike over the previous weeks had been due to the staple of Argentinean culture known as the siesta. Coming down Ruta 40, when the clock hit twelve each day, 99% of businesses would close, not reopening until 5p.m.. This covered all shops, the majority of petrol stations and most restaurants and meant that if I wanted to buy something during these times, often the only thing available would be an overpriced meal, as local restaurateurs would be able to charge high prices for the luxury of being open.

With towns dotted roughly only every fifty miles, it meant that I had to plan when I was going to arrive, as otherwise I'd be sat around waiting to buy food.

Ten days before arriving in Mendoza I'd mistimed my distances and arrived in the town of Belen at five past twelve. Needing something to accompany my evening meal I asked around if a shop was open only to be told that despite the town's reasonable size the only place doing business was a small, expensive restaurant and if I wanted anything else I would have to wait another four hours and fifty-five minutes. After paying £5 for a meal of little more than canned spaghetti, I cycled out of town and dined that night on a meal of rice and sugar. Breakfast was leftovers from the night before.

Evening meals like that made it easy to get frustrated and on the bike there is very much a *go go go* attitude, but when taking a step back you could see that whilst not much ever got done, people did at least enjoy life and the emphasis was far more on being happy as opposed to doing anything else.

Another time I entered an internet café an hour before it was due to close for its siesta, only to be ushered back out the door along with a group of disappointed children.

"Sorry ninos, I know the internet café is usually open, but today I am closing early so I can meet a friend for lunch."

A relaxed attitude to work, or simply an allergy to it; regardless, the people seemed content, but it did leave me wandering, how does anything get done around here?

Back in the bar our night died down. Anna and Kris left a few days later, as did Simon and Adrienne, whereas I stayed until into the new year, first with Graham, the QPR fan, and then with Alejandra and Cecilia, two local girls and their families. During these times I saw the best of Argentine culture: the closeness of family, the celebrations of both Christmas and New Year, which consisted of exploding as many fireworks as possible long into the night, and also what would be, by quite some distance, my favourite feature of Argentina, the asados.

Spanish for 'barbecue', an Argentine asado was like no other I'd ever been to. Much like anything else in Argentina, it took an absolute eternity to get done, with meals lasting at least four hours and sometimes as long as six. But as one piece of meat at a time was cooked and then served, in terms of quality, the beef for which Argentina is famed was second to none, and when washed down with some of the local wine, hanging around wasn't that hard.

During my time in Mendoza I saw the best Argentina had to offer, although the reason I stayed so long was due to the more frustrating side to Argentine life: the difficulty in getting the most simple of tasks done. My parents had sent a package containing my new bike parts, which should have arrived for Christmas, but had been held up at Customs. Graham did his best to help release it, and now Alejandra had taken the reigns, saying it should be easy, because as a local she knew how to get things done. Two hours later, her confidence and patience were gone and I watched as she screamed down the phone in frustration, repeatedly being made to jump through hoops and still making absolutely no progress. Having already spent two weeks doing this, I knew how she felt. A few days later, I gave up on the package that contained my desperately needed bike parts and left town, heading towards Chile.

The ride from Mendoza to Santiago consisted of close to three days' torture, riding into a headwind as I climbed to over 3,500 metres of Andean altitude. However, the very moment I crossed the border the descent kicked in, first through a tunnel - which I was frustratingly forced to put my bike in a van for - and then along what is one of the most enjoyable downhills I would ever traverse: the switchbacks. Famed throughout South America by cycle tourists, I emerged from the darkness of a passageway cut into the hillside to be greeted by the sight of a series of thirty hairpin turns, which drop for over ten miles, losing over a vertical mile in the process; the ultimate reward for the pain of having got there.

Santiago was the most modern city I would visit in South America and wouldn't look out of place if it were picked up and placed anywhere in Western Europe, but I moved on quickly towards the long, boring 1,000 kilometre stretch to Puerto Montt, a stretch that was brightened up by bumping into Kris and Anna. We would cycle together for a week, which was quite a common occurrence, although what made it more interesting was the lifestyle that these two lead.

By this point of the journey I had come to accept I was being ridiculously tight with my money; it led to embarrassment, selfishness and, often disgust towards myself as I balked at the idea of paying for anything unless absolutely necessary. I hated my miserly ways, but it was something I had come to accept about myself. Travelling with Kris and Anna, it soon turned out that by comparison I was a complete squander-bird, as here were two people who lived off far less than me and who also flat-out refused to ever pay for accommodation. Not only this, they also refused to wild camp.

Now if you're not paying for accommodation but at the same time you're not wild camping, what option does that leave?

Every evening at about five o'clock, when there's still a good couple of hours of daylight, they would arrive in a small village or anywhere with a population and simply ride around asking the people in the street:

"Hello, we are from Poland. We are travelling on our bicycles, we have tents, is there somewhere safe we could camp, for example, in your back garden?"

Every day, for the past eighteen months they had been doing this.

Every day, for the past eighteen months, with just one exception, they had succeeded.

For the week I spent with them, they, of course, found us a place to sleep every night.

For me it was an interesting experience: I'd been invited into people's houses wherever I'd been on the road, had enjoyed hospitality from people all around the world and had often been truly humbled at the kindness shown to me wherever I'd been.

What I wasn't sure about though, was that whilst I appreciated people's hospitality, was it ever OK to rely on it?

I talked to Anna about my concerns and I was told a couple of things: I was not the first person to have asked this, but rest assured, they never force themselves into someone's home; and most of all, the number of people who have thanked her for letting them help has been one of her favourite experiences. I asked what she meant by this

228

and she told me how - especially in the US - people had been scared to help them and cited the American media in particular as creating a so-called fear of 'the other' (something I can wholly agree with from my time in the States), which had left a lot of people hesitant to invite strangers on bicycles into their homes. As a result, she told me how they had often struggled to find places to stay, but what they had also found was that when people who were originally fearful of taking them in did so and the night went by without a hitch, the 'hosts' had always been thankful for having had their opinions changed about the dangers of strangers. Anna especially took a lot of pride in having helped change the way some people saw the world.

In truth it wasn't a way I felt comfortable living, but as we stayed with several people who clearly loved having us in their homes, I could see her point.

In Santiago I booked my flight to Cape Town and this left me with a clear schedule for the next few months; I needed to cycle to Ushuaia and then find a way to get back up to Buenos Aires for my flight, which would be on the 21st of March. This left plenty of time and with relatively few obstacles in the way, I headed for Puerto Montt. With no direct road south through Chile, at some point I would have to take a ferry to join the Carreterra Austral, a road built under the order of Pinochet in the seventies and the only route through the south of the country, so I decided to take a detour via the island of Chiloe and to get my boat from there.

With cold weather and a lot of rain, Chiloe provided the place that felt most like Britain climate-wise and I arrived at the port to do what I thought would be the simple task of buying my ferry ticket, only to find that boats were booked up for the next eight days. I asked if any of the other ports back on the mainland had tickets, and I was told that there were none available anywhere.

A part of me had expected this, so rather than moping, I embraced the challenge; cycling had been a little dull of late and now here was something to get my teeth into. I needed to find a way to the mainland without using public transport.

I went straight down to some of the stationary boats and asked about fishing vessels that were headed to Chaiten, a small island en route to the mainland. I was told there were some but the town we were in was the smaller port on the island, and that 100 kilometres further south was Quellon, a bigger port and also a better bet as anything that would be going to Chaiten would be going via Quellon.

Wasting no time at all, it was back on the bike, camping just outside of Quellon that night and descending to the waterside the following morning. Having been so enthusiastic about the challenge of finding a boat to the mainland, it was a slight anti-climax when the first captain I spoke to said '*yes, no problem*' and told me he had a cargo boat going to the small island of Melinka the next day, and from there I would easily be able to get across to the mainland and onto the Carreterra Austral.

My hot streak was further confirmed when, as I was preparing to sleep rough in a bus stop on the edge of town, a local family started talking to me, took me back to their house, fed me and even insisted on washing my clothes.

The boat left at midday and much to the amusement of the crew, I started vomiting the moment we left port. We spent the first night picking up the ship's cargo (twenty tonnes of seaweed bound for Japan), arriving on the island of Melinka late the following evening.

Another night was spent on the boat before my new friends left me on the island the next morning, where I was to search for a lift over to the mainland. The morning's search didn't yield any results, but in the afternoon I met someone who told me to come back to meet him the following morning.

I showed up for my ride, only to find that he and his boat had disappeared, but whilst there was no sign of him a new vessel had arrived. I knew exactly what the words 'Armada' meant in English, but playing the dumb tourist I walked up to the captain, explained what I was doing and asked if I could have a lift back to the mainland in their boat. Noticeably unsure at first, just as I thought it was the expected 'no', I was invited on board and taken downstairs, where I would spend the next few hours in the ship's canteen, a guest of the Chilean Navy.

I arrived back on dry land in style, in a pristine behemoth of a boat, and all that separated me from Ushuaia and the end of my South American journey was a mere thousand miles. I was in the clear.

I flew down, covering the first 600 miles with the strong South American wind on my back and was just a kilometre from the Chilean border to Tierra Del Fuego when it happened.

A click, a grind, a snap.

I knew that sound.

I was just a few hundred miles from my goal when the chain went over the top of the gears, snapping the derailleur in the process. It was the fifth time I'd done it, but recognising this didn't make me feel any less foolish.

The nearest town with an available part was seventy kilometres away and I pushed the bike to the border, hoping to leave it there whilst I went back to get a replacement. My only memory of Argentinean border guards to this point had been on first entering the country, when one had asked me what I had thought about the Falklands, followed by an awkward moment's silence, only for him to burst out laughing and then welcome me to his country.

I hoped I would meet someone with an equal sense of humour.

I didn't.

With no help forthcoming, I eventually found someone who let me leave my bike at the border in an unlocked room, and hitched back to the previous town. Buying a £5 derailleur, which simply needed to get me to Ushuaia and nothing else, I made my way back to the border and the following morning took the boat to Tierra Del Fuego.

Nothing else could go wrong now. I was going to make it.

In many respects, South America is little more than a giant cyclist's playground. The mountains are huge, the roads are good, the cost is cheap and the food is exquisite. It's no wonder so many cyclists choose to come here and I had met dozens throughout the seven months I'd been on the continent. I spent the night before arriving in Ushuaia in the town of Tolhuin at another Casa De Ciclista, this time conveniently located in the town's bakery and the last I would stay in, where I met more travellers on wheels and once again found Simon - one of the best friends I'd made on the road. We had all come a long way and would all finish in Ushuaia. The end was so close and we knew that life, in some way or another, was set for a major change upon reaching the city that lay in front of us.

There was an air of quiet excitement, as Simon and I rode out the next day to complete South America together.

Ten kilometres from Ushuaia the skies opened; two kilometres from the campground, a bolt sheared off my front rack, causing the pannier on this rack to fall into the wheel, ripping out three spokes. To top it all off, as I pulled into the campsite I found that the rain had somehow got inside my odometer causing water damage. All the while this had been going on, Simon had ridden ahead of me, only to get lost; he would eventually show up to the campground a full hour and a half after I did.

Soaked head to toe, our steeds falling apart and failing at the simple task of riding in together, our *crossing the line* could not have been any less glorious.

But it didn't matter: we were here. I was here. I'd started riding in Alaska on the 8th of August 2009, I'd finished 29,700km later in Ushuaia on the 25th of February, 2011.

Simon and I celebrated that night and were joined the next day by Dylan, a cyclist I'd met first in Bolivia, who had just ridden from Seattle to the tip of South America on a single speed bike. To have cycled *that* far on *that* bike, Dylan's achievement dwarfed anything I had accomplished and he was welcomed by Simon and I in the proper Argentinean way: with an asado centered on a *vacio* - a boneless piece of beef the size of my arm and the staple of any good asado - and a bottle of red wine that Graham had given me for Christmas, which had been with me since Mendoza.

Back when I'd arrived in Cambria for the first time, before heading up to Alaska, I'd bought a cigar that would be my reward for reaching Ushuaia. It was now battered and falling apart, but made the perfect accompaniment to the meal that night as I delighted in blackening my lungs.

The following day we would go our separate ways: Dylan would go back to his native Alaska to save for a longer bike trip, whilst Simon was flying back to Buenos Aires and then onto England, where he planned to quit his job and move to Canada to be with Adrienne. Within six months they would be married. By the time I would return to England, Adrienne would be pregnant. Back in the present, I had a flight to South Africa to catch.

But for that one night, none of it mattered. We had all made it to Ushuaia.

I awoke to find the celebrations over, and with Buenos Aires airport still 2,000 miles away, I needed to ensure I caught that flight. Riding to the edge of town I passed a Swiss couple who were starting their trip in Ushuaia, heading north. I wished them luck, although I secretly pitied them, as I knew they were about to cycle 2,000 miles into a headwind, whereas I was fortunate enough to only have to cycle three miles to a service stop.

Being nearly blown off my saddle, I pulled into a petrol station and began asking around for lifts north. I was offered one from a trucker straight away, threw my bike in the back of his lorry and climbed aboard. I would be hitchhiking to Buenos Aires.

South America had been cycled.

23: The Cycling Chicken

I had left myself ten days to hitchhike the 2,000 miles from Ushuaia to Buenos Aires and even then I had wondered if this would give me enough time; in reality I had nothing to worry about. In Ushuaia the first person I asked gave me a lift: by the end of the first day's hitching I had travelled 400 miles; the longest I would wait at any point was two hours and whilst I would make the last leg to Buenos Aires by train, this was more for logistical reasons, as opposed to not being able to get a ride. Hitching proved easy, cost effective and I made it with plenty of time to spare.

Just as London is in no way representative of the rest of the UK, and Los Angeles is in no way representative of the rest of California, Buenos Aires proved to be nothing like the rest of Argentina. The streets are bustling, the pace of life is rapid and, most amazingly, between the hours of twelve and four o'clock, the people are awake and the shops are open. After twelve days spent in various parts of the city, I rode to the airport and, much like in Japan, found myself with a day to kill before I left another large chunk of my life behind me and began a new phase.

I had thought I would use this time, again, like I had in Japan, to reflect on the ups and downs of the previous leg of the journey. However this was too easy: I knew I liked Canada, Mexico and Colombia above all the other countries, and likewise couldn't see any reason why I might return to El Salvador or Honduras any time in the future. Instead, I had something altogether different on my mind.

Without the ego going overboard, it's fair to say I'd had a lot of plaudits over the last three years: 'inspirational', 'brave' and 'adventurer' are all adjectives people had very kindly bestowed on me. On the flip side of this coin, in Buenos Aires I had met a British girl who had repeatedly told me how anyone who travels for a period of over a year is hiding from something and that whilst she didn't know me well enough to tell what it was, she was adamant that being on the bike was a safety zone for me and I was only out here as a way of running away from whatever problems I faced back home.

This proved a far more interesting question to ponder; was I this 'brave adventurer' as some had said, or merely a chicken living in a safety zone, running away from the horrors of reality?

Well to start with, I knew I was most certainly not the former. I despise the word 'adventurer' and as for 'special' or 'brave', I have little time for people who do the same sorts of thing as I had done and label themselves as such.

I was doing what I was doing because I enjoyed it; every day I saw new things, at no point during the previous three years had I stopped learning and I had both seen and done some amazing things, yet I never considered myself anything more than an average guy. Before I left on this trip I led a normal life and in terms of both intellect and sporting prowess, I could at best be described as 'OK': on the sporting front, I played football at university in the Men's fifth team and could run the 100 metres in around 14.5 seconds; in academic terms I got one A-grade in GCSE History and hadn't seen a similar mark since. My degree is a 2:1 in a meaningless subject from an ex-Poly.

The point I wish to make is that I am nothing more than an average person, so when people say to me 'I wish I could do what you do', the truth is that they could. Anyone with the same resources could have done what I'd done and granted, whilst if I were female or, depressingly, of another ethnicity, it would have added extra challenges and dangers, with the right preparation it still would have been entirely possible.

236

Since the beginning of the recession, the skyrocketing numbers of cycle tourists prove this, as the affordability and pleasure level attract more and more people like me to the road.

So no: I was not a 'brave adventurer'; I was on the road because I enjoyed it and if I didn't enjoy cycling I would have packed up the bike after a month and gone home.

I could not class myself as any of these positive things people had labelled me, which left me with option two: the 'Chicken in a safety zone' option.

Now this was a far more interesting idea.

When I'd left home, one of the main goals had been to get outside of my safety zone; to challenge myself in far-off lands, to see how I'd cope with not knowing where I'd sleep each night and to see what I'd do in places where I didn't speak the language.

In truth, most of my questions about myself had been answered within the first six months; it turns out I was more than happy not knowing where I'd be sleeping each night and was perfectly content roughing it in shop doorways if necessary. I'd shown myself I could learn new languages - or become decent enough in mime to get by where I couldn't - and mentally I'd not only found myself thriving, but truly at peace when on the bicycle.

What had become apparent though, was that as I'd removed myself from one safety zone, in being able to learn the tricks of wild camping, the joys of riding the bike and the lack of responsibilities of my new found lifestyle, I was busy creating another.

I began my own routine and settled into life on the bike; I became comfortable with not showering daily, I liked the fact I would only do laundry every so often, I enjoyed that I only had to shave monthly and as for the lifestyle - well a friend once said of me: "If he's not sleeping, he's eating". Not a truer word has ever been spoken, and on the bike I got to eat 6,000 calories a day whilst sleeping ten hours a night.

When combined for a daily routine, if all of that isn't a safety zone, then what is?

On the road I had picked up new skills: I couldn't fix a puncture when I left the UK, but now I was travelling on a machine that had two wheels I had built myself. And I had taught myself to speak Spanish.

But whilst these appear positive achievements, I could also argue that I'd not learned these things through choice: fixing a puncture was something I was forced to learn (quickly); I'd be doing well to be around Spanish speaking people for fourteen months and not learn any of it, and the same could be said for my world knowledge - it would be impossible to travel and not take in facts and information about the places I'd visited.

Indeed, when it comes to things that have taken effort or have been non-compulsory, at certain times I've struggled. I was the first to admit I didn't take as good a care of the bike as I should and there were occasions when I'd failed to take advantage of all the opportunities presented to me. The example that stuck out most was the number of days wasted sat on the internet, as opposed to visiting local museums and taking in tourist sites.

I was being hard on myself, but these aspects definitely needed addressing when it came to answering the question of whether I was simply a chicken living in a safety zone or not.

In the end, the truth lay somewhere in the middle.

Perhaps a part of me enjoyed the safety zone of being on my bike, but at the same time I reasoned that living in a tent, continually travelling to different places and never knowing where I'll be sleeping the following day, removes some of the 'safety' from that so-called zone.

I acknowledge that yes, I did sometimes struggle to take up all of the opportunities offered on this trip, but at the same time this is nothing new. I have always been someone who has preferred to 'learn through doing', so with this in mind I would say that the best way for me personally to learn is to put myself in a situation where I have no choice but to do so. In this case, it meant getting on my bike, going out into the world and putting myself out there.

Finally, as for the things that require effort: perhaps I should have taken more opportunities but it really wasn't that easy. When I first started cycling, everything had been new. It was easy to find enthusiasm, as my life had been turned upside down and I was always encountering fresh experiences, new sights and different ways of living. Three years down the line it was undoubtedly still fun, but the one-off cups of tea I'd had with locals, the oddball conversations with random people and the constant near misses I was continuing to have with cars were nowhere near as exciting as they had previously been.

These things still made up the bulk of my days, but they were no longer new to me.

I was still eager for the journey, but it's hard to deny that I often settled for being content just to ride my bike each day and stick inside my safety zone. What I really needed was a situation that forced me out of it.

There are only two things that would be able to remove me from the little bubble world I'd created, and as the introduction of a female was relatively unlikely, it was only a grand change in environment that would cause anything to alter.

A boarding call for a flight to South Africa was announced.

The idea of going from Argentina to Africa may not sound like a massive deal, and admittedly I would still be cycling. However, as I landed in a different world, with a new culture and the people of the Rainbow Nation, I would, for the next few weeks at least, be forced to come a little out of my shell.

Having deliberately stayed up late the night before, I boarded the plane, we took off and I closed my eyes. I was later woken by a stewardess's prod to alert me that the plane would shortly be landing. I looked out of the window, over the sea and in the distance I could see Cape Town.

Leg two: Alaska, USA – Chile, South America

Dates: July 9th 2009 – March 21st 2010

Countries visited: 17

Alaska (USA), Canada, USA, Mexico, Belize, Guatemala, El Salvador, Honduras, Nicaragua, Costa Rica, Panama, Colombia, Ecuador, Peru, Bolivia, Paraguay, Argentina and Chile.

Kilometres cycled: 29,700

24: Different World

From the moment I touched down in South Africa there was only one place I looked to on the map; I may have been 10,000 miles away but from now on each pedal would be in the direction of home.

I was nervous as I arrived in South Africa. Whilst by this point I knew not to listen when someone told me a place was unsafe, I had been given so many warnings about the dangers of both living and travelling in the country that, even with all my experience, I still felt apprehensive. As always, my worries proved to be moronic.

I'd thought I'd be out of my safety zone in this unfamiliar environment, yet in Cape Town I found a city that for large parts felt as though it had been transferred straight from England. There were some obvious differences: Table Mountain, at 1,084 metres, is higher than any English peak and dominates over the city, whilst Britain has neither a penguin nor baboon population prospering so close to its cities. But on the most basic level, the language was the same, people drove on the left, many of the shops bore the same name as their counterparts in the UK and I could get so many of the brands - *Cadbury*, *Heinz*, *Weetabix*, to name a few - that I'd not seen in so long. If I still felt hungry after that, I could even visit the main fast food store in town: Wimpy.

I quickly settled and began to immerse myself in Cape Town life. I was staying for three weeks and it was during this period that I began to form my opinion about the aspect of life in South Africa that I had previously feared: racism.

South Africa's past is well documented and I had been concerned about some of the unpleasant racist people I may meet out here; it was an opinion based on some of the white

South Africans I'd met when living in South-West London and an anxiety only exacerbated after meeting an openly racist Afrikaner at the airport in Buenos Aires. In reality, I only came across one explicitly racist person in the entire time I spent in the country. Granted, it's one too many and I am sure that there are still numerous bigots out there, but given where South Africa was twenty years previously it was clear to me a lot of prejudices had been eroded. In particular, it was noticeable how the younger generations mixed together and during my stay I enjoyed the company of people from all walks of life.

What I found to be the big divider amongst South African communities was class. I'm not an expert on South African history and I wasn't going to pretend that a few weeks cycling through meant I knew everything about their society. However, everywhere I went, the noticeable divide between people wasn't between black and white, but, particularly in the cities, it was between the people who lived in the Townships and those who didn't.

Townships were the places where non-whites were forced to live during Apartheid and whilst Apartheid was now gone, the people who were affected remain. The majority of these places remain on the poorest end of South African society; they are pretty much exclusively black or mixed-race areas and, particularly at night, are known to be dangerous. Many locals would advise me against going to these places, both in Cape Town and in several other cities on my ride up to Lesotho, warning of what might become of me should I enter.

Whilst I never visited at night, I cycled through several Townships and the standard of living was noticeably different. Compared to how people just five miles down the road were living, the gulf in lifestyle was spectacular.

South Africa has a well documented high-crime rate and the link between social status and crime is obvious. I'd assumed that the biggest challenge facing the country would be the question of race, which I now knew I was wrong; from what I saw the big challenge for the future of South Africa is eliminating the divide between the Townships and the rest of the social order.

My hosts in Cape Town were people my father had put me in contact with: Rob, Dawn and their two sons Ryan and Glenn. Ryan was an aspiring cricketer who at the age of ten was already a far more proficient batsman than I had ever been, whilst eight year old Glenn was a child with a natural showmanship that constantly made for entertaining company. Just like with several other families previously, they had taken me in as one of their own. A few days before I departed my father forwarded an e-mail in which Rob had described me as 'the older brother the boys had always wanted' and when the time did come round to leaving I felt lower than usual, desperately sad to be saying goodbye. The familiar pangs of loneliness were beginning to kick back in.

But I had to go.

The end was in sight and the target for this leg of journey was a simple one: home.

On the 12th of April 2011 I rode out of Cape Town, into the rain, in the direction of England.

After ambling through the South African countryside, Maseru, the capital city of Lesotho, was my first real stop on this continent and coincided with something that had not happened to me since October of 2008: I got ill. My throat glands were swollen, I had small ulcers on my tongue, my gums were twice the size they usually were and the skin from large portions of my lips had flaked off. It was horrible, but fortunately for me, by complete chance, the family I was staying with happened to consist of a nurse and a doctor and they were happy to offer their help.

They were never quite sure what I had; scary words such

as scurvy were used, but no conclusions were ever made and instead I was given a crash-course of antibiotics. Within four days the infection had gone, I could both eat and talk again, and was now ready to get on my way, aiming for the 2,873 metre Sani Pass which would take me out of Lesotho and back down into South Africa, to the city of Durban.

I knew very little about Lesotho before I arrived, but learned quickly; it's a small country of about two million that's landlocked by South Africa on all sides. The people are known as the Basotho, the local language is Sesotho, and in turn this means you can say the fun yet factual sentence of 'The Basotho in Lesotho like to speak Sesotho'. The history of it becoming a country in its own right lies with the British, who turned it into a protectorate and amongst other things it's known for its mountains, the fact that it used to have a ski-resort and for holding the distinction of being the only country in the world entirely above 1,000 metres elevation.

The ski-resort had long since closed down but the fact it *had* a ski-resort and the fact that I was now here at the beginning of winter set alarm bells ringing. The Sani Pass was 330 kilometres from Maseru, I had given myself six days to get there and I had figured this would be plenty.

The ride out of Maseru was easy enough, however it was shortly after I'd turned off the main road towards the town of Thaba-Tseka that I learned a quick lesson about Lesotho; I knew the Sani Pass was a tough climb, which several people had been quick to warn me about, but none of them had warned me about the seven mountain passes I would have to cross in order to get there in the first place, the smallest of which was 2,200 metres, the tallest a rather more imposing 3,200.

The first of these, the 2,263 metre Bushmen's Pass, was a blunt lesson in what riding here would be like; if there's a mountain, we'd be going straight up over it on a gradient which at a minimum would be around 10%. At the end of my first day it had taken me five hours to crawl sixty kilometres and my legs were really feeling the effects of those steep climbs, but it was now time for an even greater challenge: finding a place to sleep.

Again, many people had given me warnings about wild camping in Lesotho, reciting stories of those who had woken to find their tent slashed and their valuables gone. I'd been given the blunt advice that if I wanted to camp then what I needed to do was to go to a local tribe, request to see the chief and then ask if I could camp in their village. If the chief consented to my request, then I would be safe for the night, as it would be unthinkable for anyone to steal from a guest of the tribe.

I was slightly nervous about this beforehand, wondering how I would be welcomed by the leader of a mountain tribe, particularly as in my head I had posed the chief as an imposing, masculine figure. After meeting a young man in the village I'd stopped in, he offered to take me to their leader; far from being what I'd imagined, the chief was a small woman in her seventies with a big smile, few teeth and a welcoming persona. Whilst it turned out I was a sexist, the Basotho certainly were not.

She was warm, friendly and not only said I could stay, but found a place for me in the house of her daughter-in-law. The rain had poured all day and we were expecting a frost, so I was grateful for the offer and enjoyed a good evening being taught how to count to ten in Sesotho by local children, eating a meal of Samp - a maize based dish with no discernible flavour - and was then off again the next morning with a warning that the tops of the mountains had been getting a lot of snow recently, so I should proceed with caution.

The gradient of the eight kilometre climb out of their village could best be described as 'ridiculous' and led to the aptly name 'God Help Me Pass', before another immediate climb took me over the 2,633 metre Blue Mountain Pass.

245

The ride was slow and the climbs relentless, but the scenery was stunning.

It was another gruelling ride, but by the end of the day, if I narrowed it down from when I'd crossed the Bushmen's Pass to where I now was, I could legitimately claim to have crossed five separate mountain passes in the space of seventy kilometres.

Alas, at the same time, whilst the mountain top snow had been pretty to look at, it had also rained constantly since leaving Maseru and as the second day drew to a close I had no intention of camping out in the cold if I could avoid it. As I crossed yet another hilltop I met a local who told me that at the bottom of the descent there was a town called Matsonyane and here I would be able to sleep at the local police station.

This turned into an experience; I arrived, was welcomed in and after the usual questions about who I was and where I was going the Chief of Police turned the conversation to the subject of AIDS. Lesotho has an official AIDS rate of 23%, but several people had told me that in reality it is a lot, lot higher and it was clear this is what my host wanted to talk about.

He asked me if we had AIDS in England, I told him we did.

He asked me if we had a cure for it in England, I told him we did not.

He then asked me if I drank beer, I told him that sometimes I did but that I couldn't at the moment as I was still on antibiotics.

"I hate this AIDS shit. Everywhere there is people dying, so what I do is I abstain. I have no wives, no girlfriends, I have no sex. I don't want a girlfriend because I don't want AIDS. Instead, what I do to pass my time is I drink. I drink, I drink and I drink and that is how I will get through life. AIDS will not kill me."

246

I didn't really know what to say to this, but just to prove he was telling the truth, the Chief subsequently left the building only to return an hour and a half later absolutely off his face, upon which he entered the room, slumped in a corner and didn't move again until morning.

In the meantime, the local secondary school headmaster had joined us in the police station, as his friend worked there and he wanted to watch an important football match on the station's TV.

We got talking about the school.

"We have about 300 children at the school. Of them, about half are orphans."

It was an eye-opening evening. Not only had I seen the effect that AIDS was having on both the community as a whole and the behaviour of individuals, but I'd also seen how even having a job wasn't the solution to poverty; it turns out the police weren't that well paid and didn't get much of a varied diet, so I ended up sharing my dinner of rice and fried vegetables with the two grateful officers who had remained with me in the station.

The night passed, the sun rose and it was back onto the ridiculous gradients, this time with the added fun that the roads were no longer paved.

A few more passes came and went, the next two days dragged by at a painfully slow nine kilometre per hour average speed and on the second day - my penultimate day in Lesotho - I turned off on the road to the border, assuming that the Sani Pass would be the only summit on this road. I pushed all afternoon thinking that, as my goal was only 2,800 metres, if I kept climbing I'd make it that day and be able to find somewhere to spend the night.

What I didn't know about was the existence of a 3,200 metre pass shortly before Sani. I pushed, kept climbing, got above the snow level - which I knew to be around the 3,000 metre mark - and then the light disappeared. Quickly.

It had been a while since I'd camped in snow. I hadn't

enjoyed it the last time, and whilst the snow wasn't as deep, it was something I'd hoped to avoid doing again. But it came, it went, I made the impressive Sani Pass, which included descending 1,400 vertical metres in the space of fourteen kilometres, and cruised on down to Durban.

Lesotho had been unlike any other place I'd visited before and the whole country highlighted both the best and worst things that the world has to offer.

To expand on this I'll start with the best things: the mountain scenery is beyond spectacular, with snow-capped peaks overlooking glistening valleys and vast rivers. Add to that the toughness of the road - the hardest climb was a 34% gradient on unpaved road - and you've got one of the most demanding-yet-naturally-beautiful rides on earth.

So the backdrop is spectacular, but add the Basotho people on top of that and you have something truly special. The overwhelming majority of people here are subsistence farmers; they are born poor, unlikely to ever leave their own land and will die poor, quite possibly from AIDS. And yet when you stop to talk to people they are still overwhelmingly warm, happy to see visitors in their country and to wish you well on your way. I knew the kindness of those less fortunate had been a common theme of my journey, but I'd never seen poverty on the scale that I saw in Lesotho, so to still be welcomed as I was a very humbling experience.

Combining the people with the scenery, it's a place that, particularly on a bicycle, I feel privileged to have visited.

Sadly, the country also offers up several examples of situations that demonstrate the 'worst of the world' section; poverty and AIDS are rampant.

We'll start with the latter: AIDS.

We all know what AIDS does, we all know how it spreads and in Lesotho it is the main reason as to why the life expectancy is around forty. I was fully aware that people suffering from AIDS is something I'd be coming across as I travelled through Africa but even so, Lesotho has been a sharp introduction to what the disease can do to communities.

I learned from the nurses I spoke to that there are programmes under way in which education about the disease and also some treatments are being introduced, particularly in rural areas, and these are having a small but positive effect. That said, whilst these offer a tiny flicker of hope for the future, in the here and now the fight with AIDS is an uphill battle.

But whilst the reality of AIDS was hard to take, one of the things that hit me harder in Lesotho was the poverty. 40% of the population live off $1.25 per day and as stated previously, the majority of people, particularly in the countryside, are subsistence farmers.

With this in mind, one of the things it is impossible to ignore is begging; here it is from everyone.

Riding past people, noticeably adults, I would hear shouts of 'give me money' and every time I sat down to rest or to have a snack, no matter how well I hid myself, it would only be a matter of time before someone would find me, walk straight up to me and more often than not, rather than say anything, would simply look at me and literally stick their hand out.

There was no question that these people were poor and I understood how poverty causes begging, but seeing people do this made me wonder about the way we give aid from outside to these countries.

In Britain we are well off and are quite right to help those in need, particularly in places like Lesotho. That said, when, as in places such as this, we've managed to condition people so that upon seeing a white person their reaction is to simply walk up to them and silently stick their hand out, it's hard not to feel that something has gone wrong.

The requests were always for one of three things;

money, food or sweets.

I never give money to anyone as, whilst it may seem cold, giving cash to someone on the streets solves nothing. As for food, sometimes I'll give a little, but so many people had asked all over the world that giving to everyone simply wasn't possible. Sometimes I'd give, sometimes I wouldn't. Finally there was the real issue in Lesotho: sweets. Or as it's pronounced in Sesotho, 'Sweeeeeeeeeeeeettttttssssssss'.

This one was exclusively down to the kids, but when riding and I heard that cry of 'Sweeeeeeeeeeeeeettttttssssssss' I knew that for the next ten minutes, I was going to have an army of small children chasing me, demanding I give them something. This was such a common occurrence that after my first day, out of curiosity, every time I had a chase on my hands I used my odometer to see how far the children were willing to follow me. The longest runners followed me for three and a half kilometres up a hill, repeatedly yelling 'sweets' and nothing else at me.

Again, much like the food, if I have, sometimes I'll give, but having a sweet tooth combined with not having been to a dentist in over three years meant that for the benefit of my own oral hygiene I rarely carried sweets and ended up leaving a fair few kids disappointed.

These were the three common things that were being requested and one of my most poignant memories of Lesotho was how a request for these led to a situation that I didn't know how to handle.

On my first night on the road I'd stayed with the chief and whilst I usually like to give sweets or something small to the kids of the families I stay with, due to poor planning, I had nothing. The second night I'd stayed with the police, whom I'd cooked for, and on the third night, in anticipation of staying with a local family, I'd bought a bag of lollipops to give to the kids of whoever I stayed with.

I'd arrived at a village, found the chief, had been told I could stay and as per usual soon had a crowd of kids wanting to stare at the freak on a bike who'd come to put his tent up in their vicinity. It didn't take long for the shouts of 'sweets' to start and I knew from experience it was best not to give any out until morning.

Nevertheless, one of the children's mothers, who it turned out was nineteen, unmarried and already had two of her own children amongst the group, came over and asked if I had anything for the kids of the village.

I gave her the bag of lollies, which she distributed amongst the kids.

After they'd all gone she promptly turned around and said "OK, now you should give me some money."

No *thank you* for the lollies, no *please*, just 'now you *should* give me some money'.

The level of expectancy in her voice caught me completely off guard. I knew people didn't have to accept me into their lives and that in letting me camp in their village they were doing me a favour, but I have to admit that for the gift I'd given to her kids to have been so unappreciated was slightly disheartening.

I politely declined, she left and I was now left cooking my dinner in my tent with twenty or so children, each with a lollipop in their mouth, watching me cook.

One of the group then came up to me: "Excuse me, can I have some of your dinner?"

This is a difficult situation to be in as, what do you do? Give the child some food? If you do that, you then have twenty more kids in front of you who you have to feed. Or do you tell these kids that one child can eat whilst the rest of them can't?

"I'm sorry little lady, but this food is for me," I said in a friendly tone.

"But please, I am eight years old, both of my parents are dead, I have no family and I am homeless. I have no home."

More than a little stunned, I asked her where she slept at night, if she went to school and a few other basic questions. Within five minutes the sun had set, the temperature entered the minuses and the crowd of twenty disappeared. The little girl who had asked for dinner stayed with a nearby family and was, at least, safely indoors for the night.

I didn't sleep well that evening, as I had no idea what the right thing to have done was; should I have given food to the child, knowing that she would not be the only orphan in that group and that if I were to feed her, I would need to feed the others as well? This was something I didn't have the supplies to do. Or did I feed that child and somehow explain to the others that she got fed because she'd asked first? Or did I do nothing, knowing that whilst she was an orphan she would have a roof over her head and a meal of bland Samp from the family which was looking after her?

Whilst I had spoken to her and tried to make friends, I hadn't fed her. It weighed on my mind for weeks.

I still think about her now; not just because of that night, but because of how she represented what was the saddest aspect of life in Lesotho; for many people, I didn't see how things were going to get better.

All around the world I've seen poor people, but before now there had always been opportunities to escape poverty: in Asia and South America it's obvious that economies are growing and those who work have the opportunities to escape. The same could be said of South Africa and even as I crossed over the Sani Pass I met a man from Gugulethu, Cape Town's infamous Township, and he told me about how he'd been born there, had worked his way to a good life and now here he was, 1,000 miles away, on holiday and viewing the famous Sani skyline.

In Lesotho it's impossible to see an escape; there isn't much industry, there are no jobs, no natural resources, AIDS is everywhere, there are high rates of teen pregnancy and, particularly if you're born in the countryside, it's hard to see how you will ever escape this life.

I could see no answers to these problems. What made it harder was that I'd never met a group of people who I'd wanted to help more.

A few days before arriving in Maseru the third anniversary of my leaving home had occurred and with so many miles under my belt I thought I had seen it all; wherever I went I was able to compare one country to another and no matter how impressive something was, I was always able to say to myself 'Oh, *that* mountain over there reminds me of *that* one in that country', or '*these* people are similar to *those* people in *this* way'.

What I'd seen in Lesotho I had no comparison for; no reference point, nothing. It was unlike anything I'd ever seen before or would see again.

The week I spent there was one of the most valuable I would ever have.

25: Uniting Factors

It is true that there are some elements of existence that bond the entire world; similar interests that unite us no matter where on the planet we happen to live. At the same time, there are also regionally specific aspects of reality, where you can witness something and think 'that could only happen here'. I was reminded of both of these truths during my first few months in Africa.

If there is one thing that unites the world like no other, it is sport. It doesn't matter, where, what, or to what standard, the thing that almost all of mankind has in common is the desire to either play or watch some kind of competitive sporting event. I had watched numerous sports throughout my journey and this had led me to meeting some true sportsmen; in Japan I had met Bobby Valentine, a major league Baseball manager who had previously coached the New York Mets all the way to the World Series, in California I had met Antonio Alonso, someone who had both played football professionally in Mexico and also went on to arrange for his family to teach me Spanish, and of course there was Tom Kennedy back in Cambria, the first ever World Frisbee Golf Champion. As I came through South Africa, another name was added to the list.

I was about thirty-five kilometres north of Jamestown on my ride up to Lesotho when, with light fading, I pulled down a sidetrack and asked some local people who I could see working on a nearby farm if there was anywhere I could camp. The farmhands were black and I was taken aback by their response of 'We'll have to go and ask the white people', but when they returned they brought with them the owner of the farm, a giant of a man, well over six feet tall, with arms the size of my legs and a beaming smile to match. After hearing what I was up to he instantly welcomed me into his home. His name was Marius Corbett and his size was explained when, after a night talking with him and his wife Anel, he told me he was a former professional athlete and had won the gold medal for Javelin at the 1997 World Athletics Championships. An obviously humble man by nature, there was a clear smile on his face when he talked about how it was Steve Backley - an English athlete famed for never winning either an Olympic or World Championship gold medal - that he had beaten into second place.

Marius and Anel now owned the farm I was staying on and the following morning gave me a proper Afrikaner breakfast of fried meat, eggs and tomato, before sending me on my way with panniers full of chocolate, biscuits, a bag of delicious syrup-coated doughnuts called Koeksisters and some borewors meat from their farm. I was glad to have met them, not just because it was another sportsman to add to the list but also for their hospitality, and I spent the following day pondering which was the more impressive achievement: World Frisbee Golf Champion, or World Javelin Champion?

Sorry Tom, you lost.

But this was how South Africa had introduced me to a new sportsman; the country also gave me an opportunity to watch more sports in person and this in turn reminded of sport's bonding power.

Up to this point on the trip, any live sport I'd seen had predominantly been football, and quite a bit of it. Three years previously in Georgia I had been to a Champions League Qualifier between local champions Dinamo Tbilisi and the champions of the Faroes Islands, where during the game, thanks to several of the Faroese players, I had been able to enjoy looking down on the pitch with that wonderful feeling inside of 'I'm better at football than those guys'.

In contrast, my football smugness had been eradicated

when, after attending a Chivas Guadalajara match in Mexico with some locals, I was asked about Javier Hernandez, who had just signed a contract with Manchester United. "He'll never make it, he's too lightweight," I had mused; in his first season in England, Henandez scored twenty-seven goals and I was glad I had moved on from Mexico.

And finally, when not making any terrible predictions, having been to a River Plate match in Buenos Aires, where my friend David and I had bought the wrong tickets and ended up in with the Ultra fans, I was simply glad to have got in and out in good health.

These had been the football events I had attended, but as for other sports, I could only count a baseball match in Japan, which I remembered most for the politeness of the crowd; both sets of supporters had brought a band with them, however they only made noise when their team was batting and the moment their last man was out the entire support sat down and it was the opposing fans turn to sing.

So, when I pulled into Durban and was offered a chance to attend a Super XV Rugby Match between the Natal Sharks and the Pretoria Bulls, I snapped it up.

The game itself was between two of South Africa's biggest historical rivals and proved unfortunate for the Sharks, by whom I'd been adopted, as after a slow start and despite a second half comeback, they went on to lose by thirty-two points to twenty-three. The home fans left disgruntled, but I had enjoyed the game and was also pretty intrigued by the atmosphere of the event; despite the rivalry between fans there was no form of segregation before, during or after the match. Before the game fans lit barbecues outside the ground and mingled with each other, whilst during the game home fans and away fans sat next to each other, both freely allowed to cheer as and when they felt like it. Having had a QPR season ticket for eleven years, I knew that the idea of transferring this policy to English

256

football would be laughable and as we left the ground I considered what would happen if they'd tried this in Argentina. *Carnage.*

Far more interesting though, I once again thought about the role of sport as a uniting factor among people; twenty-five years previously, Apartheid meant that people of different races would not have mixed in such a way and most certainly not at a sporting event. But at the rugby I saw white, black and Asian families coming together and all enjoying the game.

A few days later, as I left South Africa, I thought back to how I had feared coming to the country in the first place; how I was warned of the racists I would come up against and also the danger of the streets wherever I went. In reality, whilst not perfect, I had found a generally peaceful and welcoming nation and throughout my three months I had barely come across any issues at all.

As for sport; I love sport and will never be able to hide that fact. Whilst legislation, laws and other such things can certainly make it illegal to segregate people, they can't bring people together; sport has the power to do that and in my opinion will play a key role in the country's future.

Just like it is doing all around the world, sport is making South Africa a happier place.

As much as watching sports is something you can do anywhere, it's fair to say that the sights I was seeing could only take place on the continent of Africa.

Having headed along the coast into Swaziland, I took the briefest of detours back through South Africa to the Mozambique border and on into Maputo, the capital city.

Maputo was my first experience of what I would call a 'proper' African city; a place that, whilst not meeting all stereotypes, was more what I had pictured when thinking of the continent's big cities prior to my arrival. The scale of the place was immense, with sprawling suburbs stretching for kilometres and with far more noise than the previous big African cities I'd visited. Animals such as goats and chickens ran free; vendors selling shrimp, fish, vegetables and all kinds of fruits were located on every street corner. Down at the beach front, the city's sewage pipes emptied out far too close to the shore, meaning that the water looked disgusting, although this didn't stop people from swimming in it on a daily basis. And in amongst all of the organised chaos of car horns, roaming animals and pot-holed streets were the people. The locals were beyond friendly, with Mozambican girls the prettiest in Africa. Warwick, the father of the family I stayed with, told me his theory: that the happiness of the locals was due to their ridiculously healthy fruit and vegetable based diet.

Whatever it was, Maputo had a positive energy and due to an unplanned bout of Tick Bite Fever and the necessity of ordering a new passport as my old one was close to being full, I ended up staying around the city for two weeks.

Arriving in Maputo really was one of those moments where I was forced to stop and think to myself 'OK, now I am in Africa.' Of course, it hadn't been the first such moment; Lesotho was an eye-opener in terms of where I now was, and Swaziland, the small nation of just over a million people and ethnic home of the Swazi tribe had also provided similar instances, the most poignant of which was being invited in to stay with a local man at his kraal. A kraal is the name given to the homesteads of men in the rural area of southern Africa and refers to the fenced off piece of land which will include the individual's livestock, houses and family. The owner said I was most welcome to camp on his land, before then pointing to the five houses around the site. In each house, it was indicated, lived a different one of his wives. As I'd arrived I had noticed a large number of children present and the following morning I counted as a total of fourteen emerged from the various houses; their existence suddenly made a lot of sense and I was left realising that I was indeed somewhere new.

Although polygamy was something that I was coming across personally for the first time, it was not something exclusive to Africa. Indeed, if I were to ask people which places they associated the practice with, many would list places other than Africa.

The aspect of everyday life which left me in no doubt as to which continent I was now in was the role that animals played in African life.

Coming through South Africa I had visited several game parks and had also stayed with Murphy, a friend who worked at the famous Jane Goodall Chimpanzee Sanctuary in Nelspruit, which had recently been the subject of a TV documentary. These made for entertaining day trips, not least because each story about an animal at a South African game park seemed to go along the lines of *"We once had this really great elephant, but one day he went crazy, so we shot him,"* and then *"This other time, we had an awesome rhino, but one day he got a bit boisterous, so we shot him,"* followed by *"And this other time we had a friendly hippo, but one day he got angry, so we shot him,"* but these trips had not felt natural; all the animals I had seen had been from behind a car window or behind a fence. In Africa I wanted to see how wild animals were living with people.

I didn't need to look far and the first instance of animals affecting human lives happened as I landed in Cape Town, with the euthanising of the infamous Fred the baboon.

Baboons roam freely around Africa and as I touched down in Cape Town, Fred's demise was front page news. The reason? Fred had made his name as the leader of a gang of carjackers.

Whilst the details were hazy of exactly how he was orchestrating it, the most common theory was that Fred's troop of baboons would hide at traffic lights and - having learnt that if the lights were red, then cars were about to stop - would bide their time, waiting for an appropriate vehicle to pull up. With the lights halting traffic and a target in place, the baboons would pounce collectively, opening the car doors and grabbing whatever they could from inside, before running off into the bushes.

It sounds amusing, but several attacks had left people needing medical attention and Fred specifically was known for an escalating level of violence. So it came to pass that the Cape Town Baboon Operation Group released the following statement:

> *"The decision to have him euthanised was not taken lightly and not without extensive discussions between all role-players involved. This baboon's aggression levels had recently escalated to the point where the safety of tourists, motorists and other travellers along the road past Smitswinkel Bay was being threatened."*

A sad day for Cape Town.

As I'd left the city I'd passed several troops of baboons; they looked just as menacing in real life and a reminder of some of the dangers that were out there came back as I entered Swaziland.

On my first night in the country I stayed with a white-Swazi family - the only white Swazis I would meet in my time there - and the head of the house told me about two events that had happened in the previous three months involving another of Africa's most notorious dangers: snakes.

The first involved the liquor store my host owned; one night a gentleman had partaken in a few drinks in the shop and as he and a friend were walking home they had seen a dead Black Mamba in the road. The snake had a flat portion in the middle of its body where a car had run it over and it now lay motionless, so the man said to his friend 'Hey, look, a dead Black Mamba' and went to pick it up. Alas, whilst the snake had been run over and was about to die, it turns out he hadn't gone quite yet. The understandably distressed snake didn't take kindly to being picked up, bit the man on the arm and by the time his friend had got back from running off to get help, the man who had been bitten was dead.

That sounded unpleasant enough, but then there was story number two; a few weeks ago my host's wife had gone to clean the stove after cooking. She had lifted up the cooking grates and been met by a Spitting Cobra, which had entered the oven to soak up some heat; upon seeing her, the Cobra had attacked and spat venom in her direction. Luckily she wore glasses, so not all of the venom had entered her eyes and after they'd been washed out, although it stung for a while, she was fine within a day. As for the snake, my host told me he had killed it there and then, but his major worry was that they live in pairs and he hadn't managed to find the other snake, which would still be around somewhere.

"Possibly in the house?"

"Possibly."

That was not an easy night's sleep.

Several weeks later, as the time rolled around to leave Maputo, with all remnants of my fever gone, it was once again animals and an 'only in Africa' vibe that would shape the events of the next few days.

"You could take the main road, but that's boring," insisted Warwick. "Far more fun is the back road. It'll be safer because there's less traffic and you'll come into the part of Zimbabwe you want to be in, saving you about four days of riding."

It was my last night with the Fletcher family and we had

a map out, discussing my route.

"A quick 'heads-up' though, on the Zim side of the border there's a game park, but don't worry, there's a paved road that goes around it and you're fenced off from the animals."

For the uninitiated, game parks are the areas of land set aside for Africa's wild animals to live in. In Mozambique, all big game had been hunted to near-enough extinction during the thirty years of civil war, but in Zimbabwe the animals lived in abundance.

Trusting Warwick's words, I left Maputo and headed for the Zimbabwean border.

"Oh Mr. Blake, you are a joker."

This was not the reaction I'd hoped for when telling the Zimbabwean customs official that I planned to cycle to Victoria Falls. He patiently went on to explain the situation; the road I was on wasn't as described and instead there was only one route, which consisted of a forty mile dirt road that ran straight down the middle of the game park. The fence that would supposedly keep me away from all the animals didn't exist.

I asked what my options were, and was told that my best bet was to wait for a car to drive me through.

"OK, when is the next car heading through the park?"

"We expect another car to be coming through on Thursday."

It was Tuesday.

Deciding that this couldn't be the only option, I spoke to some other officials at the border and after twenty minutes a consensus was formed; all of the animals, particularly those most likely to eat me, would not be active during the day, so from the hours of 9 a.m. to 5 p.m., it would be safe for me to ride through. It was also likely that they would not have seen a bicycle before and as such, would act in fear of it.

However, unless I had a death wish I should not go into the park at night, as that's when the animals come out to hunt.

By this point it was three in the afternoon, so a plan was made; camp early tonight and then ride the fastest forty miles I'd ever ridden the next morning. I'd already crossed the border and the only buildings on the Zimbabwean side were the police houses, the same guys who had just told me not to enter the National Park at this hour.

"OK, so I will ride through in the morning. I have my tent, would it be possible to camp here tonight? I have food, water and everything else; I just need a little space for my tent."

"No, you cannot stay here, not on police property."

"But I can't go back over the border."

"No, you cannot."

"And the other way is the National Park. And you just said that I'll die if I go into the National Park at night."

"That is also correct, but you cannot stay here. Not on police property."

A few further discussions followed, but with the police failing to see the problem and with my face fully embedded into the palms of my hands, I ended up riding fifty metres down the road, pulling off on a footpath that bordered the police compound and camping there for the night.

Luckily, my logic that the lions would not come so close to humanity paid off. I survived the night uneaten and was woken by three police officers the next morning who had come to check up on me before I ran the gauntlet. I ate a hardy breakfast, put some extra air in the tyres and, clearly not having learnt any lessons from my previous escapades with it, attached my bear mace to my right wrist. Ready to pepper-spray any lion who fancied a lunch of cyclist, I rode out into the game park.

As with most of my travels, the fear proved greater than the reality and despite coming across fresh elephant dung as well as a few footprints, the only animals I saw were springboks. Legitimising that these were easier to catch, and therefore a more appealing meal to any day-walking lion, I relaxed and made it to the end of the game park.

Carrying on through Zimbabwe I saw numerous bits of wildlife from the road, including a baby crocodile swimming where children cast their fishing nets, before, on my penultimate night prior to arriving in Victoria Falls, I camped by the side of the road.

After climbing into bed I could see the silhouettes of four elephants as they walked past the outside of my tent, with them stopping to graze from the nearby trees. It was near enough pitch-black outside, but from the thud of their feet every time they moved I could appreciate their size. I lay still, part in fear - for if they took a dislike to my tent I was in massive trouble - and part in awe, as they ambled about filling their stomachs, before eventually wondering off.

A crocodile by the road, riding through a lion's patch and now lying in my sleeping bag, listening intensely as elephants wandered by. I now had a massive appreciation for where I was: I was in Africa.

26: What Do You Think Of Africa, Mr. Blake?

Zimbabwe had once been a well run country; not perfect, but with an economy heading in the right direction to the extent that the nation had been able to sustain a profitable export industry. As I rode through, the country was now a sorry state of affairs.

The forced removal of white farmers had been implemented with the government proposing that the taken land would be passed on to the indigenous people. All ethics in removing the white farmers aside, the main problem had been that instead of the skilled labourers of the country receiving the land, it had gone to Mugabe's cronies, who had in turn run the country into the ground. With a failing economy the government had started printing money, hyperinflation soon followed and by mid-November 2008 - when I would have been back in the snow of China - the inflation rate was estimated to be 89,700,000,000,000,000,000,000%. Now as I entered Zimbabwe, according to Wikipedia, the country had the lowest GDP of anywhere in the world.

Their currency had since been ditched and in its place people used South African Rand or US Dollars. This system worked, except for the fact that no coins had made it into the country yet, so whenever I went to a supermarket I was forced to round the cost of whatever I wanted up to the nearest dollar by purchasing additional small items. Matches were six cents a pack and as I left I had around forty boxes.

Away from money, I passed numerous empty or derelict farm houses and could only speculate as to who used to live there, whilst in the towns unemployment was high, power cuts seemed to be expected and lack of organisation at Government level was apparent when, of all things, I rolled into Bulawayo at the end of June, I passed under what appeared to be the town's Christmas lights still up.

For all of their suffering, the Zimbabwean people I met were surprisingly upbeat and very welcoming, but as I came to leave the country I just felt incredibly sad at what had become of the place. A country with the people, natural resources and fertility to succeed was now a ghost town; destroyed by a thug.

My first birthday on the road was in Trabson, Turkey, my second had been in Tokyo, Japan, I'd arrived in Panama City for my third and after crossing Victoria Falls, I would spend my fourth and final birthday on the road in the town of Livingstone, Zambia.

Having been ill just once in the first three years of my trip, I was now on a bad streak and became sick for the third time in two months as, cruelly, a virus hit me the night before my birthday, hung around for the day itself and then left the following morning; being twenty-five had gotten off to a bad start.

But that would be enough moaning. Having spent two weeks in Zimbabwe, I would spend a further five weeks riding through Zambia and its neighbour Malawi as I recovered from sickness, got back on the bike and headed at a snail's pace to the Tanzanian border.

The ride through Zambia was quiet. I stopped briefly in the capital Lusaka and then made my way to Chipata, which was always going to be a special place for me, as it was where the money I was raising for SOS Children's Villages was going. I had no previous affiliation with the town and had only known of the place because when I'd contacted SOS saying that I wanted to fundraise, they had told me that Chipata needed help and was also on my route home. I'd instantly read up about the project; Chipata has an orphan rate of 10%, one in six children wouldn't live past their fifth birthday and life expectancy was somewhere in the forties.

With many children in need, working with both the local people and government, SOS was in the process of building a new village which would contain fourteen houses that would each home eleven children. Upon completion, 154 children would have a new home and to look after them fourteen women from the local community would give up their lives, move permanently to the village - one into each house - and live as the children's mother. Meanwhile a local school was also being expanded to help give the kids an education. I was instantly on board with the project.

At the time of my visit building was well under way, with completion expected a year later. Being shown around the site by the man who was running SOS Zambia, the excellently named Golden Lwando, was one of those memories will stay with me forever; it was probably the humblest day of my life.

Chipata itself I also took to heart. I stayed with Sebastian, a German friend I had met back in Cape Town, and after overcoming the joy of seeing a familiar face, I found a big city with a small town feel and a place that can claim to have the best golf course I've ever seen.

Golf can be a boring sport, but the Chipata Municipal Golf Course knew how to make it more interesting by having holes that crossed a busy main road. With cars driving through the course, it is the golfers though, who were given priority, meaning that drivers are warned of the risks and told that if any stray golf balls hit their car then it's their own fault. I never saw a car get hit, but I saw a few near misses.

I had vowed that I would return to many places on my travels, but with Chipata I really meant it and having made that promise I moved across the border to Malawi.

My crossing was delayed by a day, as riots over a national petrol shortage meant that the president, Mr. Bingu wa Mutharika, a terribly corrupt politician labelled a

'Mugabe wannabe' by people I met, had closed the borders. Sixteen people had died in the riots and it was clear that political change was coming soon, but in the mean time, whilst I had no doubt that anger dwelled in certain places, I found the majority of people to be just as calm and as welcoming as they had been in Zimbabwe. For my part, a petrol shortage meant I had clear roads all the way to Tanzania and as I arrived at the frontier I was mulling over the question I had been asked the week before.

Outside of Lilongwe, the Malawian capital, I stayed with Minhye, a Korean Couchsurfer who was working as a volunteer at a refugee camp and whilst there I got talking to some of the camp's inhabitants. One had asked me a simple question: what did I think of Africa?

It may sound straightforward, but it wasn't one I had a good answer for and I spent most of the following week thinking about it.

Having spent five months on the continent, I was now at a stage where I had my own views on Africa, what I thought of the people and also what I thought were the big issues for the future. As I rode I began to piece them together.

The first thing to state was that what I thought of the people of Africa was consistent with the view from the rest of my travels, and my time on the continent had only cemented my opinion; without a doubt, the poorest people in the world are always both the happiest in life and most willing to give to others.

The African people were by quite some distance the poorest I had come across. Despite this, as I travelled I found that they were by far the most welcoming; I stayed with many local families, was always treated with respect wherever I went and even though they lived in abject poverty, I found the people to be consistently smiling to an almost infectious level.

Granted, there was begging from many, most notably

children, but it was never aggressive and was done with the most common personality trait I found the African people to possess: optimism. The African attitude was one that said *'sure, I'm poor now, but some day I am going to be a king'*.

So the African people were easily likeable, but with their attitude of living in the moment, it made me worry for what the future held, as no-one seemed to be planning for it. From my vantage point though, both the clear target and necessity was to lift people out of poverty and I could see four distinct obstacles in the way.

The first of these was education.

Not just the education of people in the sense of work or career skills (although these were vital), but also about bigger issues such as sexual health, AIDS, healthy eating and the effects of overpopulation. On ground level a lot was being done, both from concerned governments and foreign NGO's, but whilst inroads were being made I met many people, particularly in the nursing industry, who told me how many of the local people didn't believe the advice given about AIDS and still placed faith in the witchdoctor.

Aside from AIDS, the sad reality is that many children are growing up malnourished as the maize-based staple foods of sub-Saharan Africa offer little nutritional value and for their part, local people are not keen to listen to advice which tells them the food they've been living off for centuries is not healthy enough. On top of this, the sheer number of African people with an army of children was shocking and from staying with local families it was painfully obvious that many of my hosts had produced more offspring than they could care for. Education on family planning was so desperately needed.

I saw many successes that had been achieved through teaching; I met numerous young people who had gained skills with computers and were well on their way to a career in this field, whilst universities were booming in several places I visited. But for all the positivity, due to the number of children being produced, the escalating AIDS rate and the scale of poverty at base level, it was clearly an uphill battle. Finding ways to educate as many people as possible is going to be one of the keys to a successful Africa.

So whilst getting the man on the street educated was important, also key to the success of Africa would be the guidance the continent's leaders could offer. Sadly, the examples of Zimbabwe and Malawi showed that this did not bode well. On the face of it, when the British left it must have been such an optimistic time for the African people; the oppressive white men were leaving and one of their own would now be in charge. It must then have been somewhat frustrating to find that when one dictatorial set of leaders had left, in many places they were replaced with others who were exactly the same, just with a different skin colour.

For a place to grow it needs good leadership, with politicians who can be trusted. In Africa I found people didn't trust their politicians and even in places with something close to a functioning democracy, widespread corruption was still expected; in Lusaka, the capital of Zambia, I had been driving round with Chitende, my host, and commented on how new all the roads looked.

"It's an election year, the Government needs to look like it's doing something," was the blunt answer I received.

Often utilising the politicians - corrupt or otherwise - were the third group that will shape the future of Africa; foreign forces. Sadly, many seem to be effectively pillaging what they can from the continent.

Africa is full of natural resources, but so much of what comes out of Africa is owned by foreign companies with little trickle-down effect to the local populace. The US are one of the main players and during my time in Lusaka, Chitende showed me the absolutely massive site that the US Embassy was about to expand on, as they had recently found a large swathe of natural resources in the country and wanted to get a firm foothold in local industry. Meanwhile the number of Chinese in Africa, particularly on road building projects, was astounding and the level of influence the Chinese politicians had over several African governments was growing to the point that it was starting to rival the US. In respect to the Chinese, their arrival also endangered another industry, tourism, as the demand for rhino horn and ivory to be used in traditional medicine sky-rocketed, meaning illegal poaching was on the rise. Tourism is relied upon for many African countries, so this trend of poaching was a worrying side effect from the Chinese presence.

The solution isn't obvious; I am not an economist and I know that governments of these countries will need outside help, but there were many occasions where I got the impression that much of Africa's wealth was not being directed to where it should have been. Surely this needed to change?

Finally, linking in with both the problems regarding education and also foreign intervention, there was the role that religion played in African society and, more specifically, the people spreading it. Christianity is very much the religion of choice and more than any other place on earth, people look to religion for answers. Given how little many of these people have, it is understandable how a higher being who will help you is something that's appealing. Sadly, whilst I will always respect peoples religious freedoms, I found that many of the foreign groups who were 'spreading their word' in Africa did so in unethical ways and more often than not their pushing of their beliefs came across as little more than bribery; believe in my God and we'll make life a little better for you.

In Livingstone, on my birthday, I met a girl who had come with a group to work in schools and had been told it was not religion-based at all. She had been enthusiastic when we met. A few months later I received an e-mail that told me that what she had been doing in Africa was not what she had been expecting and that the organisation had been constantly pushing its religion.

"I felt very frustrated and lied to by my friends... being forced to listen to religion everyday all day was not something that I was prepared for," was how she put it.

I'd had run-ins with religion in before, but in Africa I got the distinct impression that several of the groups were exploiting the people, seemingly saying to the locals they were offering to assist 'sure, we can help you, but here's our religion, we hope you like it'.

Add to this the significant amount of disinformation regarding sexual health issues and the often flat-out refusal to teach safe sex and I left feeling downhearted, for it was clear these organisations were only here to push their own ideologies, as opposed to teaching things that would actually help people.

I met many good people working for religious charities, doing good work that was vital to local communities. What I wasn't sure about, was why they needed to push religion forward whilst doing it.

All of this left me confused as to how to answer the question of 'What did I think of Africa?'

I liked the people but also felt that many of them needed to take more responsibility over their own lives, particularly through having less children. At the same time I knew that due to the history of poverty and the levels of ignorance among many people, that outside help - the correct kind of help - was needed to educate the population and in turn achieve prosperity. But then so many of the groups who were in positions of power had vested interests and if assistance were to come, how could they be sure it was from the right people?

The place was a battle ground; it had been for a while and it would be long after I would leave, thus I found answering the question I'd been set nigh on impossible.

What did I think of Africa? It was a place that had the potential to prosper, that much I knew. Did I think it would? I had absolutely no idea.

As Africa busied itself with not deciding whether to succeed or fail, my own mental health was fading. I didn't feel depressed or sad, but what I did begin to feel again was alone. Whilst my feelings for her had gone, the recent discovery that Bella was pregnant had not helped and I couldn't lie; female company would have been most welcome. But it ran much deeper than that; I no longer wanted to meet new people, or even to try new things. I started to turn down offers of places to stay if I thought I might be able to find a place to wild camp alone, and my only desire was to be around people I knew. Having £5 a day was also proving tiresome and I missed the feeling of having money in my pocket.

I had known it shortly after arriving in Africa, but refused to acknowledge it. Now, after several months, I was forced to accept it: my enthusiasm had gone. Far too stubborn to quit, all I could do was get back on the bike and tell myself the same nine words: *Every pedal is now in the direction of home.*

27: Things You're Not Prepared For

There are moments that change your life. Sometimes you know these moments are coming, such as the build-up to a big exam or sports match, and sometimes they just come out of thin air, completely unexpected; after moving from Malawi into Tanzania I was about to experience one of the latter.

Since crossing the border my mind had been elsewhere; I'd been tricked out of £8 by the money changers at the border in a scam which I really should have known better than to fall for and when I hadn't been cursing myself over that, I'd been trying to think of my own suggestions for a theme I'd seen on Twitter called 'Books with a letter missing', whereby you take an existing novel and remove a letter to make your own title and book description. Having spent twenty-four hours trying to come up with something clever (and with my best efforts being the feeble 'Casio Royale - a book in which a British spy uses the calculator function on his wristwatch to beat the odds and win millions at poker' and 'The Girl with the Drago Tattoo - a mystery novel in which a young Swedish girl must find out why she's woken up with the face of the Maltese Snooker legend tattooed across her back') it's fair to say that as I was riding along, my mind was anywhere but on the road. As I was coming up a hill and saw what I thought to be a dead animal up ahead of me, I didn't really bat an eyelid and instead did my usual routine of what I do every time I come across roadkill; think 'oh, that's sad', put my head down and take a deep enough breath so as to not have to breathe in the immediate vicinity of a rotting carcass.

Except as I got closer this time it became apparent that this was not roadkill.

A body lay slumped on the road, about a metre in from the kerb, with only one or two people standing around, and as I was about twenty metres away downhill on a steep gradient I still couldn't see if the person was alive or dead.

From looking at the people standing around him, it was obvious none had any medical knowledge and as I approached I knew that I would also have very little clue as to what to do, should the situation be as bad as it appeared. As I pulled up next to the victim, the sight I saw was something that will stay with me for the rest of my life; a young man - I would guess fifteen to twenty years old – unconscious on the ground, blood pouring from his head, with no movement in his body, but still breathing.

Definitely still breathing.

Although the time from first seeing the scene to actually arriving on it could have been no more than a minute, a small crowd had started to assemble. This told me that the accident had only just taken place, that whoever had hit him hadn't stopped - *welcome to Tanzania* - and given how much blood he had lost, he needed medical assistance quickly.

Nobody in the crowd spoke any English and after some desperate attempts to communicate it became apparent that whilst the gathered group had called the police right away and had made the scene safe by putting bushes in the road to guide oncoming traffic around the victim, nobody present had any idea on how to help the guy who had been knocked down. I realised that with the nearest hospital thirty kilometres away, if I didn't do something, nobody was going to.

All I could remember from the first aid courses I'd taken at school was that a) I needed to stop the bleeding, b) I needed to make sure he could breathe, and c) we needed to get him to a hospital as quickly as possible.

I got an old t-shirt from my panniers and ran to the victim on the road. He was slumped face down on the ground, with the wound resting on the asphalt. I adjusted his body to put him in the recovery position and supported his head, with my t-shirt applying direct pressure to the wound to stop the bleeding.

I've never before felt a human body so lifeless and limp.

The only other thing I knew to do was to keep talking to him. He was unresponsive, but I did it anyway and by this time a large crowd had gathered as we waited for the police car to arrive; during this time, as I was supporting the man's head and talking, other locals - who knew seemingly less than I did about first aid - did what they thought would help; one man took off the victim's shoes to allow his feet some air, another wafted him with a large coat to keep him cool. I didn't know if these things would make any difference.

Eventually a police car showed up to take the man to hospital and this brought the next challenge; how to get him into the car. An ambulance or a stretcher was wishful thinking and instead we had an old car that looked a very sorry sight. I knew from old TV shows such as *Casualty* and *999* that it can make things worse to move someone who's had a big accident, but at the same time I knew he needed medical attention, that he wouldn't get it here and also if a foreigner such as myself was seen to be trying to keep someone who was dying away from the police car, then if he did die there was a big chance I would be in serious trouble with the local law.

People had been reluctant to come close to the injured man and of a crowd of around thirty, only three men other than myself had offered any help, but I knew when it came to moving him that if we were going to do it, then we needed to keep his body as flat as possible.

Upon arrival the policeman had joined us, a couple more men came forward and we soon had enough people to lift him. I did my best to convey that we needed to keep his body as flat as possible as we were moving him, however the moment we picked him up several people instantly backed off leaving me and one other man holding the body which was now slumped at the hips, with me holding his shoulders and the other guy his ankles. For his part, the policeman had forgotten to unlock the car doors on the back seats and more valuable seconds were wasted trying to get him into the car.

As we held the man, he sneezed blood and a white snot-like substance was dribbling out of his nose down his chin.

The door was opened, the two of us bundled him into the back of the car, I lay him in the recovery position, put my t-shirt on his bicep and rested his head on top of it so there would be at least some pressure on the wound as he was en-route to the hospital, got out of the car and the police drove away.

The whole incident from first seeing the scene to the car driving off could not have been more than twenty minutes.

As the car drove off I was still shaking. A local man brought me water to wash away the blood that was now on my arms and legs, but one thing still shocked me; whilst the mood was sombre, of the thirty-plus people who had been present and watched all this unfold, only two or three had actually done anything to help. The rest, I assumed through ignorance, had done nothing and would have stood around whilst the man died.

The moment the man was driven away, mud was kicked over the blood stains on the road, the crowd began to disperse and life carried on as normal: if you had arrived ten minutes later, you would have had no indication that anything had ever taken place there that day.

After cleaning myself off one man came up to me, shook my hand and as loud as you can go without shouting, in his best English, said 'God bless you'. This was then followed by another man coming up to me and in basic English he said 'Time to go now', indicating that I should leave.

From the moment I'd first arrived I'd felt useless and that I should have been able to do more to help and now I was supposed to leave? Still with the empty feeling of wishing I could have done more? It didn't feel right.

Since arriving in Africa I had found that a consistent factor of riding on the continent had been people constantly shouting 'Give me money' at me, as more often than not I was seen as little more than a walking wallet. As I was about to leave, a young woman in the crowd began to shout 'GIVE M...' , but before she could finish her sentence the same man who had said 'God bless you' to me had put his arm across her to stop her mid-speech. Several pairs of eyes shot directly at her. I've never seen an African person scowl before, indeed, I'd rarely seen an African angry, but in a strange way the piercing looks she got from all around her were the best kind of reassurance I could have got that day; *'This man has just done what he could to help save one of us who's just had a massive accident and you're still going to shout this at him?'*

For the first time in Africa I felt like a wall had been broken down, that I wasn't seen as just a walking wallet and for that brief moment I didn't feel like an outsider anymore.

With that I rode away.

The next couple of hours were horrible. My hands were shaking, my helmet was tightened faster than I've ever worn it before and when I'd calmed down I had several horrible realisations: I'd done what I could, but I had no idea whether what I'd done was the right thing to do.

I cursed myself for not having known more.

A few metres down the road another realisation hit me; when the police had arrived on the scene I'd breathed a big sigh of relief as I thought they would take control and as such I'd not really even thought about going along in the car to the police station. As I replayed the events over in my head, I realised how even with my basic education I'd seemingly known more than the local policeman and the sickening thought hit me that they hadn't seemed to know to put pressure on the wound; I felt nauseous at how much blood would have been lost by not applying extra pressure on the thirty kilometre trip to the hospital.

278

I stopped early that night, set up camp and thought of little else.

I got up the next morning, descended fifteen kilometres down to the town of Mbeya and frantically e-mailed all the friends I have who work in the medical field, telling the story and asking if I'd done the right thing; as the replies drifted in it seemed as though I'd generally done what I could and that whilst there was debate over how best to have moved him, given the circumstances it seemed I'd done OK.

I also received an e-mail from a friend in Lesotho who happened to be a Tanzanian doctor. He told me frankly and honestly about the quality of hospitals in Tanzania and also warned me about things I hadn't even begun to consider at the time; he told me how the AIDS rate in Tanzania is 7% and that I needed to be careful as if I'd got blood on me there was a chance of infection (I got myself tested three months later - thankfully I was OK). His other warning was that people have been known to steal from victims of accidents out here, so I needed to be careful when helping people not to be accused of theft. I was grateful, if not downhearted, for the advice.

As I pulled away from Mbeya I knew it would have been possible to find out if the guy pulled through or not, but I also accepted I had no desire to know. I had done what I could and had also educated myself on what I should do if I were ever to find myself in the same situation again.

That was enough for me.

28: A Way Out A Dead End

When QPR were relegated from the Premier League I was nine years old. I had been there that day in 1996, when a 3-0 victory over West Ham had not been enough to keep us up, and had kept on returning to Loftus Road for the following years of depression and mediocrity. If I had one vice in life, it was Rangers and now, after fifteen years in the lower leagues, the club had just been promoted back to the top flight. As I left Mbeya, pushing the distressing scene of the previous day to the back of my mind, I shifted my focus to the fact that the new season was just five days away. QPR would open at home to Bolton Wanderers and, conveniently, I was five days from the next big town on my map. Knowing that I would rather have been in West London for the event, I accepted that if I couldn't be there I was at least going to splash out on a hotel, get comfy for the night and find a TV on which to watch our return to the big time.

I didn't just hope that I would be able to watch the game, I was adamant that I would.

Knowing I would have to rush in order to get there on time, the road out of Mbeya knocked the wind out of my sails as a steep climb on roads that were a combination of sand and rocks meant that my afternoon's riding only garnered a measly ten kilometres. The views looking back down the slope may have been spectacular but I really wasn't in the mood. *Didn't whoever put this mountain here know I've got a football match to watch?*

I camped near the pass that night, before the following two days saw more slow, mountain riding. I was behind schedule, but I was sure I could make up the ground. What I was unprepared for though, was what was about to get me; I had been attacked by numerous varieties of blood-suckers, primarily mosquitoes, wherever I'd been, but I had never before come across tsetse flies.

Two or three times bigger than the British housefly, they were capable of sucking blood through two layers of clothing. Unlike mosquitoes, they were difficult to crush and if you flicked one who happened to be gorging on you, rather than being paralysed or dying, they seemed to take the attack personally and would come back even more determined.

I first came across a swarm on the Thursday morning; they would stay with me until Saturday and for these days, despite the thirty-five degree heat, I rode in jogging bottoms and with sleeves, scarves and a mosquito hat, in order to protect my body. It made little difference, as the flies could bite through the layers.

After two stressful days, as I lay in the tent at night I looked at my arms and the side of my stomach to see fifty or sixty bite marks, but knew I had far more on my back and shoulders; counting them would have been impossible, but touching these areas felt like running my finger over a slice of cold pizza. Scratching them proved irresistible and I drew blood repeatedly as I dug my nails in to stop the itching.

The tsetse flies fast became my most hated foe and the only cure for them was to smoke them out; whenever I stopped to rest or to set up camp my first action was to start a fire which would see them disappear. Unfortunately this only worked for when I was stationary; when I was cycling I was stuck with them and my only plan had been to cycle so fast they couldn't keep up. The flies though, proved smarter than me and just sat on my panniers, enjoying a free ride and jumping on my neck whenever they wanted a meal.

It was horrible and the mountains, the poor roads and the constant need to stop and scratch my bites meant time was continually lost, so much so that by the time kick-off of the football came round I was still twenty kilometres from the nearest TV. Vowing I could still see the second half, I rushed on only to find a road that turned to sand. Unable to ride, I pushed the bike on and as I did the light disappeared, time ticked over and I accepted I'd missed the game.

When I finally arrived in town two hours after full time I found that my efforts would have been in vain anyway; a power cut meant nobody had electricity.

Given the effort I'd put in to get there and how tired my body was, I treated myself to a hotel anyway and in candlelight, had my first proper shower in over two weeks. After washing I examined my back to find hundreds of red bites all over. Dejected and in pain, I walked to the town's market and had a dinner of the local staple food, chips omelette, a dish that was exactly what it sounded like. Battered, bitten and tired, I overheard some locals talking about English football teams and saw that they had a phone with internet, which they were using to check the scores. Excitedly I rushed over and the man offered to look up the result for me.

This was it; after the week I'd had, all the effort I'd put in to get to the game, the energy used, the beating my body had taken and the bites I'd received, even though I'd missed the match I would at least find out the score.

We'd lost 4-0.

Bollocks.

The following day I awoke to aching muscles, a rare occurrence for my super fit body, which let me know I had been pushing it too hard. Unable to cycle even if I had wanted to, I took another day off and after getting back on the bike, the following days saw me leave the mountains and plod along an ambling, dull road towards the Rwandan border, powered on a diet of chips omelette.

The border, marked by the impressive Rusumo Falls and notable for a large number of wild baboons and small number of security guards, was another whereby crossing, even though I had only travelled a few metres, I instantly knew I was in a different country. Known as 'The Land of a Thousand Hills', as I approached from the flat roads of Tanzania I could see the slopes in front of me and knew I would see no even riding in the country. Cars drove on the right, as opposed to the rest of the African countries I had visited and whilst Tanzania had been relatively deserted, as I came into Rwanda there were now people everywhere, working in the rice paddies that swamped the valleys or the banana plantations that loomed over every hillside.

Rwanda was not just different from Tanzania, but from the whole of Africa and it was immediately apparent why this was from the moment I crossed the border: there was no litter in Rwanda.

Africa had always had its appealing factors, but the cleanliness of the place had not been one. The cities were covered in litter and roadsides would be smattered with whatever unwanted rubbish drivers had felt the need to throw out of their windows. It wasn't small amounts either and to say that Africa was filthy in many places was no understatement. This made Rwanda's cleanliness all the more remarkable.

A small country, it took just two days from the border to the nation's capital Kigali. As I arrived my odometer clicked over 40,000 miles and I was in the most developed African capital I would visit.

The reason for the cleanliness was attributed, by the locals at least, to Umuganda. On the morning of the last Saturday of each month Rwanda stopped, all businesses were closed and each citizen was legally required to take part in community service, usually in the form of cleaning up their neighbourhood or partaking in a community building project. This was known locally as Umuganda and it was hard to disagree that it helped keep Rwanda clean, but this was just for three hours a month. How Rwanda stayed so clean the rest of the time, I believed, lay deeper in the national psyche.

In 1994, after generations of tension between the Tutsi minority people who had controlled power for centuries, and the majority Hutu people who had recently come to power, following the assassination of the Hutu leader at the time, all hell broke loose. A retaliatory genocide followed and over the following 100 days at least 500,000 Tutsis - an estimated 20% of the country's population - were killed, in what would be one of the bloodiest purges of an ethnic group in history.

How did this link to how pleasant a place Rwanda was now?

I'd been to several places that had experienced genocide before, most notably Germany and Cambodia, and when it came to history, the way these countries had told their stories had been with a mixture of shame and defiance; shame that it had happened and the defiance that the country would never been seen in that light again. Through tragedy, the survivors appeared to have vowed to make their country the best it could possibly be for the future. Rwanda was no different.

Since the genocide, Rwanda had been helped massively by outside aid money, but many other African countries received financial help as well and none in the region prospered as Rwanda did; not only was the place clean, but an improving economy and an education programme which aimed to make Rwanda a technological hub of Africa pointed to a place with a bright future.

The people I met showed so much pride in who they were, where they were from and what their country was becoming. In the past was a sickening event; whatever happened, nobody could change that. Now though, the people wanted to show that their country was being the best it could be. Keeping the place tidy was just the start.

I had first seen it in Zimbabwe. Thinking I was mistaken, I had ignored it and carried on, but I had kept on seeing it and Rwanda and Uganda were the capitals of it. I talk of men holding hands. For guys who were as macho as the Africans undoubtedly were, to see them walking around arm in arm as they did their grocery shopping, played pool, or simply sat to eat lunch, was one of the great childish pleasures I never grew out of.

Saying goodbye to Jacob, a former college basketball player (yet another sportsmen met!) who had been my host in Kigali, I made my way to the Ugandan border. As I crossed over and on into the mountain roads, shadowed by an active volcano on the Congolese side, I came across a work team and about an hour after I'd passed, one of their vehicles caught up and then pulled over in front of me.

"What are you doing? Don't you know about the people around here?" was the opening sentence of the man who had got out of the 4x4, before he told me how he was a Serbian working for the UN on the local road projects. After expressing his anger and disbelief at the fact that I was riding my bike through Uganda and that I planned to either wild camp or stay with a local family that night, he eventually realised I was going to do it anyway, got back in his vehicle and drove away, signing off with the volatile line "When you get to the bottom of the hill, the people there won't let you stay. They'll just kill you."

I descended the hill and on my way down, with darkness due soon, I realised I wouldn't find a place to camp so instead stopped at the first family I saw. I went up to explain who I was and that I was looking for someone who would be willing to let me put my tent up in their garden. The man spoke no English but his daughter was fluent and acted as translator; with a beaming smile he said yes and welcomed me in. Explaining I needed to go and retrieve my bike from the side of the road, I went to shake the farmer's hand to show my gratitude. Rather than shaking it back, the man saw it as an invitation and we walked back to my bike, hand in hand, for the duration of the thirty metre stroll.

I wish my Serbian friend could see this.

Crossing back over the Equator, I made my way to Kampala and arrived to a return of the organised chaos I was more used to in Africa. The city sprawled for miles, mud roads, combined with the rainy season, left traffic at a standstill and as I arrived I was passed by a motorbike that on its back carried not one, but two Nile Perch, a breed of fish that weigh around seventy kilos each. The organisation and order of Rwanda had been relaxing for a few days, but this place was far more fun.

Though I was now in a spot of bother; not since Kazakhstan had I been stuck without an obvious route in front of me, but as I arrived in Kampala I now appeared to have hit a dead end.

My original route through Africa had seen me heading from Uganda, to Kenya and then up through Ethiopia to Sudan. Now I had found out that for the previous year the Ethiopian Embassies had not been issuing visas to overland travellers, which meant that anyone who wanted to visit the country had to fork out to courier their passport home to obtain a visa via that method. By now I had so little money that this wasn't an option and even if it had been, whilst known for its natural beauty, to cyclists Ethiopia is also known for its stone-throwing, hassling children.

Whilst in Kampala I met Ken McCallum, an English cyclist heading from Cairo to Cape Town, who summed it up quite nicely when he said "If there's a country that's going to break you, then it'll be Ethiopia." I would have loved to have visited, as the mountains are something I'd only heard good about, but I knew that in my fragile mental state I wouldn't have coped.

What did this leave? West into the DRC and up through the Central African Republic and Chad was a no-go, so this left just one other option, the world's newest country: South Sudan.

South Sudan had only become a country five weeks previously and was also, in places, little more than a volatile warzone. That said, having the opportunity to be the first person to ride through a newly independent country proved alluring and I gingerly began to ask around those in the know as to whether it'd be possible to make the journey overland from South to North Sudan. The first responses weren't encouraging, with people pointing out the political unrest, the closed borders and the general instability of the region. Aside from these things, I was also told that cycling was a non-starter as September to November is rainy season and the roads are washed out, so not even cars or trucks can make the journey from north to south at this time.

Things looked pretty bleak until I got an e-mail from a friend of a friend who worked in Juba, the South Sudanese capital, who told me that whilst cycling was not possible, I could theoretically make the journey from South to North Sudan on one of the many cargo boats that go up and down the River Nile. These boats leave regularly, but the downside is they are very slow and have a habit of stopping at every port possible, meaning the journey time can be around two or three weeks. The contact also raised safety concerns over getting off the boat in these ports, meaning that food could be hard to come by.

He may have had concerns, but all I needed to hear was that it was possible; as fortune would have it, the people I was staying with in Kampala had previously lived in Juba and they reassured me that this journey was a viable alternative. They were kind enough to put me in contact with a friend of theirs named Peter, an Australian who lived in Kampala but whose job took him all over the Sudans. I met Peter within my first couple of days and he was brutally honest with me; the boat would be a difficult trip to make but was most certainly something I could do, however there were concerns over safety. He said he was off to Sudan in the following days and would find out the situation on the ground.

Upon his return, he gave me the lowdown: the UN mission in Sudan had been asked to move from Khartoum to Juba and this meant they had 2,700 containers of equipment that needed to be shipped from the port of Kosti, 300 kilometres south of Khartoum, to Juba ASAP. This meant that boats were leaving Kosti fully loaded, dropping the delivery off in Juba and rather than meandering at a slow pace back to Kosti, were instead returning directly.

This direct journey would take nine days and as there was so much equipment needing to be shipped, the number of boats on the water meant that there would be direct departures from Juba to Khartoum near enough every day.

And the cost of this nine day voyage? £25.

Peter also allayed my security fears, giving me up-to-date information on where the troubles were ongoing and where they were likely to be in the future, with the answer being nowhere near anywhere I would be going.

Organising all of this, as well as the accompanying visas and travel permits, ate up nearly three weeks, but I was now officially moving again. Having spent so much time on the bike, a boat ride was something to look forward to.

In Kampala I stayed with Bill and Sue Farmer, an English couple in their sixties who over the previous thirty years had lived all over Africa, including long stints in Juba in the seventies and Swaziland in the eighties. With some fascinating stories to tell and with Bill having a voice identical to Richard Briers, I left feeling not only indebted for the help they'd given in letting me stay, but also for the privilege of having had their company.

The ride up to the South Sudan border went quietly. I passed a few zebra herds, was fortunate enough to be a guest at a rhino conservation park (a place where I was forced to tip my cap to their genius in naming a rhino born to an American mother and a Kenyan father 'Obama') and came across my first wild python, a full grown adult coiled up by the side of the road who slithered into long grass before I could get a picture. But I thought of little else other than catching my boat.

On the South Sudan side, the ride up to Juba was through a luscious green landscape and on arrival I met with Peter's friend Paul, a local man with a larger than life personality. Everything Paul ever said was accompanied with a smile beaming from his face and he explained to me that the company they all worked for (an NGO which helps farming projects in rural South Sudan) was transporting fuel via boat to the north of the country so I would be welcome to travel on this boat, which after dropping off its cargo would head on up to Kosti. As everything on the boat had been paid for by the NGO I would be travelling for free. There was plenty of room onboard, so I would have a private cabin to sleep in and as the journey would be pretty much direct (and with the place where we'd be stopping having no facilities) I was advised to take fifteen days worth of food, even though the journey shouldn't be more than nine days.

I bought fifteen days worth of food and waited. And waited. And waited. It quickly became apparent the boats weren't leaving as regularly as we had thought and each day I would see Paul, who with a big grin on his face would tell me "Mr. Blake, do you know what we mean by an African promise?", before stating that whilst he thought it would have been today, he was sure it would be tomorrow.

After over a week of twiddling my thumbs the day came and Paul told me to get my stuff together as we were going to the port. The curse of the African promise was in full swing; the security at the port would not let me travel on the private boat and told me that the only way for me to go north would be to take the public barge, which by chance would leave the same day.

This would cost 80 South Sudanese Pounds (about $20

US) and would take an estimated twenty days: just like that my journey time was doubled, my comfortable cabin was lost and better yet, my visa was due to expire in ten days time, so now I would be illegally in the country for half the trip.

Downstream I could see the empty UN boat getting ready to leave. As I looked at the public boat I was being directed toward I saw no floor space for my tent, but could see piles of bricks, shopping trolleys of people's possessions and a heard of twenty goats tied to a tether at the rear of the ship, crapping all over the place and creating a foul smell.

With all other options offering dead ends I had little choice; thanking Paul for his help I paid the $20 and climbed aboard. Six hours later, we set off down the Nile.

29: The Best $20 I'll Ever Spend

We didn't get far that first day, only going around two kilometres to pick up some more cargo from a dock a little downriver. With Juba still visible in the distance, I decided to keep a low profile and went to bed early. When I woke I found that whilst we had moved, it hadn't been far as a further twenty minutes downstream we'd beached ourselves. We were only stuck for about half an hour and as I'd been in bed the moment it got dark the previous evening, with our freight now complete, I took the time to examine what would be my home for the next three weeks.

The 'boat' consisted of three cargo laden barges; one large barge with two smaller barges lashed to its right hand side. None of these barges had the propensity to move on their own and instead the whole bundle was pushed along by a small but powerful boat from behind. Inside this boat was the crew's quarters and, for the public, three squat toilets and two showers that operated with water pumped direct from the river.

The boat would be stopping at four main ports along its route through South Sudan (nothing would be being exported to the North) and on its way, from examining what we had aboard, it appeared we would be delivering among other things: minibuses, sacks of maize, bundles of clothes, beer, an incomprehensible amount of rich tea biscuits, bundles of six foot long sticks (I couldn't say why) and of course the goats, which were now being supplemented by several live chickens. In amongst all of this, sleeping wherever space allowed on deck, were my fellow passengers. They were as eclectic as the cargo; Kenyan and Ugandan businessman who had come here as prices were so high for their products, families migrating from Juba back to their more rural home towns, soldiers on their way to their next call of duty and even that rarest of things, some

South Sudanese migrating to North Sudan.

I settled quickly to life on the boat and made friends with Zakariah and Milka, two Kenyans who were travelling to our second port of call Adok, a tiny port in the middle of nowhere, from where people would alight to travel to Bentiu, the region's biggest town. They were businessmen who were selling bundles of clothes and with their tent next to mine, I spent the first two days enjoying their company and otherwise hiding in the shade of my tent from the ridiculous heat.

I began to plan ahead for the journey, most specifically how I would get by with what I had. I'd bought with me enough food for potentially fifteen days and enough petrol to use my stove for around that time, provided I used it conservatively. This covered food and water; for entertainment, I allotted myself to read only eight chapters of each book I had per day. As long as I could stick to this I felt I would make it through. I would be able to stick to the reading schedule, but as for my stove fuel rationing, that was thrown into jeopardy on the second day, thanks to what could now officially be labelled my biggest waste of money: my Katadyn Mini Water Filter.

I had originally paid £60 for the filter, thinking it would be something I would use frequently on my travels. In reality, I had used it once in Georgia three years previously, decided pumping was too much hassle and had instead cleaned it and stored it away, thinking I may use it again someday. Now my plan was to filter water direct from the river each day and it was the Katadyn Mini Water Filter's chance to shine.

After pumping roughly a litre of water through, the damned thing snapped.

It hadn't been misused, it had been cleaned and stored correctly over time and when it broke I could see no reason why. But it had snapped. I was now stuck with no source of clean water, meaning my only option was to boil river water. I had nowhere near enough fuel to do this for the whole journey, but we would be stopping at Malakal, a big town on the ride north and I was sure I would be able to get some there. For the time being there was no problem, but the issue weighed on my mind.

Having successfully managed to build a rapport with both the people around me and the crew, I was happy with my new environment, and after three days afloat we arrived in Bor, the first of our four major stops.

We arrived on the Saturday and would leave on the Sunday night, however on Sunday afternoon we experienced a very sad event.

At each stop the routine would be the same; the boat would stop and local labourers would come aboard to manually move the cargo onto land. The work was all done by hand and the men were paid by the amount they took off; more money for heavier stuff, less money for the lighter stuff.

By the evening of our second day in Bor and with about an hour of daylight left, I was sat cooking dinner. Due to a storm, I had moved my tent and was now camping about halfway down one of the side-barges. As I sat, a flurry of activity started at the front of the boat and a crowd began to form. It didn't take a rocket scientist to work out that someone had fallen in, but with the crowd gathered I was sure someone would be helping whoever had gone in and I felt that despite the danger, my rushing to the front of the boat to see what was going on wasn't going to help anybody. My view was only reinforced when, from the back of the boat, one of the crew ran to the crowd at the front carrying a life ring.

Feeling the situation was now under control, I returned to my cooking when a couple of minutes later the crowd at the front of the boat suddenly turned and ran; first towards the side of the boat and then to the back of the boat. The rubberneckers on shore, of whom there were now a sizeable number, changed location as well.

I did not see the man who had fallen, but within a couple of minutes it became apparent we would not be seeing him again and as the crowd began to disperse I found Zakariah, who had seen the whole affair. He filled me in: a labourer had fallen in, however he couldn't swim and in panic had been thrashing around in the water. Someone in the crowd had thrown him a rope which he'd managed to get around his arm whilst he waited for the life ring to arrive. When the person with the life ring had arrived he had bravely jumped in as well to try and help the drowning man but unfortunately, in his panic, the man being rescued had made a fatal mistake and had taken the rope off of his wrist before attaching himself to the life ring. He'd been sucked straight under the boat.

A few people hung around at the back of the boat waiting to see if a body surfaced but within a couple of minutes all present knew that we wouldn't be seeing the man again.

No body was found whilst we were there and with only half an hour of daylight in which to look, combined with the area being known for crocodiles and the current of the river being far too dangerous to swim in at night, a proper search would not have been possible.

Later that night we left Bor with a somewhat more sombre atmosphere over the boat.

Zakariah was a Kenyan clothes salesman who spoke fluent English and even before he informed me of the sad events above we had become good friends, so when he told me that the next challenge we faced would be from bribe-hungry soldiers I was definitely listening.

"The next stop of the boat is Cadok, it's a military point. The soldiers come on the boat and are supposed to be checking the cargo, but all they do is make us give them

294

money. It's not legal but we have no choice. Don't pay more than 20SSP (South Sudanese Pounds)." This was the equivalent to about £3.

I'd only ever paid one bribe on this trip - around 10p to an Azeri policeman which I only paid as if I hadn't my host was going to on my behalf - and with no intention of changing that record, we approached Cadok.

A couple of soldiers came onto the boat, nodded to me and carried on with their business, before a soldier in a different uniform came aboard, asked for my passport and travel permit before saying "OK, give me ten SSP."

Politely and with a genuinely friendly smile that screamed *I'm an idiot* I asked "What is the money for?"

"Ten SSP, you need to give me ten SSP."

"Yes, I understand that but what is the money for?"

"Ten SSP or you have to come to the office."

I pretended not to have understood the threat.

"We need to go to the office? OK, let me just close my tent," I said, conveying that I had no idea that what he'd just said was supposed to be intimidating.

Still with the big friendly smile on my face I began to put my belongings in my tent and as I was zipping up the door I sneaked a quick look at the guy. An interesting sight met my eyes; a soldier staring at me with absolutely no idea what to do. It was obvious he wasn't used to coming across people who weren't particularly scared of him and before I finished zipping up the tent he muttered "I'll be back later" and walked off to harass some other people.

I went to search for Zakariah, who I found sat hiding between two bundles of sticks. He told me just to stay in my tent, keeping a low profile until we left and that he was hiding because they'd already taken 20SSP off Milka and he didn't want to get found either.

I decided the best plan would be to wait it out in my tent. I wanted to close the doors for ultimate privacy but the heat meant I'd suffer if I did, so I lay with the doors open, waiting to see if my friend would come back. About an hour later, he did.

"Do you have the 10SSP?"

"But I thought we needed to go to the office."

"10SSP."

"Yes, let's go to the office."

"I'm not your brother you know, I am not your friend, I am not your brother."

Assuming this wasn't a lesson in basic genetics and with his temper getting noticeably more wound up, I kept a blank look on my face and politely and calmly replied "I don't understand."

By this point he was getting pretty agitated but, again, he left saying that he'd be back.

This time I was taking no chances; the temperature was thirty-five degrees of humid heat, but I got a couple of litres of clean water and shut myself in the tent with the doors closed. It was sweltering and for two hours I hid. During this time, out of necessity, I drank all two litres of water and when I was close to giving up the engines of the boat roared and out of the tiny air hole I'd been using I could see land begin to move. I knew it was safe to come outside again and I went to find Zakariah.

"Hey man, I made it; I stayed in my tent and didn't have to pay!"

"No one had to pay. The army chief heard rumours that his men had been asking for money and he came on the boat and asked to speak to the people who had been taken from. Milka and the others who had paid were taken on shore and asked to say which men took their money. Then, when they said which guys it was the chief made them give the money back. I never saw anything like this, the chief then started shouting at the guys '*What right do you have to take these people's money?*' and things like this, right in front of everyone. I never saw anything like it."

"Really? That's amazing. Wow, that's really good.

Congratulations for Milka, when did this happen?"

"About an hour and a half ago."

He hesitated; Zakariah had a naturally broad smile anyway, but at that moment it snuck out an extra couple of centimetres at the side, a school boy smirk forming on his face.

"Have you been in your tent the whole time?"

My reaction told him that I had and the smirk turned into a laugh before returning to a smile which stayed on his face for the rest of the day.

I was happy as well. Not at spending two hours in what equated to a sauna, but at the day's events. Visit Juba and you will see how big the fight against official corruption is; all newspapers repeatedly say it's key to South Sudan succeeding as a state, the UN backs their sentiments, billboards around the city encourage people to report instances of abuse of power and even the president had been on TV stating the punishments for corrupt officials would be severe - potentially even death - and that for South Sudan to succeed it needed officials it could trust in.

I'd been in Africa long enough to know that the fight against corruption probably wasn't being won, but it felt good to know that it was being fought.

The next stop, a day or two later, was Adoc, a destitute port but a point where anyone going to the bigger city of Bentiu would be departing. Here, again, we were asked for bribes; this time a couple of soldiers came on and told all foreigners (whilst the only white guy, I wasn't the only foreigner on board, many of my co-travellers were Ugandans and Kenyans) to go and register in the small office in port.

My strategy this time was far simpler: take my passport and travel permit and simply leave all my money safely stashed away in my tent on the boat. I was taken to the office, along with a group of about five or six which by chance included Zakariah and Milka, but I was dealt with first and taken in on my own, again being asked for 10SSP.

I said, "OK, but my money is on the boat."

The man behind the desk, who was far friendlier than the last guy I'd dealt with and who had found it hilarious to find a westerner on a Sudanese cargo ship, gave me a wink and told me not to worry about it, but as I left he gave me a stern warning. "Don't tell the others outside that you didn't pay."

I went outside and straight away, told Zakariah I hadn't paid and went back to the boat. Twenty minutes later Zakariah, Milka and the group returned; they hadn't paid anything either.

Zakariah and Milka said goodbye at Adoc, which left me more or less on my own for the ride up to Malakal and at noon on what was our twelfth day on the boat we arrived in port. Malakal, I had been told, was of a similar size to Juba and would have all the facilities you'd expect of a major city.

What I found was the poorest city I had visited anywhere on earth. Without an inch of paved roads, thanks to the rainy season, the town's main drag resembled a ploughed field. Sewage drains flowed over into the streets, the only electricity was from generators and aside from the odd NGO 4x4 or countryside delivery truck, there were absolutely no vehicles on the road.

Back in Adoc, arriving on the boat had been Paul, a ten year old South Sudanese child whose parents had put him and his five brothers and sisters on board with the directions for them not to get off until Kosti, where someone would meet them and send them to school in Khartoum. Despite his young age he was a streetwise kid, fluent in his tribal language, Arabic and English and liking his cocky style I enlisted him and his brother Sudande, who spoke no English, to help me in finding petrol, which I now vitally needed to boil drinking water.

We found none, and checking my fuel bottle I was confident I had enough petrol to be able to cook each day and get to Kosti, but I knew I would not have enough to be boiling water to drink. Instead, I would now be drinking straight from the Nile.

The first two days of this didn't go well. We were in Malakal for three nights, as the ship unloaded the vast majority of its cargo, and by the end of the second day I'd done my best not to drink any water. Alas, the result of this was a horrible feeling of weakness and dehydration, whilst any urine I did produce was coming out a healthy shade of bright orange.

I gave in and began doing what I'd seen the more health-conscious locals doing; most were just drinking straight from the river, but the more cautious were filling up their water bottles, putting a sock over the drinking hole to act as filter and drinking through this.

Pretty much every person on board had been drinking straight from the river for the previous two weeks and given the questionable water I'd been drinking over the past three years, I was hopeful my stomach would survive. Wrong.

I managed to survive two days before the dysentery kicked in, and when it did, it came with a disgustingly literal tidal wave. A sleepless night, many toilet dashes and the beautiful discovery that I could no longer urinate without losing control of the other aspect of my excretion system at the same time made for a stressful few days.

The sun beamed down, the boat plodded on, I kept soiling myself and we arrived in Renk, our last port of call before crossing the border into North Sudan.

It was here I said goodbye to Abraham, a South Sudanese soldier who had been on the boat since Juba. Due to South Sudanese independence, Abraham had joined the army and was now destined to be stationed in Renk for the next two years. With the border being a warzone in several places I wished him luck, shook his hand and returned to the boat. We now carried no cargo, only around fifty people who were all making their way into Sudan, and those of us who were left all felt good that we were now nearing the end of our trip.

Unbeknownst to me, we arrived at the border around eight o'clock at night. It was pitch black by this point and having gone to my tent to hide from the mosquitoes I was surprised to be woken by soldiers asking to see my documents. Only when I got out of my tent and saw different flags on their uniforms did I realise we were no longer in South Sudan.

I also realised very quickly that I now had a slight problem; in sub-Saharan Africa a frequent form of alcohol consumption is in the form of *sachets*. These sachets are made of plastic, available on every street corner, cost about ten pence and usually contain 100 millilitres of vodka/gin/whisky that would be far better for stripping paint than anything else. In Zambia, a German friend had given me one and told me to take it with me back to Europe so we could drink it together upon my arrival to his house. I was now at the border to a dry country - where the penalty for alcohol ownership was usually forty lashes - with a sachet of 40% vodka in one of my bags.

I'd been meaning to make up my mind for a while what to do with it; whether to dispose of it and apologise to my friend or attempt smuggling it through regardless. However, having spent the last couple of days doing little else but running to and from the toilet and using the time in between to rest in preparation for the next sprint, I had forgotten of its existence. Arriving at the border like this had caught me unawares.

No other border in the world has required me to empty all of my possessions, but as the soldiers rifled through my neighbours' belongings it was apparent I was now going to be subjected to this. The vodka was stored in the zip pocket of my rain coat and whilst I did consider quickly going through my stuff and throwing it overboard there simply wasn't time.

A lone soldier came over.

That small problem I wrote about with the bribe request in South Sudan? It is worth acknowledging that the boat had stopped at around a further eight ports, where I'd not only been treated well by the authorities, but had also found them to be friendly, courteous people.

In comparison the soldier now approaching didn't even try to hide his personality: he was a complete tool.

I stood outside my tent awaiting his arrival, but he still felt the need to come over and aggressively grab the canvas to gesture he wanted to see inside. I opened the door, he shoved his torch inside and demanded that I bring my bags out. As always when dealing with authorities, I did my best to keep my decorum. With a polite 'OK' and a friendly smile, I reached inside to get my panniers.

Whilst I had a calm look on my face inside I was shaking. It was pretty clear that this guy thought I was a spy/terrorist/enemy - as, it seemed from his viewpoint, was everyone else on the boat - and he was determined to prove it.

The first bag I was asked to empty was my front right pannier. This pannier contains a sleeping bag, a wash kit and a couple of books. No problems there.

Next up was my front left pannier. This pannier contains a first aid kit, some spare razors, shaving foam, my bear mace from Canada, all of my clothes and one waterproof rain coat.

The man made me empty the bag out on deck and after moving the razors and foam to one side and asking what the mace was (apparently having something that was designed to blind bears was no problem), to my horror, he not only emptied the bag of clothes, but pressed them all in his palms to make sure there was nothing hidden inside. He moved rapidly and after finding nothing picked up the rain jacket, padded it down, put it to one side and moved on.

I had no idea how he missed it and having watched out of the corner of my eye I knew for a fact that he would have felt it, but I suspect he was so sure that I had something big, like a gun or a bottle of vodka or some form of spy documents, that a small bit of liquid in a coat pocket didn't register. I was a very lucky boy.

After he'd been through these two panniers I was allowed to return the contents to their place and we moved onto to the rear panniers. With the alcohol gone undiscovered I relaxed and began to enjoy the experience; the soldier had found the photo album I'd had printed out and that I used to show people around the world about my trip. By this point he'd been told the story as to why I was here and whilst he'd done his utmost not to believe it, as he flicked through the photos he really didn't know how to accept that I was just a cyclist coming through. His face was a picture of anguish already, but the highlight was when he came to a photo I'd had taken of myself riding my bike with a tame lion in Zimbabwe. His face contorted, the frustration rose and he stared blankly at the photo, with absolutely no idea of what to make of it.

Irate at me being who I said I was, he took great pleasure in dumping the rest of my belongings all over the deck as he went through them, spilling my neatly packed bags into a heap. His frustration rose as I simply smiled it off and took my time placing everything back in its rightful place.

After the search had been completed, he disappeared for a few minutes and when everyone else had been inspected the same soldier, now accompanied by his superior, came back and asked me to come on shore, bringing my laptop, camera and travel documents with me. I was told by Paul that this was because they needed to register me. Much fuss then followed; my passport was taken, many phone calls were made and with the time now nearly midnight, despite a lack of English, it was explained to me that it was bedtime and that the rest of the formalities would be sorted in the morning. I had changed the dates on my visas so I appeared to be in the country legally, and thinking I was OK I turned to go back aboard when I was stopped.

"No. No sleep boat."

I was asked to leave my belongings with the army and then taken around the back of the hut that served as an office, only to see several other members of the army sleeping on the floor outside. I was given a rug and it was gestured that I sleep on the dirt next to them. Having no intention of doing this when my tent and mosquito net were so close I told the soldier that I would not sleep here as I did not want malaria. The beauty of coming across hard-line military types is that despite their aggression they will always play by the book, so he disappeared, confiscated a bed from another soldier and gave it to me to sleep on.

Given our location in the middle of nowhere, I didn't really understand why I wasn't allowed to sleep in my tent and I also didn't really see it as necessary for me to be woken so crudely by a soldier shaking the bed frame the following morning (although maybe it was his bed I had taken). But woken up I was, at which point I was made to get up, taken to a different, empty hut and gestured to wait.

Half an hour passed, the sun was coming up, my belly was yearning for breakfast and with boredom entering I got up out of the chair I'd been given, walked outside to find the senior army official and it was only after I was quickly bundled back inside by the first soldier I came across that it began to click: I was under arrest.

My initial reaction of smirking was probably the wrong one, but as the predicament set in, the main thoughts going through my head were a) I hope they're not on the boat going through my things again, and b) deary me, being under arrest is boring.

After about two hours, a soldier came in, stated the word 'breakfast' and pointed to a small boat. Our boat had since been moved further away from the river bank so the small vessel was for him to escort me to my tent, where I was to retrieve my breakfast. Whilst on board I saw that the rest of the army were examining the cargo holds of the ship and going through paperwork. Having got some food I was then sent back to the room and back to my boredom.

Another hour passed and my mind was melting, when a thought occurred; they were trying to treat me properly as a prisoner, something they'd shown by getting me a bed and by allowing me breakfast, and this meant that theoretically I should be able to wash, something which the soldiers had done by swimming in the river that morning. I'd never swum in the Nile before and realised that I may never get a better or safer chance than this; more in hope than expectation I asked the guard outside if I could bathe.

Spectacularly, he didn't see a problem with it and I stripped down to my undies and ventured into the water, where I spent fifteen minutes splashing around. The water was beautiful, swimming was far more fun than being stuck in the hut and as the sun was now up and out it also offered a way to cool down from the heat. Unfortunately I made a mistake; my swimming had caught the attention of the boat and Paul was sat on the edge watching me paddle. When I swam over towards him and tried to ask if he was OK, it was at that this time that the guard realised I was not taking my detention as seriously as I was supposed to and ordered me back in the hut.

Another hour passed and whilst I'd regained the ability to urinate without soiling myself, the dysentery was still prevalent. Explaining the situation to my guard, I was taken back to the boat and allowed to use the toilet. When I came out I saw Paul, the only English speaker now left, and asked him to ask the guard if I could make a phone call; I had now been held for about sixteen hours and given that I had the contact details of the UN's Head Of Security for South Sudan I figured it wouldn't hurt to see if I could make contact.

It was at this moment I discovered something; every person on board of South Sudanese origin was petrified of the soldiers. Paul, for example, was the most confident ten year old I've ever met; fluent in three languages, he had spent his time on the boat speaking to anyone and everyone, joking with the drivers and generally walking around as if he owned the place. But when I asked him to ask my guard if I could make a phone call, it was clear he didn't want to talk to the guy. Without me pushing him and with it being clear he didn't want to, he asked the guard. The reply came that I couldn't make a phone call as there was no problem and I was to be released soon.

It sounded ominous but it proved true and an hour later I was returned my camera and my laptop, and put back on board. Somewhat unexpectedly, a welcoming party awaited. Paul sat me down and a crowd gathered around as Paul, acting as translator, asked all the questions that the people wanted to know; Had I been looked after? Why did they arrest me? Was I scared? Did they beat me?

To me it had been a fairly boring seventeen hours, but to these people they couldn't believe that someone had been arrested by people they viewed as their enemy, and was now here safe and sound. Some people were less than impressed and wished I hadn't been on board, but Paul found my story hilarious.

The boat moved along and knowing that my bags were likely to be checked again I decided the risk wasn't worth it and threw the sachet of booze away.

A day and a half later we arrived in Kosti. The port itself was now a refugee camp, with thousands of displaced South Sudanese people waiting for boats going south to take them home. As we docked, I spoke to people living in the camp and found there to be a five month waiting list for a ride south. Coming north had been stressful enough, but going south would have been far harder.

305

But I had made it. Looking around, I could see evident relief on the faces of those few who had been on the boat since Juba. We had made it. Twenty one days on the water, but we were now here.

Paul, the charismatic young man who I could tell was going to grow up to be an accomplished individual, left the boat and went straight to downtown Kosti, shepherding his family on the way. Sadly he left before I realised I hadn't exchanged contact details with him, but he was a remarkable person and despite his age I knew he would be fine. I wished him well.

As for me, I said goodbye to the boat's crew, met a contact who had arranged to greet me at the port and looked forward to my first proper meal in three weeks.

When first coming up with the idea of travelling through South Sudan I had been fearful. Having made it through, a few weeks later I e-mailed the UN Security guys who had helped me, asking if the journey would still be safe for others to make.

"Recently some barges moving on the Nile have been shot and many UN equipments and vehicles that were on the barge were damaged. The Militia activities in Upper Nile is increasing and I do not think it will be safe in the coming weeks and months, it can only get worse."

Looking at the timelines and the local news, it became apparent that terrorist groups had been opening fire on boats whilst I had been on the river.

I had a lot to be thankful for; not only had I made it through safe and sound, but the last big obstacle was now out of my way. I had a clear run at home.

30: I Don't Love You Anymore

Sub-Saharan Africa had taken its toll on me. The lack of infrastructure or organisation had become infuriating, but the aspect of life I had found most difficult to deal with was the constant attention I received. Wherever I went, be it a big town, a small village, or even a roadside stop, from the moment I got off my bike it would only be a matter of minutes before a crowd, predominantly of children but often containing adults, would gather round to stare at me and my bicycle. This was nothing new: In China I had been the Laowai, in Latin America I had been the Gringo and now in Sub-Saharan Africa I was the Mzungu. *The White Man*. Before though, I had possessed the patience to deal with it.

Now, I was fed up.

In Malawi, I had been woken one morning by a goat farmer who had found my tent; he spoke a little English and gestured that it was no problem for me to stay where I was. He then spent the next two and a half hours sat outside with his goats, watching me; he showed no aggression, declined attempts at conversation and simply smiled at me, curiously watching my morning routine. Before, I would have accepted the lack of privacy as part of the lifestyle, and his curiosity would have appeared charming. Now my facade had changed; I wished the outside world would sod off and leave me alone.

Moments like this led me to realise that I wanted to be somewhere different and as I got off the boat in Kosti, having left Sub-Saharan Africa behind me and now entering the Arab world, I hoped that I would leave the stresses in the past and be in a place where I would feel myself again.

Time would lead me to look back fondly on my months in Sub-Saharan Africa, but having got out of there, I heaved out a sigh of relief.

Back on land after three weeks and having cycled just seven days in two months, my response to an open road was one of 'go go go'. Alas, things did not run smoothly; first the Sudanese Police - who I had gone to see as a matter of courtesy - would not let me leave Kosti for a further twenty-four hours, and when I finally did get back on the bike I managed to lose my Primus stove, which had been my best piece of equipment over the course of the journey. To top it off, after a day and a half and just 100 miles from Khartoum, after 40,000 miles and with its replacement waiting for me in the Sudanese capital, my front hub gave up, the bearings fell out and I was forced to arrive in Khartoum via bus. I had cycled every centimetre possible in the Africas so far and the boat had been unavoidable, but with only a short-term visa that I wasn't able to extend I had no choice other than to accept that those hundred miles would be added to the cheat sheet section of the diary.

With the goal of cycling every step in Africa gone, my best piece of equipment lost and my digestive system still feeling the effects of drinking unpurified river water for the previous weeks (I weighed myself after getting off the boat and found that I had lost ten kilos in this period), I arrived in the city feeling deflated.

Khartoum would be a big test for me. It was a city many of the blogs I'd read had raved about; a city of culture in the middle of the desert, located where the two Nile rivers meet and populated with people who, amongst the organised chaos of street markets and dusty roads, were warm and welcoming. I knew if I liked the city, my first in the Arab world, then maybe I would have the enthusiasm to carry on the ride with a smile on my face and realise the old romance which had first made travel exciting. Conversely, if I didn't like the place then it meant it was time to go home.

I hated it.

I arrived on the day which marked the beginning of Eid,

a Muslim festival where farmers from the countryside bought sheep to the city and slaughtered the animals to give meat to the poor. It was a noble gesture, but the killing was done in the street and all leftovers were thrown to the side of the road. With no rain and a daily temperature well into the forties, none of the leftovers went anywhere, leaving behind a city in which several streets were covered in blood and large areas stank of rotting carcasses. Meanwhile throughout the day the *Call to Prayer* rang out over the city. It's not a pleasant sound when it's just coming from one Mosque, but with hundreds simultaneously blaring out different calls, the resulting bulge of indecipherable sound amounted to little more than noise pollution.

Staying with ex-pat teachers at the local International School, they told me how Sudanese culture centred round family life, so making friends or even finding local social hubs was very difficult. With not much to do, many of my new friends either smuggled alcohol in or simply brewed their own booze and during my week in Khartoum I drank more than I had in the previous two months combined (although this wouldn't have been a massive amount).

I stayed for a week as I needed to register with the immigration authorities and had to wait for Eid to finish before I could do this. In the interim I managed to replace my front hub, Primus kindly sent me out a new stove for free and eventually, with my documents signed and my attitude to the outside world frosty, I cycled off north into the desert. Ironically, given the emotion I was portraying, the day I left Khartoum the temperature was forty-seven degrees.

There is only one way of getting from Sudan to Egypt, a boat crossing which leaves weekly on Wednesday afternoons. By the time I got my documents sorted I had nine days to cycle the 1,100 kilometres to the port in Wadi Halfa and I did my best to crack on. Thinking a flat desert road would make this possible, I ran straight into a strong southerly wind which meant that cycling all day would garner barely eight kilometres. This was inconvenient, but far more stressful was what was going on with my insides.

Given that I'd now had close to a month of chronic diarrhoea, I decided to invest in anti-diarrhoea pills. These certainly stopped me crapping myself, but they also dried out my throat, preventing me from eating anything but *fuul,* the Sudanese staple of mashed fava beans. The beans were readily available at the truck stops I would see every fifty kilometres or so and were passable as food, but not being able to eat my beloved bread and jam - or anything else - in between left me frail.

I slept rough each night, woke at six each morning and rode through the daytime heat, often until I physically couldn't pedal anymore. After seven full days I limped to the halfway point to Wadi Halfa, the town of Dongola, and knowing I had to be on Wednesday's boat in order to avoid overstaying my visa, dragged myself to a bus stop. For the second time in Sudan, I boarded a bus and took a miserable six hour ride to the port.

I had cycled over 40,000 miles to this point, but every kilometre post I saw from the bus window laughed at me. They each represented a different failure in my efforts.

With just the one entry from Sudan to Egypt, all who wish to make this crossing get bottle-necked into the same place and among those making the boat journey were some fellow overland travellers; Jiten, Ria and Imraan were three South African cyclists of Indian descent who had cycled from Cape Town and were heading to Cairo, Kirsty and Simon were two doctors from Scotland who had been working in Zambia and were now driving home, and then there was the ten-strong Voetspore team, an Afrikaans language TV crew making a documentary about driving from South Africa to Egypt. It was pathetic, but being around people who were 'like me' made me feel much better and having arrived a day early for the boat, with our tickets sorted we all made our way five kilometres out of town, set up camp in the desert and had a barbecue.

During this night it also became apparent that I wasn't the only overlander who'd picked up an illness on their travels and as the evening wore on, an orderly queue formed outside Kirsty and Simon's 4x4. They were generously patient and thanks to their leftover medication, with my spirits up and now a clean bill of health, I looked forward to Egypt.

The boat came and went (having spent three weeks on a boat, one night was easy), entry into Egypt ran smoothly and accompanied by the Saffa cyclists, I took a couple of rest days in a youth hostel in Aswan for £1.40 per night. Seeing other cyclists on the road had been the key to combating loneliness on the ride; I owed much to Nick and Alex back in America, as well as Simon in South America and the fact that I'd met barely anybody on the road in Africa is one of the things that had made life there so difficult.

Being around these guys picked me up and hearing that their stories were so similar to mine left me feeling reassured that I wasn't going crazy. After three days of trying to put some of those ten lost kilos back on, and with my new friends staying in town for a more relaxed pace, I was forced to say goodbye. I didn't tell them so, but both I and my sanity owed them a lot.

My cousin James, he who I had stayed with back on the first night of my ride, was to fly out to meet me in Cairo and was going to ride with me for six weeks. Now all that stood between me and a travel partner was nine days of Egyptian riding.

My first impressions of Egypt weren't great; in Aswan I'd found myself being continually ripped off - something that simply hadn't happened at all in Africa - and I was sad to see how little shame there was in the practice, as though because I was foreign it was everyone's duty to try to double prices.

Aside from this, I was also surprised by the aggression levels of the local people in everything they did. Not just in dealing with me (although this was done very aggressively) but also in dealing with each other; communication was via shouting, driving was done as if life depended on it and kids fought, punching and kicking each other in the street. It wasn't what I was expecting and despite meeting several kind people, including Mohammed, our hostel owner, who after hearing we'd been ripped off at an Internet Café insisted on giving us his laptop for the night, I felt slightly intimidated.

I thought here would be more relaxed than Sub-Saharan Africa.

I initially chalked these things up to being in a tourist area, although after three days of riding I realised I was wrong. The ride was characterised by kids and teenagers seeing me as a target to throw rocks at, by once again being used as a dartboard for people to throw English words they knew towards and also frustratingly, as someone to beg for money from. The stone throwing, apart from the odd kid every few months, I'd never really had to deal with, but in Egypt there was a constant bombardment of rocks heading my way, whilst in terms of the begging, having just come from one of the poorest areas in the world it felt almost shameful to be approached by twelve-year olds riding motorbikes who demanded money; demanded being the operative word: in deep Africa the begging had been done with optimism, here it was done with aggression and expectancy.

These experiences weren't fun, but neither were the following three days, during which I had a police escort forced upon me. I had been told to expect one if riding in

312

Egypt and the idea is that they're supposed to protect you from any terrorist gangs who wish to harm tourists in the country. Whilst I was certainly safe, I was also effectively under arrest; I was not allowed to speak to anyone, I was not allowed to choose where I ate, I was not allowed to use the internet without a policeman standing directly behind me and when I rode I had a police car tailing me, never further than a metre away at all times.

I hated every second of it and as my protestations that I wanted neither their presence nor their help fell on deaf ears, on my third morning I woke at sunrise and made a break for it. I didn't get far; I had slept in a church and the police had stationed a man at the front gate of the complex whose job is was to make sure that I went nowhere and spoke to no one without police present. I had been monitored whilst I was asleep.

I finally managed to persuade my escort to leave me a little over two days from Cairo. I'd slept six hours a night on the previous three nights, whilst having cycled eight hours each day. I was tired, getting cranky and just wanted to be left alone.

As darkness approached, I looked for a place to sleep. This wasn't easy, as Egypt has severe problems with overcrowding and Mohammed, a man I'd met on the boat to Aswan had summed it up quite well with his statistic that whilst there are eighty-four million Egyptians, only 7% of the land is liveable. With people everywhere, finding a place to get my head down proved quite a challenge, but I eventually pulled off down a side road and decided to sleep rough at the foot of a fence. By this time I'd had enough of the stresses of riding in Egypt and just wanted to get to Cairo, so my plan was to sleep rough, get up at day break and go as fast as I could to the capital.

I knew I wasn't safe where I was, I knew people would find me, but I was exhausted; physically, emotionally and mentally. The best I could do was move down a footpath and sleep rough on a verge underneath a tree.

A few hours passed, I thought I was safe and then suddenly I sensed footsteps.

I inhaled sharply. It must have been noticed as the next thing I knew I heard a gun being cocked and I had an AK47 pointed at me. I was marched into a small office, close to the main road. My possessions were rifled through; I was a suspected criminal. A couple of minutes later an English speaking man arrived and my story was explained.

I apologised profusely and this new man, with a confident, welcoming nature, laughed it off, offered me tea and asked if I'd like to sleep on the floor of their office for the night. All my worries disappeared, the loaded gun was put away and having spent the previous week either being pelted by stones, shouted at by locals, being physically grabbed hold of in the street or being followed by police, I finally felt good about Egypt; I'd met some good people, had been taken in by them (despite me being entirely in the wrong) and had enjoyed their company.

After a brief discussion about Egyptian football they let me sleep; my head hit the floor and I was out like a light. That night I had a strange dream whereby I was with my bicycle camping somewhere and when I'd woken up all my possessions had been stolen. Snapping back to reality, I woke the following morning, thought nothing of the dream and packed up ready to leave.

The group on the farm was now down to two. The English speaker had left and one of the guys, who I had clocked the night before, was a bit odd. He asked to see my camera and then said he wanted a dollar for him to give it back. I wasn't sure if he was joking or not and not really on my guard I gave him a dollar from my spare wallet - a wallet they'd seen the night before when inspecting my things - as an act of kindness. It was something I had never done previously, but his co-worker was apologising to me

314

about the man's behaviour and implying that he was a bit slow, so given their hospitality the previous evening I didn't mind sharing the souvenir. The more intelligent of the two men then said he wanted to show me something around the back of the office. I went with him and whilst trying to keep one eye on my bike, he showed me what he wanted to show me. As the sun was now fully up I rode off, stopping a kilometre down the road for breakfast.

As I sat eating, the less intelligent of the two men ran up to me, handed me back my spare wallet - now devoid of any money - and started to leave. It took all of half a second for me to register what had happened.

I went for him.

I chased after him, shouting loudly and he ran to a parked bus. This wasn't good for him, a small crowd soon gathered, I was gnashing at the teeth, amazed at the fact I appeared intimidating, and his partner came to the commotion, apologised profusely and took me back to the office.

It was as we walked back I checked my money in my wallet that sits in my bar bag; that had gone too.

I desperately wanted to call the police but knew my story of 'I was kind of trespassing on someone's land and then this stuff happened' wasn't going to go down well. Additionally, given that I'd spent three days actively trying to get rid of them - claiming throughout that I didn't need their help - doing so would have involved swallowing an insurmountable amount of pride.

Thankfully, due to my accounting for every penny I spent, I knew exactly how much money had gone and I refused to leave until they'd returned all that was stolen. It was only when I calmed down and started riding that what had happened sank in: I'd been taken in by people, they'd laughed and joked around with me, they had been my friends to my face and then, at the first chance they'd had, they had gone through my personal possessions and stolen from me. Twice.

They had gone through my bags whilst I was asleep, then the following morning they had distracted me (it was only about forty kilometres later that I realised that the men had been working together) and stolen from me again.

The only thing I couldn't work out was why they had come back and returned my empty wallet, because if they hadn't it would have been a long time until I'd realised its disappearance and they probably would have gotten away with it.

Overall though, as far as I was concerned with the Egyptian people, that was it: I'd had enough.

That day I had more rocks thrown at me and even had twelve year olds on motorbikes ride alongside me and kick me as I rode through one town. Drained, and just one night away from Cairo, I caved in and went to a hotel.

I asked about vacancies and they told me they only had rooms available which were well out of my budget. They tried to sell me one of these, I politely told them I couldn't afford it and they then went on to tell me that there were no cheap hotels in town; they were the best and the only place I could stay. I said 'thank you', told them I couldn't afford it and turned to go.

As I was about to leave they chased after me. *"Oh Mr. Blake, there is one more room we forgot about."*

It may sound petty, but it summed up so much of what dealing with Egyptians was like; I'd told them what I wanted, in return they'd spent ten minutes lying through their teeth.

I was too tired to argue, and at least managed a good night's sleep.

The following morning I left town, feeling rested, although still just as miserable. Within thirty minutes I'd had a rock the size of a tennis ball thrown at my rear wheel, leaving a large dent on my rim. This time I lost it completely and chased after the little bastard who'd thrown it. After thirty metres of running I heard the boy of about twelve years screaming as he ran ahead and I stopped in my tracks. *When did it come to this?*

I was running after a twelve year old boy.

And what exactly was I going to do, even if I caught him?

I got back on the bike and arrived in Cairo a few hours later. I met Dagmar, my host; she took me to her apartment and left me to shower. Before I washed I looked in the mirror; looking back was a ghost. Unshaven, dust in my hair and with black bags around my eyes.

Usually when I have just completed a ride, particularly a tough one, the first thing I do before washing is look at myself in the mirror and see the twinkle in my eye. It had been with me ever since my first practice ride, long before the trip and it was a spark that would say to me 'That was tough, but you made it. Well done'. I talked to myself way too much throughout the journey, but these conversations with mirrors had happened wherever I'd been. They allowed me to see the fire inside of me.

Looking now, my eyes were vacant. I had no emotion, no pride, nothing.

All previous milestones - arriving in Tokyo from home, or completing Alaska to Argentina, for example - had been met with celebration.

In eight months I had just cycled from Cape Town to Cairo; I felt nothing. I looked knackered.

See me in the street and ask me if there's any country I didn't like cycling in, I will give a liberal answer of 'well, I couldn't choose a country that I didn't like, as I always look for the positives and can find things I enjoyed in every country that I visited'. This is simply so as not to offend anyone, but the honest answer to this question is Egypt.

Granted, I was in Egypt at an unfortunate time; protests

following the previous year's revolution were in full swing and this led to an unstable environment.

I should also state that I did meet several people I liked and found that the country, in this sense, was similar to Azerbaijan (although Egypt was definitely more extreme) in that often people were either ridiculously kind to me, or massively aggressive.

But I could not say it was a pleasure to ride through; I was ripped off wherever I went, I had stones thrown at me, I had been kicked several times in the street by children and had insults hurled at me throughout the ride.

Much as I didn't like it, I could (begrudgingly) understand why certain people ripped me off. What I couldn't get my head around though, was the aggression.

If the anger was over the political situation it would make a little sense, but I found the overwhelming majority of it had come from people in the twelve-to-sixteen age range; not exactly a demographic known for their political activity.

I didn't know why, but the youth of an entire nation was angry.

Arriving in Cairo I thought that maybe someday in the future I would come back, but for that week I was determined to stay indoors.

Whilst I maintain that Egypt was not a pleasant place to ride, I had been the architect of my own downfall.

It had been me who had done his best to avoid the police escort, it had been me who had ignored their advice about where to stay and whilst I couldn't condone what they did, it had been me who had been inadvertently trespassing, which led to me being stolen from.

Looking back on that incident, I was disgusted with myself. I had camped where I'd known I shouldn't, I had shown that I had money on me when I knew I should hide it and I had fallen for one of the most basic scams of the book.

How had I ended up in this situation? Simple.

Throughout the previous months all I had wanted to do was go home. I never once considered quitting and knew the only way I would get home would be via bike, so I had cycled longer and harder each day, focusing on nothing else.

I was incapable of focusing on anything other than cycling in the direction of home. This was why I'd been out on the roads late at night, why I hadn't taken the time to find a proper sleeping place and also why I'd lost focus and been stolen from.

As I'd left Kosti back in Sudan my stove had fallen out of my pannier; I hadn't gone back to look for it as the idea of doing something which wasn't heading towards home made me feel sick inside.

I was fixated with this idea. *Home*.

In my week off in Cairo, I looked at how my own behaviour had changed over the previous months of my obsession; I had become inward, a loner and now, in Egypt I had become both rude to others and a nuisance to the people whose country I was in. In ignoring the kindness that several of the Egyptian people showed me, I had also become arrogant.

All other sections of the ride had been completed with me feeling proud and with my enjoying life on the bike. Looking at who I was now, I had come full circle; I wasn't happy on the bike and I didn't like the person I had become.

With the two year anniversary of when my parents had said goodbye to me back in California approaching, I caught a bus to the airport and went to meet James.

If there was a silver lining to all of this, it was that I was no longer alone.

319

31: Standing On The Edge Of A Dream

James landed and two days later we left Cairo, a city that earned the joint top spot along with Istanbul in the 'World's Most Dangerous City To Ride In And Out Of' competition. Negotiating the traffic, we crossed under the Suez Canal, in the process going from Africa to Asia, rounded Sinai and made our way to the Israeli border.

From the moment James arrived the ride had ceased being any kind of a challenge. Where loneliness had been my undoing, travelling with someone who was family made it easy and not only was I with James, I would now also see several of the Israeli friends I had made previously on the ride.

As someone who usually got so wound up by perceived injustices in local issues, now, as we entered Israel, I simply turned a blind eye. I didn't take an interest in the Israeli colonisation of the West Bank, I bit my tongue regarding the abhorrent policy of giving all Israeli teenagers a gun and forcing them into a minimum of two years national service in an army that did highly illegal and immoral things and I didn't even get too upset at the big news of the day, which was that an Orthodox Jewish group had been told they couldn't segregate their public buses by gender and so had taken the entirely rational response of dressing their children up in World War II Concentration Camp uniforms and parading them about town, as if desegregated bus travel was on par with the Holocaust.

Instead, whilst the old me would have been fuming at these things, all I cared about now was seeing my friends; on Christmas Eve we arrived in Jerusalem at Roy's, a cyclist I had met over three years earlier in Aktau, Kazakhstan. We stayed with him for Christmas (including a trip to Bethlehem for Christmas Day - I'm not religious but it was worth seeing what all the fuss was about) and headed on to Revital's, a girl I'd met two years previously in Argentina, before a visit to a Kibbutz with Yasmin and her family, who I had met back in Rwanda.

Life was easy and making our way to the island of Cyprus we stayed with Rahme, a backpacker of Turkish-Cypriot descent whom I'd met in Guatemala, before finally seeing the people I'd longed to see most since we'd said goodbye back in California, November 2009: my parents. Mum turned sixty in mid-January and as a surprise birthday present my father and sister flew her out for a long weekend. The visit rounded off a month that had consisted of cycling from one friend's house to another's.

Before James had arrived, I hated myself. Literally; who I was, what I was doing, what I'd put myself through. Over these weeks, seeing friends and family, I found myself coming out the other side.

The closest thing I could compare it to is getting over a bad break-up; for so long you are angry at yourself. But as you get over it you accept that you got into such a stressful situation in the first place because of love and now, as you realise that you're going to be OK, it all comes flooding back; why you made these choices and why you lived like this. You can even accept that whilst you wouldn't want to go back, there was a time that you loved and you are grateful for the happy memories. The moment you realise a break-up is final there is a sudden appreciation for the experience you've been through; I was now at this stage.

Seeing friends and - especially - my family put a lot of things into context; where I'd been, what I'd done and how long I'd been away. I was no longer annoyed at myself and instead took satisfaction in the fact that I had been so low at times but had still found the means to carry on.

They had seen them countless times before, but showing Mum and Dad the pictures of where I'd been since I'd last seen them was one of my proudest moments. It was only then that what I'd done for the previous four years sank in.

321

I'd never once considered that I'd fail on my journey, but what I'd never quite got around to accepting was that one day it would be over. Now with a date, the 7th of April 2012, set in the diary I needed to get a shift on.

James and I got a boat over to Turkey and after a final night camping in freezing temperatures, James decided to leave to catch his flight. He wasn't sure if he wanted to carry on for a few more days or not, but as we passed a sign which indicated an eighteen kilometre climb that would end above the snowline, his mind was made up for him. He hitched to the next town, from where he departed to Istanbul and on to the UK. He'd made a wise choice, as the following morning, having camped in snow, a blizzard blew in and held me up for most of the day.

I was grateful for the six weeks of James' company and equally so for the fact he left his tent behind. The zips had gone on mine and the underneath was worn through, which left it poorly insulated and leaking. With James' tent close to new, I was able to use the old one as a ground sheet and it proved vital; I had previously associated Turkey with only warm weather but as I made my way to Ankara, the snow got continually deeper and on the last night before arriving in the Turkish capital the mercury went down to minus sixteen as I camped on a foot of solid snow. Arriving in the city I met with my hosts and the evening news reported that Ankara was currently experiencing its coldest ever recorded temperature of minus twenty-four degrees.

It was hard not to laugh, the local people seemed to be struggling but I wasn't. The only slight issue I'd had was with my feet getting wet, so I bought a pair of wellies and set off again. My feet got cold in the day but they'd warm straight up on a hot water bottle at night and of all the things I'd tried, wellies were the most excellent attire for snow riding.

Some days I camped, other days I slept in petrol stations

and one night I was even taken in and allowed to kip on the floor of a teahouse. Turkey had been one of the most beautiful countries to ride though on the first leg of my journey and, as I returned, I got to experience it all again, this time with the country covered in a striking white. It didn't matter that the daytime temperature didn't get above zero; I spoke to anyone I could, played games of backgammon with locals and was reminded just how wonderful the Turkish people are. All of my enthusiasm had returned and as I neared Istanbul my excitement grew.

In one of my panniers I carried with me an inflatable globe and throughout the journey I had been drawing my route on it with permanent marker. I did it country by country; slowly, methodically and with a stringent rule that I would never draw a line on a part of the map that I hadn't yet cycled. I'd been looking at it more and more over the previous few weeks as the line that had snaked up through Africa was getting perilously close to the fading stripe that had gone off in the direction of Tokyo. When I got to Istanbul, the two would collide.

With over 100 kilometres of industrial area coming into the city, I slept the night prior to arrival on the floor of a petrol station café, where I was fed and allowed use of the showers by a man who rebuffed all attempts at payment. Up early the next morning, I got to the waterfront at lunchtime.

Having crossed the Bosphorus in June 2008, I made the return journey in February 2012. The last time I had been here it was baking hot, but as I docked on the European side of the city I was reassured to see that the fishermen who adorned each and every bridge were still there in spite of the cold. I rode alongside the Besiktas Football Stadium, past the Turkish Military Museum that I'd visited on my last visit and revelled in seeing things that I recognised.

I made my way to meet Ekin, a friend I'd made on my last visit to the city and who had stayed in contact. That night we met with Ozhan, the man who had hosted me, also on my last visit to the city, and the bear hug he gave me upon our reuniting rivalled the one that he'd given me when Turkey had beaten Croatia. How long I'd been away was also put into context when, with Ozhan, we went to see another of his friends I'd met before, Samir. Back in 2008 Samir had just returned from his honeymoon, now as we met him, he had just finalised his divorce. Much had happened while I'd been gone.

I stayed for a week and had never felt happier.

The adrenaline rush of arriving in Istanbul - being somewhere I knew - would top any emotion I had ever felt before and would ever feel since; *I had made it*. No matter what now happened in my life, I could say that I had cycled around the world. I could get ploughed down by a lorry on my way out of town - a distinct possibility on Turkish roads - and on my tombstone they could write 'Matthew Blake: Average guy, not great at school, mediocre footballer, but did once cycle round the world' and no one would ever be able to take that away from me.

It was beautiful.

If since seeing James the ride had no longer been a challenge, once I got through Istanbul it was unbelievably easy. I was back in Europe, the roads were clear and all I had to do was get to Luxembourg, as my dad had arranged to ride the final two weeks with me. I left my friends, the Efes beer, the kebabs and the oh-so-beautiful women of Istanbul behind and headed for Greece.

I'd been told that, due to their part in the European economic meltdown, not only was I more than welcome to punch every single Greek adult I met in the face, but that it was also my social responsibility. I was thus slightly surprised when, as I sat on a park bench using some local wifi, despite having my laptop out, with my unshaven look and my bike out of sight, I was mistaken for a hobo and a local came up and forced a couple of Euros into my hand. When he realised I wasn't a homeless person, it was he who was definitely more embarrassed and as I made my way to the Macedonian border I thought two things: 1) maybe paying taxes instead of hobos would be a better start to solving the money issues, and 2) if all homeless people in Greece have their own laptop, then maybe that's where part of the problem lies?

The snow was a metre deep at times in Macedonia but the roads had been ploughed and it was a privilege to be riding through in winter. From the border to Albania, which proved another hidden gem, I looked over a lake and in all directions I could only see snow and tree tops in the clear air.

Thinking I'd been through the worst areas, the Albanians made a successful late bid and managed to pip the Turks and the Chinese to take the award of 'World's Worst Drivers', whilst the ride up to Austria took me along Croatian and Montenegrin coastline that could rival any across the globe for beauty.

As I travelled through these places it began to dawn on me how many of the things I was so accustomed to being part of life I was now doing for the last time. My first day in Croatia would be the last time that I'd wild camp overlooking the sea. Further up the coast I would camp in snow for the last time (admittedly, I wasn't going to miss urinating into an empty can each night, with the first job each morning being to defrost my frozen piss, but it was still something that I wouldn't be doing again). Entering Montenegro I would have my passport checked for the last time. As I came through Vienna I would visit an International School - which was how I'd been fundraising for SOS - for the last time. Prior to arriving in the German town of Speyer I wild camped for the last time. Once in Speyer I stayed with Myles and he took me to a football match of his beloved Hoffenheim; it would be the last sporting event I would attend. And from Speyer, I was accompanied by Seb and Sarah, a German couple who I'd met in Cape Town and who rode with me to Luxembourg: Dad aside, they would be my last riding partners.

All of these things only confirmed that the end was nigh and I was nearly home.

Meeting Mum and Dad, Mum had something with her that only finalised it.

I possessed few things that I was emotionally attached to. I cared about my bike, about my tools, about my camera, and even about small things such as a child's toy that I'd been given in Japan. But whilst I cared about having them I wasn't overly sentimental and when things had gone missing or been stolen, even important items such as my stove, any ire I felt was directed towards needing to replace said item, rather than that I'd lost the old one. Throughout the journey, perhaps with the possible exception of my passport, there was only one physical item that I cared about.

I have always loved flags and upon leaving the UK I had set myself the challenge of getting a small flag patch - the six-by-four inch variety that are sewn onto uniforms - for every country that I visited. With this project already underway, when I was in Cambodia SOS Children's Villages had sent me out a white t-shirt with their logo in the middle. With nineteen flags already purchased and with a mostly blank t-shirt emblazoned with the cause of my ride, I made the logical step of sewing each flag onto the garment in the order that they had been ridden. Over the following years, in what had been a trip haunted by obsession, completing this t-shirt was my most severe. Now as the journey neared completion, the t-shirt was nearly full and each flag had its own story.

Many of them had been easy to collect; simply arrive in said country's capital city, head to the tourist zone and I could find any number of retailers. Others had been given as presents by hosts and these were a great reminder of some of the people I'd met. Some though, had far more interesting tales and my favourite was South Sudan's; In South Sudan the sale of patch flags was banned, as people had been sewing them onto camouflage clothes and were causing trouble by pretending to be the army. This had left a conundrum and I had gone to a local market, where for $3 a local tailor had sewn me my own flag from scratch; it stood out on the t-shirt and was by far my favourite. And finally, if I really couldn't find a flag, on the rarest of occasions, I was forced to ask for a flag to be sent out from home. Through this I received a home-made Sudanese flag from my sister and also a Swazi flag from Luke, someone I'd never met in real life but who had followed me through the online Football Forum - back where my whole journey had started - and who wanted to help.

Not only did the flags have their own back story as to how they'd each ended up on my shirt, but each had their own story as to their creation and learning about these had been a joy; the Mexican flag consisted of an eagle with a snake in its mouth and was an emblem of the myth surrounding the creation of Mexico city. South Africa's flag had been formed in a post-Apartheid competition and among other things consisted of a large black triangle that represented the indigenous population, a thin white stripe which showed the white minority and a green filling which represented the freedom and peace between the different groups of people. Meanwhile, next to the South African flag, I loved showing others that neighbouring Lesotho had their tribal symbol of a Basotho hat on their crest, next door Swaziland had an Assegai, a tribal shield used in war on theirs, but next to these two symbols of African history the bordering Mozambicans, had chosen to have an AK47 on their flag.

The t-shirt of flags was my prized possession and whilst

I had long since grown tired of talking about my trip, showing my t-shirt was something I never got bored of. The reason for this was that telling people in words about my journey was not easy; I could never articulate what I had done.

The t-shirt though, was the perfect summation. The sheer number of the flags showed just how far I had been, whilst the story of how I came to own each flag gave a summary of what life was like on the bike. For most of them I had been able to get them on my own, just like my ride had been solo, but whilst most had been sorted this way, there were those that were given as gifts and this symbolised how on my ride, whilst never expected, the help of others had always been appreciated.

The South Sudanese flag showed that when I'd had problems, I had found a way to overcome them and by having flags from people who weren't on my ride, it was the perfect reminder that there was no way I could have completed what I'd done without the help of others. Additionally, in having a flag from my family and some from strangers who I only knew through the internet, it summed up perfectly how I relied on both those close to me and people I'd never even met.

Finally, the stories I'd picked up about the history of each flag showed the main reason for my travels; to learn. I had learnt so much and as I looked at each flag, I could single out a country and think of all the lessons that the place had taught me.

Having left Istanbul, on my way to Luxembourg I had passed through Bosnia for a mere ten miles and then, as part of a successful ego boosting effort to ride through four countries in a day, I had passed through Slovenia for a paltry six. In both countries I'd tried and failed to gain flags in the few shops I'd seen. As I arrived in Luxembourg I met my parents and Mum gave me the Bosnian and Slovenian patches she'd ordered online. In front of me I had a t-shirt

328

containing sixty flags; fifty nine countries and the State flag of Alaska. As I sewed on flags sixty-one and sixty-two, in doing so filling up the entire t-shirt, I looked down at the completed garment and could think of no better way to finish it.

I may not have been able to get the flags in their countries of origin, but this was much a better representation. My t-shirt, much like my ride, would have been impossible to complete without my parents.

As the last stitch went in, my biggest fixation was complete. The ride was now due to end.

We set off the next day. Dad cycled with me and Mum drove, meeting us each evening. Having spent four years living off £5 per day, the final two weeks were spent sleeping in fancy hotels, eating exclusively in good quality restaurants and showering daily. I wasn't complaining.

Arriving in Calais on a clear day, looking across the water I could see it.

England.

It was almost over.

32: Curtainfall

On the last morning of the ride I was joined by twenty-six friends and family at Reading Station and we all rode the sixty miles home together. Among the group were Dad, a load of old school friends, people from the village I had grown up in, my old art teacher, Abe - a motorcyclist I'd met in Kazakhstan, and also six guys I had only ever known as Boris Ignatievich, Buttered Senseless, Laertes, Gobsh, Guyster, Spasy Paddy and PNev. That last set of names were people from the Football Forum and were probably the group I had spoken to most over the previous four years; it was a fitting end that they came along and I enjoyed finally being able to put usernames to faces, and in turn, faces to actual names.

The day was one of celebration and at around four o'clock the billowing smoke of Banbury's coffee factory came into view. I live just outside of town, in a village at the bottom of a hill. At the top, our group stopped and we all descended together. Heading straight to the pub, all the other friends and family who I hadn't seen in four years were waiting there, as well as several people I had met along the ride; Jake and Mai, who I had stayed with in Vietnam, Tim, a forummer I'd met in Bogota who had timed his return to the UK especially to make this day, and Rahme, who James and I had seen in Cyprus. Chitende, who had hosted me in Zambia, would also have been there but for the inconvenience of his wife going into labour.

The pub stayed open late and sleep didn't come until four o'clock the next morning, but when it did, it had been earned.

On the 29th of April 2008 I had cycled away from my own front door with the aim of trying to ride to Vietnam. 46,180 miles and sixty-one countries later, surrounded by friends and family, I returned on the 7th of April 2012.

I was home.

Leg three: Cape Town, South Africa - Banbury, England

Dates: March 22nd 2010 - April 7th 2012

Countries visited: 30

South Africa, Lesotho, Swaziland, Mozambique, Zimbabwe, Zambia, Malawi, Tanzania, Rwanda, Uganda, South Sudan, Sudan, Egypt, Israel, Cyprus, Turkey, Greece, Macedonia, Albania, Montenegro, Croatia, Bosnia, Slovenia, Hungary, Austria, Germany, Luxembourg, Belgium, France, England.

Kilometres cycled: 18622

Epilogue

After the celebrations died down my mood at returning was one of relief; I had loved the ride, but was definitely ready to stop.

I spent the following weeks seeing all the friends and family I'd not been around in so long, whilst I was also introduced to the people who had entered the local realm in my absence. My cousin Helen had been six months pregnant at the time of my departure and upon my return that child, a boy named Charlie, was rapidly approaching his fourth birthday. He now had a bright little sister called Isabelle and meeting these two was one of the many highlights of my homecoming.

Meanwhile I began working almost straight away and throughout the year, aside from getting back on my own feet financially, I laboured continuously to raise funds for SOS Zambia to the extent that by the time the first children moved into the village in October 2012 my journey had raised over £18,000. As for Chipata itself, 154 orphaned or abandoned children now live in the community and it is one of the first places I plan to return.

With regards to cycling, I still use the bicycle as my main form of transport. A bicycle to me has - and always will be - a way to get from A to B. I have never been a Sunday cyclist and find the idea of cycling a thirty mile loop flat out on a Sunday morning for fitness purposes to be utterly tedious. But when it comes to getting from one place to another, the simplicity and joy of two wheels will never be matched and just because I am now home I see no reason to change. Alas, whilst I still cycle, due to a reduction in the amount, coupled with keeping the same level of appetite, I have quickly put on weight and by the time Christmas rolled around I tipped the scales at eighty-seven kilos, up twenty-five kilos (and 40%) from the previous year, when I'd still been recovering from the South Sudanese stomach bug.

Having returned to normality, with my fitness - the one thing I'd hoped to have kept - gone, given my efforts of the previous four years, physically all I was left with was a full passport, a battered bike, some muddy gear and a t-shirt of flags.

Of course what I also possessed were the lessons that the journey had taught me.

If there was one thing that I never stopped doing on the bike it was learning. In each pedal I would find a new challenge or discovery and even though life was not always easy or exciting, after four years of continual cycling, even as I returned home I was still finding out new things about both myself and the world around me.

It's fair to say that not all of the lessons I gained were things that are applicable to everyday life, such as the discovery that as long as you aren't in anybody's direct way then it's entirely possible to sleep on pavements, shop fronts or bus shelters around the world without anyone caring. Meanwhile other lessons, such as that the poorest people were always the most willing to share, were things I had expected to find out all along and as such, were no great surprise.

So for all of my efforts what was I left with that was practical? What had the bike ride taught me that I could take into everyday life? What hadn't I known before? There were so many things, but two always stood out.

The first was that whilst away I began to realise just how lucky I am in life to have been born to both a loving family and also in Britain. Through working with SOS I have become more aware of just how many orphaned children there are in the world and from the ride I came into contact with extreme poverty levels on such a large scale that they would be incomprehensible in the UK. Even the worst off in Britain have it better than many people around the globe and having viewed these things first hand I have since found a new appreciation for the fact that I have always had a family who looked after me and that I am from a country where the support networks are there for people who fall into trouble.

One of the main motivations for the journey had been that I had become disillusioned with so much of life in the UK - the materialistic culture surrounding mobile phones and other such items, the rise of reality TV shows which rewarded a lack of talent with fame, *The Daily Mail's* continued existence - but since going to other places and having seen how we have social support systems for the poorest members of our society, proper healthcare for all, a true sense of equality when it comes to immigration and integration, and even things as basic as freedom of speech, I now feel a great pride in being English. Of course my country is not perfect, but it is my home and I now have a far deeper respect for it. I controlled neither where I was born, nor whom I was born to, but my journey taught me just how lucky I have been in both these regards.

The other thing that the journey taught me was to feel secure with who I was.

It sounds such a basic idea but we each have our anxieties and particularly in youth can be unsure of ourselves. I couldn't single out a defining moment, but more throughout the entire journey, by putting myself into situations in which I'd never been before I was able to continually learn about myself from how I personally dealt with each differing circumstance. I learnt how few possessions I needed to get by in life, how to cope in countries where I shared no language or culture, what I could do physically when on my bike and perhaps most importantly, what my mental limits were when put to these tests. Via these constant challenges I was able to shape a clear view of who I was, what I could accomplish when I set my mind to it and also what I wanted from the future.

Through failing at certain challenges, I was also able to clearly define what I couldn't do.

Having left four years previously looking for some kind of guidance, I returned with a clear notion of who I was, what I could achieve and what I wanted from life in order to make me happy. This feeling of confidence and contentment was the greatest gift my bicycle would ever give me.

I am often asked if I'd ever do it all again; if tomorrow I could wake up and go for another four years. The honest answer is no. I have neither the energy, the patience, nor the desire.

This usually then leads to the question of whether I was glad I went in the first place; the answer to this is an unequivocal yes. Even right up until the moment I had originally left the UK I had been unsure about it; I had no cycling experience, was unfit, could fix very little on my bike and had no travel or language skills. It turned out I didn't need these things and that I could still cycle around the world without them.

Four years later I could say without doubt that leaving on the bike was the best decision I ever made.

Acknowledgements

There are so many people who I could not have completed the ride without and there isn't enough room to mention everybody, but here are just a few people I would like to specifically thank.

I would like to thank everyone who hosted me. There are far too many to name here, but I am grateful to you all. Specifically I would like to single out Phil, Misuzu, Alex and Liam Ryan in Tokyo, Scott, Beth and George Kendall in Cambria, the Alonso's in Mexico, Rob, Dawn, Ryan and Glenn Jones in Cape Town and Bill and Sue Farmer in Kampala; all of you took me in as family and made my journey complete. The help you gave and the warmth of your company was never forgotten.

During the journey I rode stretches with, among others, Alvaro Neil (AKA the Biciclown), Bella (for whom I am grateful to have met) and Jean Gosselin, Nicholas Carmen, Alex Dunn, Simon Whitehead (good luck in Canada with Adrienne), Sabine and Uli Sertl-Wenzel, Dylan Kentch, Kokoro Ito, Katerina Holaskova, Josh Corliss, Greg Penderghast, Jiten Magan, Ria Moothilal, Imraan Saayed, Sarah Konopelska and Sebastian Gaissert; I would like to thank all of you for your company and each of you did more for my sanity than you realise.

For the times the bike broke I need to thank Michael Pearson, Stephen Lord, Daniel Wolman and most of all, Luke Loren Thomson for sending me out spare parts to fix it (Luke, I especially owe you a drink), and for the times when my mental health was falling apart I owe a big debt of gratitude to Robert Seto in Canada, Beatriz Arroniz in Veracruz and Caro in Bogota. Thank you all for looking after me.

For keeping me company throughout I need to thank the gentlemen of the Football365 Forum; you chaps were always there to help, especially when feeling down, and I'd never have made it without you. I'd especially like to thank Caketaster and Hello Kitty for Tokyo, Tino's Jockstrap for the company in Bogota, all of the South African lads I met, Murf for the trip to Chimps, Myles for the fun in Speyer and Boris Ignatievich, Buttered Senseless, Laertes, Gobsh, Guyster, Spasy Paddy and PNev all for coming along on the last day; it made the ride complete. Smoggy, thanks for the map and we're waiting for you down at QPR.

I'd like to thank my close friends; Greg, Joe, James, Dan, Woody, Craig, Tom, Sarah, Claire and Chris for being there to welcome me home and I'd also like to say cheers to Natalie Parrish and Marc Sylvester for employing me upon my return. Also Sandra Nicolics, you probably don't realise it but without your help I would never have settled at home as easily as I did and I'm grateful for you guiding me back to reality over my first months back in the UK.

As for the book; Nigel and Debbie at Beaten Track, thanks for not getting wound up at my constant extending of deadlines. Alex Whitehead, ta for an awesome cover.

And finally I'd like to thank my family; of all the people who helped, you were the most important. James, thank you for coming to see me, Jo, thanks for your supporting sister role and for making the contest to be '*the favourite child*' competitive and Nan, our conversations on Skype were one of the things that kept me going.

Of course, none of this would have been possible without the support and encouragement from my parents. I am blessed and extremely grateful to have you both.